Enhance Your Garden with Japanese Plants

Enhance Your Garden

with Japanese Plants

A PRACTICAL SOURCEBOOK

JUDY GLATTSTEIN

KODANSHA INTERNATIONAL
New York • Tokyo • London

Kodansha America, Inc.
114 Fifth Avenue, New York, New York 10011, U.S.A.

Kodansha International Ltd.
17-14 Otowa 1-chome, Bunkyo-ku, Tokyo 112, Japan

Published in 1996 by Kodansha America, Inc.

Library of Congress Cataloging-in-Publication Data
Glattstein, Judy, 1942-
    Enhance your garden with Japanese plants: a practical sourcebook / Judy
    Glattstein.
        p.   cm.
    Includes bibliographical references (p.   ) and index.
    ISBN 1-56836-137-8 (pbk.)
    1. Plants, Ornamental—United States. 2. Plants, Ornamental—Japan.
    3. Landscape plants—United States, 4. Landscape plants—Japan. 5. Native
    plants for cultivation—Japan. I. Title.
    SB407.G56 1996
    635.9'5152—dc20   96-4677

Maps of Japan on p. 10 by Charles Davey. Based on illustrations in Owhi's
Flora of Japan, published by the Smithsonian Institution Press.
Illustration on p. 26 from *Amoentiatum exoticarum,* by Engelbert Kaempfer, from
the Collection of the Library of the New York Botanical Garden.
Illustration on p. 32 from *Flora Japonica,* by Philipp von Siebold, from the
collection of the Library of the New York Botanical Garden.
Illustration on p. 35 courtesy of the Herbarium of the New York Botanical
Garden.

Book design by Chris Welch

Printed in the United States of America

96 97 98 99 RRD/H 10 9 8 7 6 5 4 3 2 1

Contents

Introduction   **3**

CHAPTER 1   The Asian Connection   **11**

CHAPTER 2   How Japanese Plants Arrived in
             Europe and America   **23**

CHAPTER 3   Trees   **41**

CHAPTER 4   Shrubs   **73**

CHAPTER 5   Vines and Ground Covers   **103**

CHAPTER 6   Herbaceous Plants for the Sunny
             Perennial Border   **123**

CHAPTER 7   Woodland Perennials   **149**

CHAPTER 8   *Plants for Rock and Water Gardens*   **187**

Appendix 1   *Nursery Sources*   **203**

Appendix 2   *United States Hardiness Zones*   **209**

Bibliography   **213**

Index of Plant Names   **217**

Acknowledgments

It is only appropriate to express here my grateful appreciation to the gardeners here and abroad who generously took the time to share their experiences in the cultivation of Japanese plants, and to one very special nongardener, my husband, Paul, sine qua non.

Enhance Your Garden with Japanese Plants

Introduction

I n this book I discuss plants of Japanese origin. Some are familiar, commonly grown, and readily available; others are, as yet, unknown to all but a handful of aficionados. How to use these plants, and in what combination with other non-Japanese plants, is a matter as personal and idiosyncratic as each of us and our own tastes. But however they are grown, the horticultural treasures of Japan offer options and intriguing possibilities for the inquisitive gardener.

When I began this book I asked several gardening friends and horticultural correspondents why they, as individuals, grow Japanese plants. Their reasons were as different as the people themselves. Edward B. Leimseider, a retired executive living in Westport, Connecticut, wrote, "Basically because I wanted to match them against American natives. There are limits to the number of small (i.e., less than 15 inches tall) American plants, and I decided that Japanese plants could easily augment them." Mr. Gusman, a physicist at a university in Belgium, suggested it was for their aesthetic appeal. Also, the climatic conditions of some parts of Japan are similar to those in Belgium, so he finds it easy to cultivate many Japanese plants, except for those that come very early into growth and are vulnerable to spring frosts.

Many botanical institutions include Japanese plants in their Asian collections. This is the case for the University of British Columbia Botanical Garden in Vancouver, the University of California Botanical Garden in

Berkeley, and the Rhododendron Species Botanical Garden in Seattle, Washington. Visitors who admire the plants often become interested in growing them at home.

What are my reasons for growing these plants? Curiosity, I suppose. Success with one plant leads me to try another. Also, as my approach to garden design is plant-oriented, I enjoy the way these Japanese plants harmoniously blend with what is already growing in my garden.

Particular plants may be associated with a specific style of design, but they often have wider applications. Yes, herbs generally belong in an herb garden, but creeping thymes are also an excellent choice for a rock garden, or as ground cover for early crocus. Silver-leaved artemisias are equally elegant in an herbaceous perennial border or an herb garden. Plants are simply the building blocks of a design; they do not control it. Some plants used in the traditional Japanese-style garden are equally suited to a range of Western design styles.

In the United States, garden design has developed predominately on the foundation of English garden traditions. A sweeping sunlit lawn, with mature specimen trees that cast pools of shade, and herbaceous borders filled with colorful flowers, we find beautiful. That this was the landscape of spacious estates maintained by a suitably large staff of gardeners is irrelevant; this British concept is one that we can readily assimilate. Our attitude toward this design style changes as we hold it up to the reality of small properties; no "staff" except perhaps someone to cut the lawn once a week; our informal, hectic lifestyle; and differences in climate. We are offered a different prototype: that of the cottage garden. Now the image is of a thatched English cottage with roses round the window and a casual melange of perennials, annuals, bulbs, and even vegetables in glorious disarray.

Glorious full-color illustrations in gardening books and magazines provoke frustration. Ours is a different country, with different climatic conditions. The Pacific Northwest is closest to English conditions, but it is only one small region. Dry Mediterranean conditions in southern California are immensely different from tropical, humid Florida. Snowy boreal conditions in northern Minnesota are different from those of arid New Mexico. It is impractical, Procrustean, to expect the idiom of a single garden style to function out of context, everywhere across the nation; nor can the same assortment of plants be expected to thrive countrywide. In Japan climatic conditions are also quite variable, from chilly Hokkaido in the north to subtropical Yakushima in the south, providing phytogeographical analogues for much of the United States.

Understanding some of the differences between Western and Japanese garden styles may suggest fresh prospects for your own garden. Contemporary Western gardens create their effects predominately with flowers. Whether the style is a formal English border, a naturalistic design in the German manner of Karl Foerster, or a simple cottage garden, the impression is one of color. Perennials, bulbs, and annuals are chosen primarily for their flowers, rather than their foliage or fruit. Whether bright and vivid, or subtle and subdued, the transient blossom sustains the Western garden.

Traditional Japanese gardens are not flower gardens in the same sense as ours are. Flowers are distracting, incidental to the overall design. Indeed, in the formal dry landscape gardens of stone and precisely raked gravel, moss is often the only plant permitted. Within the walled confines of Zen temple gardens, nature is presented in abstract. Arguably the best known of these is the famous temple garden of Ryoan-ji in Kyoto. Walled in creamy, peeling plaster exactly the color of a pigeon's breast feathers is a simple rectangle with fifteen stones set in a sea of white gravel. Only from above can all fifteen be seen at once. Years ago the Brooklyn Botanic Garden had a replica of the Ryoan-ji stone garden; one could sit on the polished wood veranda envisioning something quite different from the surrounding commotion of urban streets.

The Brooklyn Botanic Garden continues to serve as home to another traditional Japanese garden, designed in the aristocratic hill-and-pond style. I was to see this style several times in Japan: at Sora-ku-en in Kobe, and at Rikugi-en in Tokyo, for example. The elements include a pond, which presents different viewpoints as one strolls around, and a gently arched bridge that allows one to cross to an island. A gentle hill will be landscaped with pine trees for winter interest, maples for fall color, and flowering cherries and azaleas for their spring blossoms. Flowering herbaceous perennials would probably be restricted to Japanese iris and perhaps tree peonies. Chrysanthemums would be displayed as container plants, and only when in bloom.

More intimate than a hill-and-pond garden, more verdant than a dry garden, the carefully planned, understated composition of a Japanese tea-house garden contains a world within limited space. The tea-house garden is meant to be viewed primarily in passage, its confined area focused on a path, some wondrous stones, a lantern, a ritual water basin, and a minimum of plants. At the heart of the concept is the mind's preparation for the tea ceremony. (Similarly, my *sumi-e,* Oriental brush painting instructor, said that one readied oneself to paint when grinding the ink. The preparation was essential to the act of setting brush to paper.) Emphasizing flowers, even flowering shrubs, is considered too distracting. A simple arrangement of a few blossoms or some foliage might grace the *tokonoma,* a niche or recess in which flower arrangements and a scroll painting are displayed.

In Japan, the tea-house style of garden design has evolved in modern times to that of courtyard gardens. Both may share the same basic elements. They differ in that a tea-house garden is meant to be walked through, in a physical passage, while a courtyard garden is designed to be viewed from a specific position, and to provide a sense of privacy and sanctuary from a hectic world. Limitations of space proscribe exuberant growth; plants must be carefully selected and trained to fit their allotted area. So ordained is the pattern that answers are given before questions may be asked. A courtyard garden may be no more than thirty-six square feet. Within such tight boundaries a flowering plant that blooms for only a couple of weeks does not pay its rent. Rather, a handsome lacy fern, a beautiful linear grass, or the sturdy bold leaf of aspidistra or ligularia provides long-term interest with elegant foliage. Spring-flowering trees such as cherries provide a second season's interest with polished bark in winter. A Japanese maple provides both superb fall color and a dainty winter outline. Potted plants will often be used for additional, temporary interest.

Japan is one of the very few countries in the world that relies heavily upon its native flora as garden material. With an intense focus on a limited selection of highly esteemed plants, it is small wonder that these plants have acquired special attributes beyond what Westerners might ascribe to a pine or bamboo, a chrysanthemum or water lily. The Japanese invest each of their plants with spiritual qualities or symbolic significance, and then group them with other plants in a horticultural epigram. What might appear simply as an attractive planting to a Westerner could have profound philosophical implications for a Japanese viewer. For example, pine is considered an emblem of constancy, endurance, health, and longevity. It harmonizes aesthetically with mist and rain, as droplets tip each needle; sea waves and mountains, as beautiful settings for a gnarled, aged pine; and the moon, against which its form becomes a silhouette. Pine also symbolizes hardiness and strength of character, silence and solitude. It is often united with flowering plum and bamboo in a triad, "the three friends of winter." Plum, flowering from leafless branches when winter is barely over (late January to March), suggests faith. In ancient times plum was regarded as the ideal of purity, virtue, and sweetness. However crooked and bent by age the forlorn bare branches of an old tree may appear in winter, it is the harbinger of spring, breaking into the most delicate bloom. Plum and nightingale, blossom and bird, are famous in Japanese poetry as the two spirits of awakening spring. Bamboo, which weathers every storm, represents strength with suppleness. It is also compared to filial piety and is a symbol for lasting friendship and hardy age, particularly since it bows to the storm but rises again when the winds have subsided, never fading in color, remaining always green. (Japanese winters must be milder than those in Connecticut, for I've often seen the green leaves of bamboo bleach to a subtle straw color against the winter snow.)

Blooming in November, winter chrysanthemum is actually the flower of autumn. Translated, its name means "they who defy the frost." When combined with pine, the chrysanthemum is considered to signify "that which survives all else." Consequently the flower has also served as a symbol for long life. As garden flowers, chrysanthemums have a front-rank place comparable to that of peonies in summer. Chrysanthemum is also the flower of retirement and culture.

The Seven Flowers of Autumn are so named because they make up the last seven flowers of the season. They include bush clover or lespedeza, *Lespedeza bicolor;* pinks, *Dianthus superbus;* patrinia, *Patrinia scabiosaefolia;* balloon flower, *Platycodon mariesii;* morning glory, *Ipomomea* sp.; a grass known as *karu-kaya,* possibly the same as *megarukaya, Themeda triandra;* and flowering grass, *Miscanthus sinensis.* Japanese poets have often used the morning glory as a metaphor for the futility of life and the transience of human existence; yesterday's buds flower for only a few short hours and then comes death and oblivion.

Sacred lotus, *Nelumbo nucifera,* is invested with religious significance. As an aquatic plant it must grow in water, whether in a natural pond or garden pool. Even when these are lacking the lotus may be grown as a container plant in large glazed bowls during the summer, blossoming from June to August. Lotus is the matchless "lady of virtue." Its symbolic meanings are many, owing in part to the central place it occupies in Buddhist art. Symbolic of noble endeavor and spiritual purity, the lotus grows unsullied out of the mud (representing the material world), through water (the emotional middle region), to emerge into the free air (the world of the spirit) where it opens its perfect flower to the sun, thus illustrating the unfolding and blossoming of the human spirit.

Each of these symbolic plants characterizes a certain season, when its flowering is at a peak and it will be celebrated in poetry, or arranged in a vase on the tea-house tokonoma. The New Year begins in February when winter cherry, *Prunus subhirtella,* blossoms. In late March to April peach, *Prunus persica,* displays its delicate pink flowers. Flowering cherry, *Prunus serrulata,* whose blossoms foreigners associate so closely with Japan, appear in early April. Next, in bloom from late April to the middle of May, peonies are "the king of flowers," and a symbol for high rank and wealth, material prosperity, and happiness. Peonies form an opulent and colorful contrast to the refined charm of the plum blossom, and to the cool magnificence of the chrysanthemum. Flower of two seasons, wisteria blooms in the first half of May, linking the end of spring and the beginning of summer. Azaleas flower in the same period. Late May to July is when iris are in bloom. Also in July the sacred lotus transforms ponds and small lakes into flower gardens. The end of summer, August and September, brings hibiscus; then, in October, the chrysanthemum festival. Maples change to their autumn hues, burning with scarlet foliage. Winter is not bare, for different types of camellias bloom in November, December, and January.

A garden's design exists independently of the plants. No matter which style of garden speaks to you, and no matter what the setting and climate of your garden, there are plants from Japan that will be eminently suitable. It doesn't matter whether your garden is large or small, located in a city or a suburb, endures cold snowy winters or hot humid summers. Perhaps you already grow some Japanese plants, such as azaleas, flowering cherry, pachysandra, peonies or lilies. They, and the other Japanese plants discussed in this book, will surely enhance your garden.

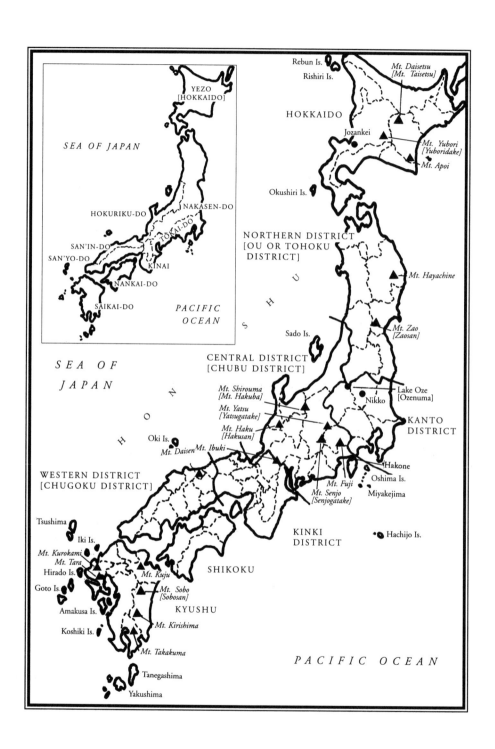

YEZO
[HOKKAIDO]

SEA OF JAPAN

HOKURIKU-DO

NAKASEN-DO

TOKAI-DO

SAN'IN-DO

SAN'YO-DO

KINAI

NANKAI-DO

SAIKAI-DO

PACIFIC
OCEAN

Rebun Is.

Rishiri Is.

Mt. Daisetsu
[Mt. Taisetsu]

HOKKAIDO

Jozankei

Mt. Yubori
[Yuboridake]

Mt. Apoi

Okushiri Is.

NORTHERN DISTRICT
[OU OR TOHOKU
DISTRICT]

Mt. Hayachine

Sado Is.

Mt. Zao
[Zaosan]

CENTRAL DISTRICT
[CHUBU DISTRICT]

Lake Oze
[Ozenuma]

Nikko

KANTO
DISTRICT

Mt. Shirouma
[Mt. Hakuba]

Mt. Yatsu
[Yatsugatake]

Mt. Haku
[Hakusan]

SEA OF
JAPAN

Oki Is.

Mt. Daisen

Mt. Ibuki

Hakone

Oshima Is.

Mt. Fuji

Miyakejima

Mt. Senjo
[Senjogatake]

WESTERN DISTRICT
[CHUGOKU DISTRICT]

KINKI
DISTRICT

Hachijo Is.

Tsushima

Iki Is.

Mt. Kurokami

Mt. Tara

Hirado Is.

Mt. Kuju

SHIKOKU

Goto Is.

Mt. Sobo
[Sobosan]

Amakusa Is.

KYUSHU

Koshiki Is.

Mt. Kirishima

Mt. Takakuma

Tanegashima

Yakushima

PACIFIC OCEAN

CHAPTER ONE

The Asian Connection

J apanese plants invite the attention of enthusiastic gardeners, for many of them are not only attractive, but also compatible with American soils and weather conditions. Where growing conditions closely match their native habitat, we expect to find plants that will grow in foreign sites. Some will be easy to cultivate, others a challenge, and a few may come to be seen as invasive, pernicious weeds.

Certain Japanese plants are so accepted as part of our landscape that it is difficult to imagine gardens without them. Dr. John Creech, former researcher with the Plant Exploration Office of the U.S. Department of Agriculture and retired director of the U.S. National Arboretum in Washington, D.C., maintains that fully 85 percent of our ornamental woody plants are native to Japan. Japanese maples offer some of the finest small trees for the home garden. Evergreen azaleas are a mainstay of American foundation plantings. Several different magnolias, from large trees to shrubs, offer magnificent, often fragrant, flowers. Sometimes a Japanese species is more suited to certain parts of our country than the native species: mountain andromeda, *Pieris floribunda,* from the southeastern United States, is hardy to zone 6, while Japanese andromeda, *P. japonica,* is widely grown a full zone farther north. It is not that we have few good plants of our own, but rather that these exotics flourish, lending diversity to our designs.

The list of Japanese plants that contribute beautiful flowers to herba-

ceous borders is more extensive than might be suspected—chrysanthe-mums, peonies, Japanese iris, lilies, platycodon, ligularia, and several ornamental grasses, to name but a few. Perennials for the shady garden include that indispensable Japanese trio of hosta, astilbe, and epimedium. The overabundance of hosta cultivars has come a long way from the original Japanese species. Take all of these away, and an entirely new palette of plants would have to be developed.

CLIMATIC REGIONS OF JAPAN

There are parallels between the climate of Japan and that of the eastern coast of North America. From the chilly northern island of Hokkaido to the temperate main islands to subtropical Yakushima, analogues for places as different as wintry Maine and New Hampshire and steamy Mississippi and Georgia may be found. Where sites are matched climat-ically, spring and fall frosts and monthly fluctuations in temperature and rainfall also are remarkably similar. What is lacking is a Japanese coun-terpart to the arid American Southwest or the Mediterranean climate of southern California.

Rainfall in Japan is, on the whole, higher than in the eastern United States. On average, Tokyo receives 61.6 inches of rain annually, compa-rable to that of New Orleans but 15 inches more than that of Hartford, Connecticut, or Norfolk, Virginia, and one and a half times as much as falls in Seattle, Washington, and Portland, Oregon. London, England, gets a scanty 22.9 inches per year.

The archipelago that comprises Japan is divided into eight regions or districts. These include, from north to south, the main islands of Hokkaido, Honshu, Shikoku, and Kyushu, and a great number of small islands. Extending over 15° of latitude, the nearly 850-mile length of Japan's land area encompasses everything from the subtropical zones of Kyushu at 30° north latitude to chilly Hokkaido at 45° north latitude. The islands belong to the easternmost part of the eastern Asian temper-ate floral region. On the whole, the country is characterized by a mild monsoon climate. *Kuroshio,* the black current, washes along the coasts of

Kyushu, Shikoku, and Honshu, flowing from southwest to northeast along the Pacific Ocean coast of the Japan archipelago. The corollary of this warm current is a warm, temperate to subtropical climate in southern Japan, with a frost-free season 200 to 300 days long. In the inner and mountainous parts of the country the climate is, however, cool-temperate, with only about 175 frost-free days.

In winter, storms constantly blow down from Siberia, resulting in colder temperatures, particularly on the west side of the northern islands, than might be anticipated for an island environment. (The continental climates of mainland countries such as the United States, Holland, France, and Germany are influenced by the land mass over which the weather travels, while maritime climates are more influenced by the adjacent oceans or seas.) Subarctic conditions occur in the highest mountain localities. On the northernmost island of Hokkaido, the climate is cool-temperate along the southern districts but subarctic elsewhere, with frost-free seasons of 150 days and less. The magnitude of the Asian continent also plays a major role in the climate of Japan. The warm current and heavier snow cover along the Sea of Japan coast of Honshu results in more favorable conditions for broadleaved evergreens farther north than along the colder, more exposed Pacific side of the island.

These variations in Japan's climate have distinct benefits for Western gardens. Simply put, if your local climate is warm and humid, choose plants from the southern regions of Japan. The colder and harsher your local climate, the more suited will be plants from the northerly islands and higher elevations of Japan. However, be willing to experiment because in gardening there are always unexpected surprises.

Ornamental trees and shrubs suited to the humid summers and mild winters of the southeastern United States come from along the Inland Sea coast of lower Honshu and the southern islands of Shikoku and Kyushu. Popular broadleaved evergreen shrubs, important elements of gardens in the Southeast, include many Japanese plants—coralberry, *Ardisia crenata;* aucuba, *Aucuba japonica;* common camellia, *Camellia japonica;* sasanqua camellia, *C. sasanqua;* paper plant, *Fatsia japonica;* Japanese holly, *Ilex crenata;* Japanese privet, *Liguistrum japonicum;* holly osmanthus, *Osmanthus ilicifolius;* Japanese pittosporum, *Pittosporum tobira;* yew podocarpus, *Podocarpus macrophyllus;* and Yedo hawthorn, *Raphiolepsis umbellata.*

Ornamental plants for horticultural and landscape use in zones 5, 4, and 3, as well as trees for forestry, were introduced from Japan long ago. Gardeners in the northern tier of states, in Canada, and even in Scandinavia, grow Japanese conifers. With its handsome, dark-green needles and bluish-purple cones, Veitch fir, *Abies veitchii,* has become an attractive addition to the boreal landscape. Nikko fir, *A. homolepis;* Japanese cedar, *Cryptomeria japonica;* Japanese larch, *Larix leptolepis;* Japanese white pine, *Pinus parviflora;* dwarf stone pine, *P. pumila;* Japanese umbrella pine, *Sciadopitys verticillata;* and Japanese yew, *Taxus cuspidata,* are equally popular. Deciduous Japanese plants such as rugosa rose, *Rosa rugosa;* Kobus magnolia, *Magnolia kobus;* star magnolia, *M. stellata;* white-leaf Japanese magnolia, *M. hypoleuca;* katsura tree, *Cercidiphyllum japonicum;* a number of maples, *Acer* species; several *Prunus* species; and some rhododendrons belong to the most popular, easily grown, and readily available of the introduced species.

After more than forty years of cultivation at the Botanical Garden and Arboretum of Gothenburg, Sweden, plants collected in Hokkaido and in the Central Japanese Alps during the 1952 Linquist-Nitzelius expedition to Japan have displayed suitable hardiness and have turned out to be very useful in ornamental horticulture. Results of an expedition nearly a quarter century later found that certain trees and shrubs of South Japanese (and South Korean) origin are unexpectedly hardy even under severe Scandinavian climatic conditions. Species currently growing under milder conditions might have a genetic predisposition that would enable them to survive harsher conditions. (This is true for some plants of the southeastern United States that migrated south in advance of the glaciers. The evergreen sweet bay magnolia, *Magnolia virginiana* var. *australis,* of the southern coastal plains, is grown around Boston, Massachusetts.) The report of the Nordic Arboretum Expedition of 1976 went on to state two main principles for the successful cultivation of Japanese plants in Scandinavia. First, the collections should be carried out on Hokkaido to match continental climatic conditions in

Scandinavia. Second, for cultivation in the milder coastal districts of Scandinavia, specimens should be collected in the mountainous parts of central and southern Japan. Plants should be characterized by good winter hardiness and, at the same time, by a genetic predisposition to leafing out later, rather than earlier, in spring.

The mountainous character of the islands, coupled with high rainfall, produces steep, fast-flowing rivers, which make flooding and erosion an ever-present problem unless the vegetation cover on upper slopes has been protected. Reforestation is an ongoing necessity. The core of many of Japan's mountains is made up of Archean rock from the earliest era of geological history. This rock is overlaid with volcanic material from different periods, with many of the volcanic peaks still active. The archetypal peak, Fuji-san, is a classic volcanic cone. In central Honshu there are granitic mountains, and Yakushima is a gigantic upthrust of the same igneous rock formed by the solidification of molten magma. As might be expected, limestone, formed from the remains of shells or coral, is extremely limited in Japan.

The glaciation of the last Ice Age, the Quaternary period, which so transformed the European and North American continents, did not directly affect Japan. (The British Isles were severely affected; England's native flora can only be described as sparse.) Flora remained rich and diversified, and today there are more than 4,000 species of vascular plants in Japan, a quarter of which are woody. There are 241 species of trees, divided among 99 genera. By comparison, in the significantly greater area of eastern North America (east of the treeless mid-continental plateau and north of Mexico, but excluding southern Florida), the figure is surprisingly similar—255 species of trees divided among 134 genera. As a result of the greatly diversified topography and climate of Japan, a remarkable range of variation has developed within a substantial number of species.

Regional Aspects

The most northerly island of Japan is Hokkaido. Hokkaido's mean temperature in the coldest month of the year is somewhat below 25°

Fahrenheit. Summer fogs are common along the eastern seacoast, a result of *oyashio,* the cold Kurile current that flows southward along the coast. Furuhashi Yoshio, a retired botanist and garden designer, explained to me that *oya* means "parent," and *shio* is "sea water." Oyashio consists of sea water and inshore melted ice. At the border of the warm kuroshio and cold oyashio, currents whirl around and ascend, and nourish microscopic plankton. (Oyashio is thus the parent of fishes.)

One plant that relishes chilly climates is the black sarana, *Fritillaria camtschatcensis.* It thrives in the cool summers and frigid winters of Kamchatka and the Kurile Islands, venturing as far south as the coastal area of Hokkaido, where the cold Kurile current curtails summer temperatures.

From the northern district of Tohoku to the western district of Chugoku, the mean low winter temperature is about 28° Fahrenheit. Districts along the coast of the Pacific Ocean generally have little winter precipitation and more days of sunshine, and progressively milder winter temperatures as one moves south. This is the result of kuroshio, the warm current, as it travels from southwest to northeast. There is little or no frost in these coastal areas, and relatively high precipitation in summer. The Kanto district, where Tokyo and Yokohama are located, has a mean low winter temperature above 0° Fahrenheit.

Along the coast of the Japan Sea winters are more humid with more snow. The forests are coniferous: fir, pine, and hemlock. Consider the diversity of conditions: montane, midelevation regions at over 5,000 feet with a cold temperate climate, and mountain peaks with elevations of 10,000 feet. These lofty sites naturally harbor subalpine and alpine plant communities on their steep slopes. To a limited extent, there are even treeless, tundralike conditions on several mountain peaks such as those of the Japan Alps. The harsh winter winds and low temperatures produce dwarfed, bushy trees. Dwarf stone pine, *Pinus pumila,* is characteristic of the alpine zone, growing prostrate, with trunk and branches flat on the ground in the direction of the prevailing wind. Where snow protects them from desiccation they thrive; in bare, wind-swept areas survival is a struggle. The boreal zone occurs at varying elevations: up to 6,500 feet in the western portion of Honshu and Shikoku; between 4,875 and 6,500 feet in central Honshu; and in the colder northern districts of Honshu the mountainous boreal forest zone creeps down to between 3,250 and 4,875 feet. In this zone can be found the dwarf stone pine already mentioned, as well as deciduous trees with a bushy habit of growth—alder, *Alnus maximowiczii;* mountain ash, *Sorbus sitchensis;* willow, *Salix reinii;* and an alpine variety of birch, *Betula ermanii* var. *nipponica.* A few deciduous shrubs, evergreen hollies, and rhododendrons, such as *Rhododendron fauriei,* may also be present. All the plants, herbaceous and woody, are accustomed to deep, heavy winter snows that shelter perennials and woody plants but weigh down pliable branches. Many trees and shrubs, even the deciduous ones, are procumbent in habit (with stems that trail along the ground) or at least decumbent (with stems that trail along the ground but with an ascending tip).

Gardeners living at high elevations in the Rocky Mountains, or the Olympic or Cascade ranges confront similar alpine conditions. Elsewhere, rock gardeners fascinated with small alpine plants attempt to grow them at lower elevations. In Japan the alpine zone descends from the northern mountains to a relatively low elevation. Wet alpine meadows and moors are a pronounced feature of the high-mountain landscape. Sedges and rushes are common in these sites, along with *Tofeldia japonica, Primula cunefolia* var. *hakusanensis, P. nipponica, Anemone narcissiflora, Trollius japonicus,* and other perennials. Many of the herbaceous plants found in these boreal regions are those with wide, circumpolar distribution, such as bunchberry and round-leaved sundew. Japanese alpine plants are also found in eastern Siberia, Alaska, the Aleutian Islands, and Kamtchaka.

Japan's Chubu district, including Hakone, has a mean winter temperature just above 35° Fahrenheit, while the Inland Sea region has a mean temperature of 40° to 43° Fahrenheit in the coldest month. This latter region includes the islands of Shikoku and Kyushu. The Southern Sea district of Shikoku along the Pacific Ocean, and the island of Yakushima, have a mean temperature above 43° Fahrenheit. Annual precipitation is often more than 60 inches per year. The climate ranges from warm temperate conditions to subtropical, roughly equivalent to zones 8 and 9, the Southeast and Deep South of the United States.

Broadleaved evergreen trees and shrubs are prevalent, including such popular plants in our gardens as camellia; Japanese ardisia; paper plant or Japanese fatsia, *Fatsia japonica;* heavenly bamboo; and *Rhododendron* species. Low-growing bamboos are found in the forest understory. Conifers such as Japanese cedar and yew podocarpus are present, as are Japanese red pine and Japanese black pine in the secondary forest belt. Deciduous trees found here include Japanese clethra, *Prunus* species, and Japanese snowbell, *Styrax japonicus.* Stately *Arundo donax* is just one of the grasses present, along with *Miscanthus sacchariflorus.* Water plants native to the region include such aquatics as sacred lotus, pond lotus, dwarf water lily, and large, prickly-leaved *Euryale ferox.*

In general, the broadleaved evergreen forest extends northward along both coasts (Pacific Ocean and Japan Sea) of the main island of Honshu, to about 38° north latitude. Here the climax forest consists of deciduous trees such as oaks, maples, Japanese alder, and Japanese hornbeam, mixed with the evergreens. The boundary zone between the warm temperate and temperate regions is usually home to sawtooth oak, *Quercus acutissima;* Japanese chestnut, *Castanea crenata;* and Japanese red pine. Continuing northward into the temperate region, a tremendous diversity of woody and herbaceous plants now common in our gardens are found as native plants. These include such deciduous trees as Japanese maple and full-moon maple; monarch birch, *Betula maximowicziana;* white-leaf Japanese magnolia, *Magnolia obovata;* Sargent cherry; Korean mountain ash, *Sorbus alnifolia;* and Japanese ash, *S. japonica.* Climbing hydrangea and gloryvine, *Vitis coignetiae,* scramble up the trees. Many conifers have their native home here, including Nikko fir; Japanese larch; Korean pine; Japanese white pine; umbrella pine, *Sciadopitys verticillata;* that mainstay of foundation plantings, Japanese yew, *Taxus cuspidata;* and Japanese hemlock. Many of these temperate-zone conifers also grow in the subalpine zone. The constant heavy shade they cast limits the undergrowth to shade-tolerant species of shrubs and perennials.

Many familiar shrubs now used in gardens across the country originally came to us from Japan. Skimmia, aucuba, and wintercreeper, *Euonymus fortunei,* are just three broadleaved evergreen shrubs native to Japan's temperate region. Deciduous shrubs with attractive flowers or fruit found in the same area include bigleaf hydrangea, *Hydrangea macrophylla;* Japanese winterberry, *Ilex serrata;* kerria; bush clovers, *Lespedeza* species; rugosa rose; and Japanese spirea.

In large part the flora of Japan is endemic, with plants native only to that country. But it is also part of the greater flora centered in China and including southern Korea, westward to the borders of Tibet, the central Himalayas, and eastern Nepal. Chilly Hokkaido shares some plants with the northeastern Asian landmass, from Lake Baikal eastward. Some of the herbaceous perennials endemic to Japan include such forest dwellers as *Anemonopsis macrophylla; Deinanthe bifida; Glaucidium palmatum;* wind-combed grass, *Hakonechloa macra; Kirengeshoma palmata; Peltoboykinia watanabei;* and *Ranzania japonica.*

JAPANESE PLANTS AND THEIR AMERICAN COUSINS

A plant is native when its place of origin and where it is growing are the same. Plants that originate from outside the region where they are growing are termed exotic. However, sometimes there is a kinship between plants, even those from widely disparate parts of the world. So it is with certain plants native to Japan and others native to the East Coast of the United States. We share woody plants—clethra, dogwood, hemlock, leucothoe, magnolia, stewartia, wisteria, and witchhazel—and herbaceous plants—jack-in-the-pulpit, pachysandra, and trillium.

Wake robin or trillium, *Trillium,* is a genus with close Japanese connections. There are a number of North American species, which fall into two types. Those where the flower is separated from the stalk by a peduncle, or stem, are called *pedunculate.* Other species, where the peduncle is absent, are called *sessile.* The three Japanese species, *T. smallii, T. tschonskii,* and *T. kamtschaticum,* are all pedunculate. Another genus, perhaps my favorite Japanese woodlander, is jack-in-the-pulpit, *Arisaema* spp. In the United States we have but two species, *A. triphyllum* and *A. draconitum,* while in Japan there are more than forty different beautiful, unusual, and bizarre species.

Perhaps the most romantic, and seminal, of these Japanese plants and their American cousins is the genus *Shortia,* for this plant led to the awareness of the relationship between the flora of Japan and that of North America.

Shortia's story begins in the latter half of the eighteenth century, in the new nation of the United States. A French botanist and collector named Andre Michaux was searching for plants worthy of introduction to gardens in France. Michaux was a thorough, meticulous workman, who prepared herbarium sheets as well as collecting live specimens. Among a group of unknown plants was an herbaceous woodland specimen whose sheet he labeled "From the high mountains of Carolina. A species of pyrola. A new genus?" Fast forward to 1838–39. Asa Gray, on leave before taking up his appointment to a chair in botany at the University of Michigan, was visiting important herbaria at various botanical institutions across Europe. In Paris he gave particular attention to the material Michaux had collected in the United States. Gray was especially intrigued by the specimen sheet among the *Plantae Incognitae,* with the growth habit of a pyrola and leaves like a galax. Deciding that this was indeed a new and distinct genus, he gave it the name of *Shortia galacifolia* in 1842. The search (which would take nearly forty years) was on to again find shortia in the wild. In May 1877, the seventeen-year-old son of a medicinal plant collector gathered some shortia from a steep hillside in North Carolina. Gray was informed of the discovery a year later, and in 1879 visited the site in the company of several friends. The type habitat where it was growing most profusely, carpeting the ground beneath mountain laurel and rhododendron, was that of deep, cool, shaded ravines. Today shortia is known to connoisseurs as a choice, somewhat temperamental plant with glossy, evergreen, rounded, saw-toothed leaves, producing bell-like white flowers in early spring. An elegant plant, it thrives in shaded, moist, well-drained, highly acid, humus soil.

Shortia's Japanese counterpart is an alpine species, *Shortia uniflora.* The leaves are quite similar to those of the American species and, like Occonee bells, Nippon bells has but one flower to a stalk, though the Japanese species has larger, beautiful, pale rose-pink, deeply fringed flowers. Although I saw positive mats of this plant growing on Mount

Nasu one May, there was still snow on the ground and the flowers were in tight bud. All my feverish breathing could not hasten them into bloom.

While he was awaiting the rediscovery of *Shortia galacifolia,* Asa Gray was obviously pondering the botanical connection with Japan. His interest expanded from Michaux's unknown specimen to other herbarium specimens and to notes brought from Japan by botanists accompanying the Perry Expedition of 1852–54 and the North Pacific Exploring Expedition of 1853–56. From this material and careful observations of his own, Gray concluded that much of Japan's vegetation could be found on the East Coast of the United States, and very little on the West Coast. The result was his theory, published in 1859, on the relationship between the flora of Japan and that of eastern North America. Once upon a time, many of these plants had a common ancestry.

For gardeners, interest in the parallels between the two countries' flora is less scientific. The close relationship means that we can find compatible plants for our gardens, simply by correlating our local climate with the appropriate region of Japan. Indisputably, the Japanese connection provides us with interesting, attractive plants that flourish in our gardens.

CHAPTER TWO

How Japanese Plants Arrived in Europe and America

THE MERCHANTS

The trail by which Japanese plants first reached Western gardens is a tangled one. The basic motivation that sent Europeans to Japan was commercial gain; horticultural and botanical interests were minor considerations. Accusations of espionage, foreign intrigue, and gun-boat diplomacy were also involved. From our perspective, the trail can be traced back to the Dutch East India Company and the extracurricular interests of three medical officers: Engelbert Kaempfer, Carl Pehr Thunberg, and Philipp Franz Balthasar von Siebold. These physicians for the European employees of the company had a passionate fascination with Japanese flora that bordered on obsession. They were not looking for new foodstuffs or medicines; nor were they smuggling tea plants out of China. They were imbued with the same ardor, the same passion for plants, that inspires all enthusiastic gardeners, regardless of the age in which they live.

The story begins in the sixteenth century, when some two hundred voyages around the Cape of Good Hope were undertaken in search of silks and spices, the treasures of the Far East. Approximately fifty of these expeditions were Dutch. A consortium of merchants from Amsterdam, Zeeland, Delft, Rotterdam, Hoorn, and Enkhuizen joined forces, forming the Dutch East India Company. Their intent was to reduce competition and trade more successfully as a group than they might have as individual merchants. By the seventeenth century the Dutch East India Company was the richest corporation in the world. In large measure, its prosperity was dependent on its exclusive trade with Japan.

Only for a brief interval of 100 years, from 1541 to 1641, did the Japanese welcome Western trade. During this time merchants in Osaka, Nagasaki, and Yokohama traded with merchants from Portugal, Spain, England, and the Netherlands. The Exclusion Orders of 1633, 1635, and 1639 began to restrict European trade with Japan. Merchants once allowed to travel freely about the country were confined to certain ports; the third Exclusion Order banned all Portuguese vessels from entering any Japanese port. Any vessel disobeying the order was to be destroyed, and its passengers and crew put to death. In July 1640 a Portuguese ship did enter Nagasaki Bay, but on a diplomatic mission requesting that the Japanese government reconsider its ban. The ship was burned, and fifty-seven of the envoys and crew, having refused to renounce their Christian faith, were executed. The remaining thirteen were sent back to Macao, with a report of the events.

It must be noted that the exclusionary policies were aimed primarily at Portugal. The Dutch, eager to secure the trade for themselves and to obtain a monopoly, had been warning the Japanese against the Portuguese, accusing them (and the Spanish) of plans to forcefully expropriate territory. The English left on their own account in 1623, before the Exclusion Orders, and the Spanish left the following year. Exemptions were made for the Chinese, as well as the Dutch.

The exclusion of foreigners was not simple xenophobia on the part of the Japanese. It was specifically anti-Christian—a political, antagonistic reaction by the ruling class to the proselytizing efforts of the Portuguese. Christianity was perceived as inconsistent with the rigidly structured feudal hierarchy of shogun, daimyos, samurai, peasants, and merchants, and ethically opposed to the samurai code.

In 1636 Japan ordered all European nationals residing in the country to move to Deshima, a small artificial island connected by a narrow causeway to the mainland, where the Dutch had established a factory in 1609, and which was to become the sole port of entry for foreign ships and cargo. Later their families were required to leave the country. Any Portuguese remaining in Japan were expelled in 1638. By 1641 Deshima, located near Nagasaki, was home to all Dutch residents, the only remaining Europeans. Trade with China and Korea was unaffected.

For the next two centuries the Japanese lived in self-imposed isolation from the West. In 1845 the United States sent Commodore Biddle and two warships to Japan with the intention of initiating trade and consular relations. Biddle was not even allowed to set foot ashore. Eight years later, in 1853, Commodore Matthew Perry, United States Navy, arrived in Japan accompanied by four warships. He made no direct threat, but certainly one was implied when he stated that he would return the following year with an even larger force, and in expectation of a favorable reply. Returning as promised, Perry signed a treaty with Japan on March 31, 1854, that opened two ports, Shimoda and Hakodate, to U.S. trade and established consular representation. It was more the overwhelming nature of Perry's naval force than the merit of any economic arguments that reopened Japan to world commerce. Having unlocked her gates, Japan then signed treaties with Great Britain in October 1854, Russia in February 1855, and Holland in November 1855.

THE DUTCH CONNECTION

Even to Linnaeus, an eighteenth-century garden superintendent to a Dutch merchant, inventor of our current system of binomial plant names, and revered father of taxonomy, Japanese plants were rare and unknown. His *Species Plantarum,* published in 1753, contained only a few, and all of these were drawn from a work by Engelbert Kaempfer, a German naturalist who served as a medical officer in Japan for the Dutch East India Company.

Kaempfer was the first Westerner to paint Japanese plants. His exquisite, accurate watercolors of such plants as camellia, tree peony, tiger lily, azalea, hydrangea, and clematis were later used as illustrations for his book, *Amoentiatum Exoticarum,* published in 1712. This reference, upon which Linnaeus relied, was the first detailed account of the habitat, history, medical, and economic use of Japanese plants.

The work of a skilled, scientifically trained observer, Kaempfer's vivid commentary (published as *A History of Japan*) included descriptions of Japanese life. In 1690, 1691, and 1692 he traveled with the Dutch merchants on their annual pilgrimage to Yedo (also known as Edo, and present-day Tokyo) to pay homage to the shogun. He wrote of ports full of ships, boat traffic on the river, the bustling crowds in the towns and villages as the embassy journeyed from Nagasaki to Osaka, to Kyoto and Yedo. This was an arduous journey of approximately 375 miles over land by sedan chair or on foot, and an additional 250 miles by boat. They traveled first by road to Kokura, then by small ship and barge to Osaka, and then along the Tokaido or Eastern Sea Road, the main highway of Japan linking the cities of Kyoto and Yedo. There was no wheeled traffic, and

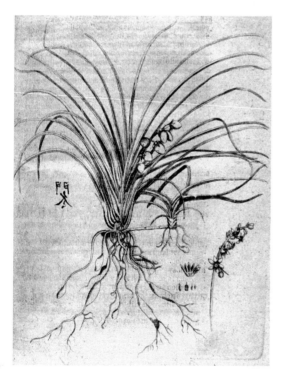

Though originally identified by Engelbert Kaempfer as Convallaria, *his eighteenth-century illustration clearly depicts the plant we know today as liriope.* Illustration from the Library of the New York Botanical Garden.

the road bustled with foot traffic, palanquins, and pack horses. On this journey Kaempfer had the opportunity to observe Japanese plants along the roadside. Lined with Japanese cryptomeria and camphor trees, pine, and fir, the roadway was defined by trees, which kept travelers from straying off it.

Nearly one hundred years later, in August 1775, Carl Pehr Thunberg, a Swedish physician, naturalist, and follower of Linnaeus, traveled to Japan. By this time Deshima Island was still the only port open to Westerners, and then only to ships of Dutch registry. Thunberg traveled from Nagasaki to Yedo and back again, and in the sixteen months he spent in Japan, collected approximately 1,000 species of plants. He described and named a number of lilies: *Lilium longifolium, L. speciosum, L. japonicum, L. maculatum.* His masterful work, *Flora Japonica,* was published in 1784 after his return, and forms the cornerstone of Japanese taxonomic botany. This work contains the first mention of such plants as

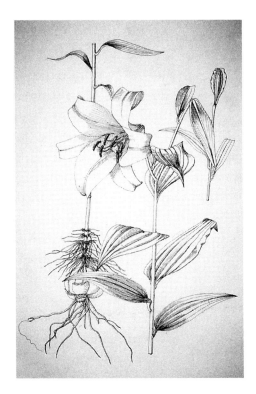

Lilium japonicum

both the single- and the double-flowered varieties of kerria. His herbarium collections, which are still held at Upsala, show the double 'floro pleno' as type specimen. (The "type" is a specimen that serves as the standard or criterion for application of the species name.) In recognition of his accomplishments, other botanists have named Japanese plants in his honor; *Arisaema thunbergii,* for example.

In addition to his treatise on plants, Thunberg wrote a popular, four-volume work entitled *Travels in Europe, Africa, and Asia, performed between the years 1770 and 1779.* The third volume describes his experiences in Japan. An English edition published in 1795 reveals an enthusiastic plantsman no different from today's botanists and horticulturists. While he intended to confine his remarks to plants that "exhibit some remarkable use in rural and domestic economy, and in the art of healing," he is also clearly intrigued by natural history. Hollyhocks are only one of the plants that engage his interest: "The *Alcea rosea* and the *Malva mauritiana* were frequently found cultivated in small gardens in the town for the sake of their large and elegant flowers." At Fakonie, on the return from Yedo, he was especially entranced by some of the roadside trees: "One of the handsomest and largest trees that I saw here, was the superb and incomparable *Thuja dolobrata,* which was planted everywhere by the roadside. I consider this tree as the handsomest of all the fir-leaved trees, on account of its height, its straight trunk, and its leaves which are constantly green on the upper, and of a silver-white hue on the under part." And, while traveling near Koijso or Odowara: "In our road we observed a pine tree (*Pinus sylvestris*) the branches of which were spread horizontally, and formed a vegetating cover over a summer-house, under which one might walk to and fro. I had seen several of these pines before at different places, but none by far so extensive as this. Its branches were twenty paces in length, and supported by several poles that were placed under them."

Thunberg was fascinated with Japanese gardens too. At Kokura he noted: "Here, as well as at all the other inns, we were lodged in the back part of the house, which is not only the most convenient, but the pleasantest part, having always an out-let and view into a backyard, larger or smaller, which is embellished with various trees, shrubs, plants, and flower-pots. At one side of this spot, there is also a small bath for strangers to bathe in, if they chuse [*sic*]. Amongst other things that were common in several places, such as the *Pinus sylvestris, Azalea indica, Chrysanthemum indicum,* &tc. I also found here a tree which is called Aukuba, and another called Nandina, both which were supposed to bring good fortune to the house." He later noted the prevalence of the azalea, writing in late May: "The *Azalea indica* stood in almost every yard and plot, near the houses, in its best attire, ineffably resplendent with flowers of different colours."

Confinement at Deshima must have been a hard check on Thunberg's horticultural ardor. It is anecdotally reported that he studied the hay supplied weekly for the animals on Deshima in order to expand his knowledge of Japanese plants. The authorities apparently took pity on this daft foreigner, for Thunberg noted in his journal: "February the 7th. Having been fortunate enough to receive from the governor a second time, his permission to botanize, I, for the first time, took a walk about the town of Nagasaki." He was accompanied by an extensive entourage consisting of several head and sub-interpreters, servants, purveyors, and others. He notes that they did not slow him down on these excursions up mountains and hills, but made his expeditions expensive: he was expected to revive his weary companions with drinks and snacks at one inn or another at the end of the day.

Thunberg's observations laid the framework for botanists who would follow him. He also saw the horticultural possibilities in the new plants: "For beauty nothing could excel the Maples indigenous to this country which are here and at other places found cultivated. They had but just then begun to put forth their blossoms; and, as I could no where get any of the ripe seed, I was obliged to bespeak some small plants in pots, which, with a great deal of trouble and expense, were forwarded to Nagasaki."

Any gardener will recognize the zeal, the acquisitive covetousness that afflicted Thunberg. I myself have been in similar circumstances as when Thunberg was in Osaka: "There was also a botanic garden tolerably well laid out in this town (though without an orangery) in which were reared and cultivated, and at the same time kept for sale, all sorts of plants, trees, and shrubs, which were brought hither from other provinces. I did not neglect to lay out as much money as I could spare, in the purchase of the scarcest shrubs and plants, planted in pots, amongst which were the most beautiful species of this country's elegant Maples, and two specimens of the *Cycas revoluta,* a Palm-tree, as scarce, as the exportation of it is strictly prohibited . . . These were afterwards all plant-ed out into a large wooden box, at the top of which were laid boughs of trees interlaced with packthread, so that nothing might injure them. This box was afterwards sent off by water to Nagasaki, from whence it was sent along with another box of the same kind, packed at the factory, to Batavia, to be forwarded to the *Hortus Medicus* in Amsterdam."

Kaempfer, Thunberg, and later von Siebold, were also interested in obtaining maps. By Thunberg's time the Japanese government specifi-cally prohibited foreigners from owning maps of the country. This was serious business, and a violation was tantamount to espionage. Not, of course, that this stopped either of them. Writing in his journal Thunberg reported: "Jedo, 1776 Maps of the country and towns are strictly prohib-ited from being exported, or sold to strangers. Nevertheless I had an opportunity to purchase several, exactly like those that KAEMPFER brought away with him (though with less trouble indeed) in his time." Next, he had to get the maps to Deshima. "Fiogo, 1776 Before we got quite to *Nagasaki* town, our chests were sealed, in order that they might pass on to the wharehouse [*sic*] without being searched." As it happened, his party and their baggage were searched but the scarce coins and maps, which he had procured "with great pains and difficulty" were not dis-covered. Thunberg was fortunate. Von Siebold was caught.

Philipp Franz Balthasar von Siebold was born on February 17, 1796, orphaned when young, and raised by his grandfather, a noted surgeon. Obtaining an M.D. degree from Heidelberg at the age of twenty-four, he practiced medicine briefly, and was then appointed court physician to King William I at The Hague. Shortly thereafter, he was appointed sur-geon-major to the Netherlands East-Indian Army, and barely a year later, on August 8, 1823, was in residence at the Deshima Island factory of the Dutch East India Company, where he promptly began to study both Japanese garden design and Japanese flora. Von Siebold gave lec-

tures on Western medicine and natural history to Japanese doctors and
scientists who, in turn, befriended him, taking him on botanical and zoo-
logical excursions in the city of Nagasaki and the surrounding country-
side, and giving him plants. He remained in Japan for six years, collecting in Nagasaki and its vicinity.

Since 1609 when the Dutch factory was founded, it had been the custom for the head of the trading mission to visit the shogun at Yedo annually. By von Siebold's time this visit was reduced to every four years. In
1826 he accompanied the Dutch resident on the mission paying homage
to the shogun. Some time later it became known that von Siebold had
obtained maps of Japan. He was accused of high treason, and deported
from the country. (It is interesting to learn that among the charts
Commodore Perry purchased in Holland in preparation for his expedition of 1853 were some brought from Japan by von Siebold.)

Upon his return to Europe in 1829 von Siebold had the misfortune to
disembark at Antwerp, where horticulture and world affairs suddenly
tangled as war broke out between Holland and Belgium. His shipment
of plants, intended for Leiden, was captured by the Belgians and confis-
cated. The plants ended up in Ghent, and thus today we know many historically important cultivars of azaleas as Ghent, not Leiden, azaleas.

Von Siebold took up residence outside the city of Leiden, where he
bought a small estate with a rather rustic country house and named it
"Nippon." Realizing the commercial potential for marketing the new
Japanese introductions, he formed the Society for the Introduction and
Cultivation of Japanese Plants, together with Karl Ludwig von Blume,
the director of the Rijksherbarium. In fifteen years of operation, aided by
government backing (and renamed the Royal Society for the Furtherance
of the Introduction of Japanese Plants), their organization imported more
than 3,000 plants of 733 species. Expenses were high, and many plants
shipped directly from Japan to Holland did not survive the rigors of the
five-month (or longer) voyage.

While Thunberg is known primarily for his descriptions of these new
plants, von Siebold actually introduced them to European gardens. It
was von Siebold, for example, who introduced the single-flowered kerria included in a shipment of 485 species of Japanese plants that arrived

in Europe in 1830. The Leiden Botanic Garden had an early lead on other botanical institutions. A catalog published in 1819 listing the botanic garden's living collections includes a number of Japanese plants still cultivated today: perennials such as *Acorus gramineus, Hosta caerulea, H. plantaginea, Ophiopogon japonicus,* and woody plants such as *Aucuba japonica, Cycas revoluta,* and *Kerria japonica.* Von Siebold's own herbarium specimens, collected while he was still in Japan, are today preserved in the Rijksherbarium.

Von Siebold co-authored several works about the flora of Japan: *Plantarum, quas in Japonica Collegit Dr. Ph. Fr. de Siebold, Genera Nova, Notis Characteristicis Delineationibusque Illustrata Proponunt* (1843), *Florae Japonicae Familiae Naturales* (1845–46), and Volume I of the *Flora Japonica* (1826–70) with Joseph Gerhard Zuccarini, a professor of botany. Friedrik Anton Willem Miquel was co-author of Volume II.

Von Siebold also operated a nursery, or *Jardin d'acclimatation,* where

Popular as grown in today's gardens, Lilium speciosum *was illustrated in Philipp von Siebold's* Flora Japonica, *published in the nineteenth century.* Illustration from the Library of the New York Botanical Garden.

he grew peonies, chrysanthemums, lilies, trees, and shrubs, selling Japanese plants throughout Europe. *Rosa multiflora,* one of his earlier introductions, was offered for sale in 1844. *Hydrangea paniculata* was introduced in 1856, and jetbead, *Rhodotypos scandens,* was introduced before 1860. Japanese maple, *Acer palmatum;* winter creeper, *Euonymus radicans;* and *Viburnum tomentosum* were introduced in the next two years, while Boston ivy, *Parthenocissus tricuspidata,* was introduced before 1867. About sixteen original specimens were still growing at the Leiden Botanic Garden in 1994. Included among these notable survivors are *Acer palmatum; Akebia quinata; Ampelopsis brevipedunculata;* a red-flowered *Chaenomeles speciosa;* loquat, *Eriobotrya japonica;* a Japanese walnut, *Juglans ailanthifolia; Rhaphiolepsis umbellata;* both *Wisteria floribunda* and *W. sinensis;* and *Zelkova serrata.* This particular plant of *W. sinensis* is believed to be the oldest specimen outside Japan.

Though known to horticulturists, nurserymen, and plant lovers, in modern times von Siebold became almost forgotten in the Netherlands. But this neglect was corrected on the four hundredth anniversary of the founding of the Leiden Botanic Garden when this remarkable man was paid tribute with the official opening of the von Siebold Memorial Garden. Designed by Professor Nakamura, the famous garden architect from the University of Kyoto, the garden was dedicated in September 1990 by the Japanese ambassador to Holland. Though it has been said that von Siebold was an impetuous, not always tactful, individual with an overbearing, despotic temperament, his accomplishments in the introduction of Japanese plants into European cultivation cannot be gainsaid.

BOTANISTS—AMERICAN AND EUROPEAN

American collection of Japanese plants began as early as Commodore Perry's expedition of 1852–54. Captain William Roberts accompanied that expedition and, according to the popular garden writer Elizabeth Lawrence, directly upon his return brought "the first red spider-lilies in North Carolina (and probably in this country)" to a garden in New Bern.

She goes on to say that his niece, Mrs. Simmons, said that the three bulbs were so dried out that they showed no growth until the War between the States broke out five years later. It is true that *Lycoris radiata,* in fact all species of *Lycoris,* are resentful of disturbance and often refuse to bloom or show top growth for a year or two after digging. However, the lengthy delay Miss Lawrence reports suggests more forceful travel fatigue than mere pique.

James Morrow, an agronomist and physician from South Carolina, collected at Shimoda, a harbor in the southern part of the Izu Peninsula, and at Hakodate in Hokkaido. He was in Japan with S. Wells Williams, both men attached to the Perry Expedition of 1852–54. Hot on their heels came Charles Wright and John Small, with the Ringold and Rodgers U.S. North Pacific Exploring Expedition of 1853–56. The work of these two voyages was important, as it formed a basis for Asa Gray's report, which later led to his theory on the relationship between the floras of Japan and eastern North America.

Various foreign settlements developed after Japan's reopening to the West. A young American doctor-turned-trader living in Yokohama, George Rogers Hall, followed in the footsteps of Kaempfer and Thunberg, and introduced to America Japanese wisteria, several magnolias, and hills-of-snow hydrangea, *Hydrangea paniculata grandiflora,* among other plants. A number of ornamental plants were named in his honor: a crabapple, a variety of Japanese honeysuckle, and Hall's amaryllis, *Lycoris squamigera* (= *Amaryllis hallii*)*,* which he introduced into cultivation. Upon his return home in 1862, most of his plants were deposited in Parsons Brothers Nursery in Flushing, New York. Two years later he planted many Japanese evergreens—at the time quite rare—in his personal garden in Bristol, Rhode Island.

Yet another American, the botanist Charles Sprague Sargent, collected in various parts of Japan in 1892. Primarily interested in woody plants, Sargent discussed the results of his study in his 1894 work, *Forest Flora of Japan.*

Meanwhile, a Russian botanist, Carl Johann Maximowicz, who was in charge of the imperial gardens at Petrograd, went to Japan, reaching Hakodate in September 1860. The Japanese authorities gave him permission to botanize within twenty miles of that city, where he remained for about fourteen months, sending about 800 herbarium specimens, many bulbs, and 250 kinds of seed back to Petrograd. Less than a week into 1862 he traveled to Nagasaki, where he became friends with von Siebold. In the two years following he collected assiduously in the area, as well as in Yokohama. Returning to Petrograd in July, Maximowicz brought with him 72 chests of herbarium specimens, 300 kinds of seeds, and 400 living plants, among which were numerous hydrangeas. The collection of specimens preserved as herbarium sheets, and live material in the form of seeds and bulbs was typical of that period; it was an uncommon achievement to successfully bring living plants through the rigors of a lengthy ocean voyage. Maximowicz introduced hydrangeas to St. Petersburg and in 1867 published the first scientific monograph on that genus, revising its classification and reducing the number of species von Siebold had described. Tschonoski Sugawa, his assistant during his

Collected during Commodore Perry's expedition to Japan, this herbarium specimen of Arisaema thunbergii *var.* urashima *is identified in elegant penmanship in the lower-right corner.* Illustration courtesy of the Herbarium of the New York Botanical Garden.

stay in Japan, continued to send plants to Maximowicz after his departure, as did several leading Japanese botanists of that period.

The U.S. National Herbarium holds a small number (less than fifty) of Maximowicz isotype/syntype material. (Isotype refers to a "type" specimen collected from the same site as the original; syntype to a "type" specimen collected at a different site.) This is still probably more than any other New World herbarium. The collection includes both woody and herbaceous material: *Acer maximowiczianum,* collected at Higo, Nagayama, in 1863; *Thuja japonica,* collected in 1862, with a notation *"vidi cultam in urbe Yedo,"* or "I saw [it] in cultivation in the city of Yedo." He collected one of my favorite perennials, *Deinanthe bifida,* in 1863, and described it in the *Memoirs of the Academy of Imperial Science of Saint-Petersbourg* four years later. Maximowicz's name has been immortalized with plants named in his honor, among them the monarch birch, *Betula maximowicziana.*

Robert Fortune, a nineteenth-century Scottish botanist who trained at Edinburgh's botanical garden, was superintendent of the hothouses at the Royal Horticultural Society's gardens at Chiswick and later curator of the Chelsea Physic Garden. Best known for his travels to China, Fortune's last voyage in 1860–62 included a visit to Japan. Though still restricted by a treaty limiting travel to ten ri, or about twenty-four miles, in any direction, he managed to amass a huge plant collection, sending specimens back to Kew. Fortune was one of the first to employ Wardian cases, glassed boxes that made it easier to bring plants back alive. One of his most notable discoveries, found in the Yokohama garden of George Hall, was the male form of *Aucuba japonica.* This shrub is dioecious: each individual plant is either male or female. Those previously introduced to European gardens were female and never produced an autumnal display of red berries. With Fortune's find and the introduction of male pollinating shrubs, *A. japonica* gained additional horticultural merit beyond its attractive foliage. He also brought to England the larger, shaggy-flowered hybrid chrysanthemums. The popular evergreen vining ground cover, *Euonymous fortunei,* is named in his honor. Another British horticulturist, James Gould Veitch, traveled in Japan from 1859 to 1862. *Abies veitchii* is named for him.

Though, like Fortune, better known for his travels to China, E. H. "Chinese" Wilson, visited Japan in 1914. He journeyed to the Far East under the auspices of the Arnold Arboretum of Harvard University. Wilson rediscovered *Hydrangea macrophylla,* which had been first discovered in 1880 by Charles Maries and introduced to the United States from England.

In December 1901 the American botanist David Fairchild made a brief visit to Japan, returning the following April for a longer stay. He sent back bamboos, cherries, even a turf of *shiba*, a Japanese carpet grass, *Zoysia matrella*, which became popular as a fine velvety lawn grass in Florida. His fondness for Japanese flowering cherries was personal as well as professional: in 1905 when he and his wife bought a property in Chevy Chase, Maryland, one of their goals was to grow these trees. *Sakura-no,* fields of cherries, and *sakura-michi,* cherry path, were made part of the developing landscape. Later, as head of the United States Department of Agriculture's Division of Plant Exploration and Introduction, he was instrumental in the introduction of ornamental cherries and their planting along the Potomac Speedway in Washington, D.C. The first lot of trees arrived early in January 1910 and were discovered to be infested with three different insect pests. All two thousand trees were burned. In March 1912 a second shipment arrived, made up of three thousand trees carefully raised in fresh soil and repeatedly fumigated. In return, several hundred flowering dogwood trees and some mountain laurel were presented to the city of Tokyo.

Exploration, study, and plant introduction continue to the present day. Dr. John Creech has led nine major plant expeditions—to southern Japan and Yakushima in 1956 and again in 1976, to Japan and Hong Kong in 1961, along the Japan Sea coast in 1978, as well as to Nepal, Taiwan, and the former Soviet Union. Creech began his explorations in 1955 with an expedition to Japan and Okinawa. At that time he had already spent eight years with the United States Department of Agriculture's Office of Plant Exploration, which sponsored the expedition. Some later trips were undertaken in cooperation with Longwood Gardens; the 1976 expedition, and those that followed, were made under the auspices of the National Arboretum. Others who investigated

Japanese plants for the National Arboretum Cooperative Explorations, either with Dr. Creech or on separate journeys, include Sylvester (Skip) March, W. L. Ackerman, F. G. Meyer, R. Jefferson, and M. Kawase.

Once a plant has been obtained, either collected in the wild or purchased at a nursery, the delicate task remains of bringing it back alive to a distant country. The most secure way to collect plants, easily transport them, and ensure their survival is to obtain seeds. However, when a plant is a cultivated variety, perhaps with variegated leaves, selected flower form or color, or a unique habit of growth, then at least a piece of the actual specimen is needed for propagation. The arduous labor of plant collection has been eased somewhat by modern technology. Less bulky, and far less fragile than a Wardian case, plastic bags have revolutionized the procedure for taking cuttings. If an entire plant is to be collected, the roots are washed free of soil and then wrapped in barely damp sphagnum moss. A plastic bag keeps the plant from drying out. Additionally, air travel is a more rapid means of transit than the slow sailing ships that von Siebold or Maximowicz were forced to rely upon. Creech often would send plants through the U.S. Embassy directly to the USDA quarantine center in Beltsville, Maryland.

Among the literally hundreds of plants that Creech has helped introduce to the United States are the crape-myrtle, *Lagerstromia fauriei,* from Yakushima. It has beautiful cinnamon-red bark and a genetic resistance to powdery mildew that has been passed on to seventeen select hybrid offspring. From the Yatsugatake Mountains near Nagano, Creech collected seed of Japanese white birch, *Betula platyphylla* var. *japonica.* It was later discovered that the trees raised from that seed have an astonishing tolerance for heat and humidity, even growing well in Florida, an area not noted for its hospitality to birches. Additionally, this birch is resistant to bronze birch borer. Today, you might find it in nurseries as a registered selection named 'Whitespire.' The tiny-leaved creeping fig, *Ficus pumila,* that Creech collected from Shikoku is now a familiar and popular houseplant often used for indoor topiary. *Deutzia gracilis* 'Nikko' is a charming dwarf shrub, and another of his introductions.

Grasses, grasslike plants, and herbaceous perennials from Japan are also available for our gardens as a result of Creech's collections. Japanese sedgegrass, *Carex morrowii* var. *expallida,* had been previously introduced in the 1800s. It was considered tender and grown in conservatories. Discovering it anew in the low wooded mountains of Honshu on his first trip, Creech found a form that is hardy from zones 5 through 9. Now the narrow, gracefully arched, evergreen foliage, delicately striped in green and creamy white, can be enjoyed outdoors in a shady garden or indoors as a houseplant.

Japanese blood grass, *Imperata cylindrica* 'Rubra' was found at the Aichi Prefecture Agricultural High School in Nagoya; *Miscanthus sinensis* 'Morning Light' was observed in the private garden of Masato Yokoi in 1976. In 1982 Creech visited the Kogoara Cooperative Nursery Bonsai Center in Angyo and found *Ajania pacifica* (= *Chrysanthemum pacificum*) grown there as a companion plant for bonsai. It is now cultivated here in gardens. One 1955 find still waiting for public discovery in the West is an orange-red daylily, *Hemerocallis aurantiaca* var. *littorea,* that Creech found blooming in late October on the face of sea cliffs at Ashizuri-zaki, on the southern tip of Shikoku. However, most daylily hybridizers are working on the foundation built by Dr. Arlow Burdette Stout of the New York Botanical Garden in the 1930s, 1940s, and 1950s, using *H. fulva, H. aurantiaca, H. dumortierii, H. middendorffi,* and *H. thunbergii,* among others.

Gardeners' interest in new plants of ornamental value is still as keen as it was when Kaempfer and Thunberg saw the horticultural riches of Japan in the seventeenth and eighteenth centuries. Enthusiasts in the North American Rock Garden Society grow a wide diversity of plants, not merely alpines. Beautiful woodland plants such as Japanese arisaema and *Glaucidium palmatum* are raised from seed, disseminated at plant sales, and seen by garden visitors. Word gets around. Perhaps first exchanged on an individual basis between friends, gradually these plants seep into the commercial horticultural trade and become available from specialty nurseries and later from general mail-order or local sources.

CHAPTER THREE

Trees

Trees are the framework of a garden, providing a backdrop for the room outdoors just as walls define indoor rooms. Of the trees that ornament American gardens large and small, an extraordinary number (such as flowering cherries, magnolias, Japanese maples, and bamboo) originated in Japan. Given the diverse flora of the different islands that form Japan, there are plants for all gardens, regardless of how unpromising local conditions might appear. Those from Japan's main islands and northward are suitable for growing conditions in the Northeast and the northern tier of states, while gardeners in the South and Southeast find appropriate plants in the southern islands of Kyushu and Yakushima, and along the coastal areas of Honshu bordering the inland sea. Even the Mediterranean climate of southern California, with its dry summers and winter rainfall, will be suitable for selected Japanese plants, though the heavy soil requires substantial amendment.

Some Japanese trees are so familiar that we have come to think of their origin as the local garden center. Understanding their natural habitat may suggest design possibilities and effective techniques for cultivation.

DECIDUOUS TREES FOR FLOWER AND FOLIAGE

MAPLES

Japanese maple, *Acer palmatum,* is a superb small tree with numerous cultivars developed and selected from the variable forms found in the wild by both Japanese and Western horticulturists. To the Japanese, this maple is a very meaningful tree as it signals seasonal changes. Spring is noted by the tender growth of unfolding buds and new red leaves, which turn green in summer and then red once again in autumn, usually late October to mid-November in Japan. Rather common and frequently planted in gardens in Japan and abroad, *A. palmatum* is native to the woods and thickets of the lowlands and mountains of Honshu, Shikoku, and Kyushu, as well as Korea. The trees can be respectably long-lived: Sometime between 1860 and 1862 a specimen was obtained from von Siebold by the Leiden Botanic Garden; more than 130 years later it has grown to 16 feet tall, and is among the original von Siebold plants still extant in the garden. Conversely, twenty-year-old Japanese maples in the Cleveland, Ohio, area died in the frigid, stormy winter of 1993–94. Consider Japanese maples useful in zones 5 to 9, but gardeners at the extremes of this range should look for particularly cold- or heat-tolerant clones.

There are forms of *Acer palmatum* with green leaves, which may have reddish margins; others have purple-red leaves, or purple leaves that fade to a dark somber green. Some have variegated leaves with white, cream, or pink markings. Leaves may have 5 to 7 lobes, 7 to 9 lobes cleft halfway, or 7 or sometimes 9 lobes, deeply divided almost to the base. There are dozens of cultivars.

One cultivar frequently offered at nurseries is 'Atropurpureum', which is 24 to 30 feet tall at maturity, with 5-lobed leaves that are a rich purple in spring, becoming darker in summer, and turning vivid scarlet in autumn. Unfortunately the name has been applied to various clones and plants raised from seed so inevitably there will be differences between one 'Atropurpureum' and the next. Another readily available cultivar is 'Bloodgood', with deep, dark burgundy-red leaf color that does not change from spring through autumn. 'Fireglow' is an improved form of 'Bloodgood', with an upright, well-branched habit and similarly rich purple-red leaf color. 'Moonfire' has a somber purple hue in summer, and turns fiery red in autumn. Possibly the best cultivar for autumn color is 'Osakazuki', as it holds its leaves for two weeks, sometimes longer, after they turn from summer's bright green to autumn's brilliant red.

There are cultivars with exotic, unusual, variegated foliage: 'Butterfly' is a small, densely branched, primly upright tree, about 10 feet tall, with small, 5-lobed, soft bluish-green leaves edged with silvery white. In autumn the white portions of the leaf turn scarlet-magenta. You'll either love 'Butterfly' or find it most peculiar. Another variegated cultivar, among the best, is 'Oridoro Nishiki'. Nearly all its leaves are variegated to some extent, and some are entirely pink or white. It grows rather quickly to a mature height of 18 feet. Variegated maples are useful in zone 6 and south.

Those *Acer palmatum* cultivars with a mushroom-shaped form, growing as shrubs about 12 feet tall and often as wide or wider, are grouped separately. Their 7-lobed leaves have a lacy appearance. Some have green leaves, others purple-red or brownish leaves. Cascading, cutleaf forms include 'Burgundy Lace', with finely divided, burgundy-purple leaves; 'Crimson Queen' with dark purple-red leaves turning reddish purple in autumn; 'Dissectum' (described by Thunberg in 1784) with a truly elegant mushroom form, muscular and gnarly branches, and deeply cut, fernlike, soft green leaves that turn yellow in autumn; and 'Dissectum Atropurpureum' (= 'Ornatum'), whose dark purple leaves become dark green flushed with red in summer, and turn an intense golden yellow in autumn; and finally the self-descriptive 'Garnet', which has good strong color. Careful placement at the top of a wall or on a bank can

accentuate the beauty of these cascading maples.

Japanese maples lend winter interest to the garden with their handsome branching frame. This is accentuated in 'Beni Kawa', a cultivar with distinctive bark—the young twigs and branches are a brilliant shrimp-pink in winter and early spring. Autumn leaf color is a clear yellow. 'Sangokaku' is similar.

Full-moon maple, *Acer japonicum,* is a common component of woods and thickets of the mountains on Honshu and Hokkaido. A counterpart of our native vine maple, *A. circinatum* of the Pacific Northwest, this species is frequently planted in Japanese gardens and has many cultivars. Some, such as 'Aconitifolium', have delicate fernlike leaves; others, such as 'Attaryi' have large, deeply cleft leaves 6 to 10 inches across. Those with an upright habit slowly grow to 20 feet high or more. Others, such as 'Green Cascade', have a weeping, mushroom form. Both 'Aconitifolium' and 'Green Cascade' have striking autumn color, turning scarlet and orange with touches of yellow or purplish red. All are hardy in zones 5 and 6.

Taxonomists have been up to their revisionist activities, and in 1984 several *Acer japonicum* cultivars, including 'Aureum', were reassigned to *A. shirasawanum*. This change is making its way into the trade. *Acer shirasawanum* is native to the mountains of Honshu and Shikoku, and is denser in appearance than *A. japonicum* with which it is often confused. Growing about 45 feet tall in the wild, perhaps half as tall in cultivation, *A. shirasawanum* often spreads wider than high to form a well-branched, shrubby-looking tree. The handsome, rounded leaves are large, up to 4 inches in diameter, shallowly lobed with 9, 10, or 11 palmate divisions. Autumn leaf color is a rich buttery yellow.

Trident, or three-toothed, maple, *Acer buergerianum,* is another of the puzzling plants possibly brought over from eastern China (where it is very common) and naturalized in Japan. Often growing as a multistemmed large shrub with a loose, open habit, this small tree reaches 30 feet tall at maturity. In autumn the leaves first turn from green to olive-green, frequently mixed with scarlet, and then turn a lovely yellow-orange. Exfoliating bark results in a pleasing display of rich brown, gold, and orange that is especially attractive in winter. Suitable for zones 6 to 8, this species is more tolerant of semidry conditions than other Japanese maples. Trident maple would be a good choice for city gardens, perhaps as a specimen in a townhouse courtyard. In his personal garden in Marietta, Georgia, landscaper and horticulturist Ozzie Johnson grows 'Mitsuba kaede nishikisiyou', a densely branched shrubby tree with 3-lobed, T-shaped leaves, and fissured, corky bark.

Amur maple, *Acer ginnala,* was first described by Maximowicz in 1857. As sug-

gested by its natural distribution in wetlands of Hokkaido, Honshu, Shikoku, and Kyushu, as well as Korea, Manchuria, and eastern Siberia, it is hardy to zones 3 and 4. A shrub or multistemmed small tree about 20 feet tall and equally wide-spreading, *A. ginnala* has pleasantly fragrant flowers, unusual in maples. Leaves turn vivid shades of red and orange in autumn, with some clones coloring better than others. However, they drop fairly soon afterward. Some seedlings of this species nearly always display white or pinkish leaf variegation. The clone 'Albo-variegatum' also exhibits this trait.

Redvein maple, *Acer rufinerve,* is commonly found inhabiting woods and thickets in mountains of Honshu, Shikoku, and Kyushu, and has an analogue in the moosewood maple, *A. pensylvanicum* of the eastern United States. The Japanese species is useful in zones 6 to 8. Growing about 30 feet tall, this so-called snakebark maple has green to silvery green bark on its branches, distinctively and handsomely striped with white. Thickish, dark green, 3-lobed leaves are paler underneath, with red-orange to orange-yellow autumn color. There is a variegated cultivar, 'Hatsuyuki kaede' (= 'Albo-limbatum'), with conspicuous white variegations, especially along the leaf margins. While some leaves remain entirely green, others are freckled with white. However, the bark on 'Hatsuyuki kaede' is not as strongly striped.

Acer sieboldianum is closely related to the Japanese maple, *A. palmatum,* and might also be confused with small-leaved forms of *A. japonicum* (its Japanese name is *ko-hauchiwa-kaede,* meaning "small-leaved form"). *A. sieboldianum* is found in the woods and thickets of the mountains of Hokkaido, Honshu, Shikoku, and Kyushu. In the more northern portions of its range this maple is found growing from sea level to 3,000 feet in more open, moister sites. As might be anticipated, this is one of the hardiest maples, thriving in zone 4 and even growing well in zone 3. *Acer sieboldianum* is grown in Scandinavia where cultivars of *A. palmatum* cannot survive, suggesting its potential usefulness in Maine or Minnesota. Frequently growing as a 10-foot tall, multistemmed shrubby tree, it may be trained as a single-trunked tree reaching 25 feet high. The glossy, dark green, rounded leaves are palmately lobed, sometimes deeply, 7 to 11 times. They turn from copper-red through brilliant scarlet to a darker, polished red in autumn. In his *Flora of Japan,* Jisaburo Owhi notes that many cultivars are grown in Japanese gardens; however, these cultivars are not readily available in the United States or Europe. 'Sode No Uchi' is a very dwarf form with tiny leaves, suitable for rock garden, container, or bonsai use. It is sometimes available from specialty nurseries.

Maples, found predominately in the temperate regions of the Northern Hemisphere, North America, and Eurasia, range from small shrubs to majestic forest giants. While different species of maples may overlap in their natural range, they do not hybridize with each other. Thus, in Japan, three or four different species may grow intermingled in small groves. This suggests a garden that includes several of the smaller maples, each chosen for its own special attributes yet still following a naturalistic design style based on plant communities.

In Japan full-moon maple and Japanese maple create a fiery scarlet display, a perfect counterpart to the blaze of vine maples in Oregon and Washington, and sugar and swamp maples in New England. Perhaps the most noteworthy garden attribute of maples is their stunning autumn foliage. The visual effect will be heightened if the trees are planted so that autumn sun can shine through the leaves, illuminating them like a stained glass window. The result of warm sunny days and cool nights, these red, orange, and purple hues will not be produced if trees are shaded, nights are mild, or skies are consistently overcast. Yellow leaves will occur in sun or shade, regardless of autumn weather. *Acer palmatum* 'Osakazuki' is said to produce splendid red color reliably in late October even in the mild climate of England, as long as it is planted in a sunny site.

Wherever Japanese maples can be grown, they are a popular addition to both public and private gardens. In the Netherlands there is a specialized arboretum just for maples, the Esveld Aceretum in Boskoop, with an extensive collection of *Acer palmatum, A. japonicum, A. shirasawanum* cultivars, and more. Japanese maples are well-adapted to the benign climate of the Pacific Northwest. At the University of California Botanical Garden in Berkeley, Japanese species of maples grow well if the site is first amended with copious amounts of organic matter to correct the often poor drainage typical of the heavy clay soil. Elaine Sedlack, curator of the Asian collection, finds that *A. palmatum* and *A. ginnala* color well, even in the mild California climate, and *A. pseudosieboldianum* is showing great promise, hardy and with red autumn color even when planted in shade.

When planting Japanese maples remember that drought can be a problem, severely stressing these trees. It can mean the beginning of die-back and perhaps eventual demise. Also avoid planting in a frost pocket. Late frosts after trees have begun to break dormancy can be a serious problem, damaging tender buds. Always handle maples with care since they tend to be bleeders: their thin bark is easily damaged and sap can leak for a long time, attracting insect pests and allowing entry to disease. In the Northeast it is preferable to plant maples in spring before their buds begin to unfold. In southern gardens, fall

planting avoids summer heat stress in the critical period after planting. As with any plant, consider mature size and allow ample room for the trees to grow. Small bulbs lend color to the maples in spring, and ferns, epimedium, and hosta create a pleasing carpet beneath in summer. Japanese maples look magnificent at the edge of a woodland, where canopy trees protect them from the strong midday sun in summer, yet allow sufficient light to reach them in autumn to produce a colorful foliage display.

MIMOSA

Why grow silk tree or mimosa, *Albizzia julibrissin,* a short-lived tree that needs cosseting? Mimosa's unique tropical-looking pink powderpuff flowers remain attractive for a month or more. Keep in mind that mimosa is a messy tree; it is also rather scraggly and brittle, subject to wind damage and susceptible to mimosa wilt, a serious disease, and (in some areas) leaf-damaging mimosa webworm. In northern areas mimosa dies to the ground in severe winters. Trees grow 18 feet high with a wider canopy. The fine textured, bipinnate foliage creates airy, open shade and drops early in autumn. In Japan mimosa grows in lowland forests and along riverbanks in Honshu, Shikoku, and Kyushu, where it is very common. Trees are also found in Southeast Asia as far west as Iran. South of Washington, D.C., mimosa self-sows into

Albizza julibrissin

empty lots and along roadsides, naturalizing and becoming something of a pest. It is hardy from zones 6 to 9; flowering occurs in mid- to late summer in the North, early to midsummer in southern regions. Native to moist soils, mimosa will grow even on dry sites as long as they are also sunny.

Bamboo

Bamboo is a diverse category. There are tall bamboos with the stature of trees, and dwarfs suitable as ground cover. Some are well-behaved while others are rampageous invaders spreading far and wide. In general, spreading, or running, bamboos are hardiest, while clump-forming species are more vulnerable to winter cold. What all of these woody grasses have in common is a buoyant quality, responding to the lightest breeze with a satisfying susurrus; an airy Oriental character that has been the subject of countless poems and paintings. Their form contrasts beautifully to broadleaved evergreen shrubs, tall conifers, and herbaceous perennials. Where hardy, and where containable, bamboos belong in the garden. Which bamboo is the question. Catalogs may be a step or two behind those taxonomists who are scurrying to revise the tangled thicket of bamboo nomenclature.

Simon bamboo, *Pleioblastus simonii* (= *Arundinaria simonii*), is a beautiful, stately species that grows as high as 25 feet. Useful in gardens, it is spontaneous in the southern Kanto district of Honshu and westward, as well as in Shikoku and Kyushu. Suitable for zones 8 and 9, and the warmer portions of zone 7, this running bamboo could be used as a hedge or screen. In large gardens it functions as a specimen, and in such settings the graceful arch of the outermost culms (the term *culm* refers to the stem of any member of the Grass family) can better be appreciated. The leaves, 4 to 12 inches long and from less than ½ inch to almost 1½ inches wide, create a bold, coarse texture. Sometimes variegated when they first appear, leaves mature to a medium bright green. There is a less robust variegated form, *variegatus,* with some white-striped leaves throughout the growing season. The same plant will have both solid green and variegated leaves.

Blackstem bamboo, *Phyllostachys nigra,* has been extensively cultivated in Japan for centuries but is native to China. The slender culms, 15 to 25 feet tall, are green their first year, become speckled, and mature to deep purple-black. The contrast with graceful, rich evergreen leaves is splendid. An elegant planting in Seattle set blackstem bamboo and wind-combed grass, *Hakonechloa macra* 'Aureola', against the backdrop of the cashew-colored stucco of a building, with large pebbles of the same color as ground mulch. The effect was superb. *P. nigra* is also prominent in the Atlanta Botanical Garden's Japanese garden. Hardy only in zones 7 and 8, it can be cultivated as an indoor plant and can reach 9 to 10 feet tall.

Narihira bamboo, *Semiarundinaria fastuosa,* is a moderately well-behaved species from Honshu's central and westward districts, Shikoku, and Kyushu. Hardy to zone 6 and growing to 25 feet tall, this running bamboo forms an erect, slowly spreading clump. Young culms are dark green streaked with a purplish brown, maturing to yellow-brown. The shiny, dark green leaves are coarse in texture, up to 7 inches long and an inch wide.

Other bamboos are discussed as ground covers in chapter 5.

Japanese Dogwood

Japanese dogwood, *Cornus kousa,* is commonly found in mountainous areas of its native range on Honshu, Shikoku, and Kyushu, as well as Korea and China. Hardy in zones 5 to 7, it is very popular in North American gardens for a number of reasons. Japanese dogwood comes into bloom in June, a couple of weeks later than our flowering dogwood, with petal-like white bracts tapering to a sharp point. If the nights are very cool when the trees are in flower, a pinkish tint may develop. Growing naturally as an oversized, multi-trunked shrub, it can be trained as a single-stemmed, more treelike specimen. Older plants have attractive, exfoliating bark. The fruits resemble dull-red warty cherries and I find self-sown seedlings on a somewhat regular basis. Planting more than one clone will not only increase fruit production, but also the likelihood of viable seed production. Most important, Japanese dogwood is resistant to the anthracnose leaf disease and bark borer that are seriously damaging our native flowering dogwood, *C. florida* of the eastern United States. Autumn leaf color is dull to bright red. At the University of California Botanic Garden in Berkeley, Japanese dogwood is a showstopper. A thirty-year-old specimen, beautifully sited above a pool, is very much loved by visitors in spring when in flower, and in autumn for its leaf color. In Japan, *amerika-yamaboshi,* flowering dogwood, *C. florida,* is sometimes planted in gardens and parks.

Giant dogwood, *Cornus controversa,* is native to the mountains of Japan, as well as Korea and China. Hardy in zones 6 to 8, this is the East Asian counterpart of our Western native, the pagoda dogwood, *C. alternifolia*. Growing 35 to 50 feet tall, in time spreading 50 to 65 feet wide, giant dogwood has distinctive, strongly layered, horizontal tiers of branches. Small white flowers in large, flattened clusters appear in late spring, followed in autumn by large flat clusters of blue-black fruits. A marvelous clone, 'Variegata', or wedding cake tree, has narrow leaves, irregularly marked with ivory-white margins. Even at a young age this clone has a striking ornamental appearance.

GINKGO

Ginkgo, or maidenhair tree, *Ginkgo biloba,* was widely distributed 180 million years ago. Older than stone age, positively Jurassic, this relic plant is known only in cultivation. Discovered by Kaempfer in Japan, ginkgo was introduced into European cultivation at the Botanic Garden of Utrecht sometime around 1727 and into the United States in 1784 by William Hamilton, who planted it in his garden at Woodlawn, near Philadelphia. The name *ginkgo* is Kaempfer's rendering of the Chinese characters for *yin-kuo,* silver nut or silver apricot. In Japan ginkgo is often associated with Shinto shrines. The trees are remarkably free of disease and insect problems, are sturdy in growth, and hardly ever need any pruning. The ginkgo is tolerant of pollution and makes an excellent urban street tree. Growing to a stately 130 feet tall, ginkgos have gray, furrowed bark, with arching older branches, and a narrow crown, widening at maturity. In winter the trees have a very distinctive, spare, open growth habit accentuated by the small spur-like side shoots. The tough leaves look like small fans, each one exactly like an individual pinnule of a maidenhair fern. Often they are notched or cleft at the apex. In autumn the leaves turn a brilliant, glowing yellow, falling to create a sunny pool at the base of the tree.

This tree is dioecious, with separate individuals either male or female. The male is generally cultivated, since the lovely, cherrylike, blush-yellow fruits about 1 inch or more in diameter that are borne on female trees give off a smell like vomit when they ripen and fall to the pavement. When I was a child the falling fruit of a female tree at the corner of our street compelled me to cross to the other side in autumn. Trees in the parking lot at the New York Botanical Garden are female, and local residents of Asian descent often gather the fruit, for medicinal use I was told. My friend Nihei Takeo is very fond of the nuts. Here is his advice for their preparation: "Gather the fruits in quantity and put them in a pail of water. While wearing rubber gloves, wash and rub off the odd-smelling peel. [The pulp contains a vesicant that produces blisters and can cause skin peeling.] Dry the nuts, which can be stored for two or three months. Keep them longer and the inside meat shrinks and becomes inedible. The easiest way to break the shell, my wife tells me, is to microwave the nuts. Their shells will burst and the meat can easily be removed. You can eat the nutritious nutmeats as is, and they are also an essential ingredient of *chawan-mushi* [a thick custard soup]."

I questioned him about possible side effects, having read an article by Peter Del Tredici in *Arnoldia* that raises such concerns. Nihei-san wrote back, "We do not consider it toxic but people do say not to eat too many as they will give a blood rush to your head. I sometimes eat as many as twenty parched nuts when drinking beer."

MAGNOLIA
Among the magnolias may be found trees for small city gardens, and others for spacious parks and grand estates. Some species are readily available; others await wider nursery distribution.

There is some controversy about the native range of star magnolia, *Magnolia stellata*. Some floras declare it to be Japanese,

others contend it is Chinese. Whatever its origins, this dainty multitrunked shrubby tree is popular wherever it is grown and is hardy from zones 5 to 9. Found in the wild in open, sunny sites on hillsides and in wet, even swampy conditions, its location in the garden should be similarly sunny. Although star magnolia tolerates some shade, flowering will be reduced and the tree will not be as vigorous. Average soil moisture is fine; simply be sure to water if natural rainfall is meager. At maturity star magnolia reaches a height of 5 to 15 feet, with a similar spread.

Star magnolias flower at a very early age, often after only a year or two, bearing numerous fragrant, white or pink-tinged or clear rose-pink flowers, each with 12 to 18 ribbonlike tepals (petals and petal-like sepals), in early spring. I find their form preferable to the larger blossoms of saucer magnolia, for when star magnolia's narrow tepals turn brown and drop, they are not so obviously apparent. In early December 1994, when milder weather followed a cool spell, I saw star magnolias with a few scattered flowers at the New York Botanical Garden. Naturally, whatever blooms appear in fall will correspondingly reduce the display the following spring. This is the case at the University of California Botanical Garden in Berkeley, where Elaine Sedlack finds that star magnolias are invariably fooled by the cool summers of the Bay Area into thinking they have already been through winter.

If you happen to bruise star magnolia's shallow roots while digging around the tree, you'll discover they have an attractive spicy scent. It is safer to mulch or use a ground cover, as digging and subsequent damage will harm the roots. Since they flower early before the leaves appear, companion planting with an evergreen ground cover such as running myrtle, *Vinca minor,* is quite attractive. Massing little bulbs such as snowdrops, spring snowflake, scilla, or glory-of-the-snow amidst the ground cover adds to the early display. Sweeping lower branches trail to the ground, accentuating the shrublike appearance. Such branches will often root where they are in contact with the soil, producing layers that can be cut and planted elsewhere in the garden.

Star magnolia suits any garden. The silver-gray bark and somewhat twisted, compact form are attractive in winter. Individual specimens can supply a formal note, set in a terrace bed edged with a clipped hedge and a precise evergreen ground cover of ivy. Conversely, a single star magnolia can grace the edge of an informal woodland garden. Massed, perhaps on a gentle slope, they add a graceful winter appearance and early spring flowers to the landscape.

Taxonomic revisions have recently shifted this lovely small tree from its own species to *Magnolia kobus* var. *stellata*. It differs from *M. kobus* in having a shrubbier,

smaller growth habit and in having a greater number of petaloid tepals. The type specimen collected by von Siebold is in the Rijksherbarium in Leiden. Political complications obstructing foreign trade frustrated von Siebold's several attempts to introduce star magnolia to the West. It was brought to the United States by Dr. George Rogers Hall in 1862, along with other plants from Japan, and given to Samuel Parsons, a Long Island nurseryman.

Kobus magnolia, *Magnolia kobus,* is fairly common in the thickets, forested hills, and mountain foothills of Hokkaido, Honshu, Shikoku, and Kyushu. Reasonably cold-hardy and adaptable to different situations, kobus magnolia can be grown in zones 5 to 9. Variable in size, at maturity it can reach a height of 25 to 65 feet, sometimes forming a fairly dense canopy. The 4-inch white flowers, often stained with a deep rose-purple at their centers, appear in March or April. Usually there are 9 to 12 tepals, contrasting with up to 33 for star magnolia. The silver-gray, smooth bark and prominent, silver-haired buds lend interest to the winter landscape. Kaempfer, Thunberg, von Siebold, and Zuccarini all mention this species. Like star magnolia, it was brought to this country by Dr. Hall and introduced by Parsons Brothers Nursery on Long Island. Though *M. kobus* seed germinates readily, such seedling trees will not flower until ten, twenty, or even thirty years old. Grafted plants or those raised from cuttings may take a decade before blooming. For this reason, early flowering *M. kobus* var. *loebneri,* a hybrid between *Magnolia kobus* var. *kobus* and var. *stellata,* is more popular. Flowers open from March to May, vary in color from white to pink, have 11 to 16 tepals, and are 4 to 6 inches in diameter. Intermediate in size between its two parents, the plant can range from a multistemmed large shrub to a single-trunked tree reaching 25 feet tall. Popular cultivars include fragrant 'Ballerina' with 30 or more pink tepals; compact, almost dwarf 'Encore' with an extended period of bloom; unusual 'Leonard Messel' with dark purple flower buds that open to dark pink-purple flowers with white insides; and 30-foot-tall, whiteflowered 'Merrill' ('Dr. Merrill').

Japanese willow-leaf magnolia, or anise magnolia, *Magnolia salicifolia,* is found growing along streams or in similarly moist areas in the mountainous forests of Honshu, primarily on the Japan Sea side, and Kyushu at elevations of 1,650 to 4,400 feet. It is hardy from zones 5 to 9. A deciduous, slender-branched, large shrub or small tree, anise magnolia grows 30 to 50 feet tall. Even relatively young trees bear fragrant white flowers up to 4 inches across in early to midspring. This close relative of *M. kobus* can be distinguished by the spicy anise scent released by bruised foliage. The long, narrow, willowlike leaves provide a finer, neater texture than the somewhat coarse appearance of other species. In culti-

vation, provide a moist but well drained soil.

Rare in the wild, oyama magnolia, *Magnolia sieboldii,* is found in the wooded mountains of Honshu's Kanto to Kinki districts, Shikoku, Kyushu, and Korea, southern China, and southern Manchuria. In gardens *M. sieboldii* might be called a large shrub since it often grows only 10 feet tall. In the wild it reaches twice this size. Large, fragrant, nodding, or pendant, cup-shaped white to pale-rose flowers, accented with maroon-red stamens, appear in early summer. Traditionally in Japan this species was planted in tea-house gardens where guests seated on the floor could enjoy the view of the pendant flowers nodding above. This species prefers shaded sites with acid soil, being less tolerant of sunny and alkaline conditions than most other magnolias. Although cultivated in Europe, it is rarely grown in the United States. Its late season of bloom and showy fragrant flowers should encourage wider use.

Lily-flowered magnolia, *Magnolia liliiflora,* is widely cultivated in Japan, but actually is native to central China. It was described, along with *M. denudata* and *M. kobus,* by Engelbert Kaempfer in 1712. The Duke of Portland introduced lily-flowered magnolia from Japan into English gardens in 1790, where it quickly became prized for its small habit and deep wine-purple flowers in late spring. Yulan magnolia, *M. denudata,* is another Chinese species that has long been cultivated both there and in Japan. Reaching 30 to 35 feet high in cultivation, and spreading just as wide, in the wild it grows 50 to 65 feet tall. Fragrant, vaselike, ivory-white flowers (sometimes tinged with pink or wine-purple at the base of each petal) open in midspring.

FLOWERING CRAB APPLES

Crab apples are just as Japanese as the better recognized flowering cherries. Some crab apples are moundlike, almost shrublike in appearance; others are narrow with a columnar form; and some have pendulous weeping branches. They offer a second season of interest with their autumn fruits, which also attract robins, bluebirds, cedar waxwings, orioles, cardinals, grosbeaks, and other birds that feast eagerly on the crab apples. The primary drawback to the trees is their susceptibility to diseases such as apple scab and cedar-apple rust in areas where there are large numbers of native or ornamental junipers within a mile of the apples. Fortunately, disease-resistant crab apples are available.

Crab apples can be used as individual specimens in a modestly sized garden or, where space permits, massed in a small grove. On an even larger scale, consider accentuating white- or pink-flowered crab apples by using dark conifers to create a handsome backdrop. Since many crab apples are small enough to consider as shrubs themselves, the garden may seem

poorly designed when they are positioned near shrubs. Spring-flowering perennials create a pleasing vignette; perhaps small rosy-pink bleeding-hearts, the blue forget-me-not-like flowers of Siberian bugloss, hostas for the sake of their tidy foliage later in the season, and bulbs. If you do choose to underplant with bulbs, remember that crab apples dislike disturbance at their roots. Choose small bulbs, hyacinths, or daffodils, which can stay in place year after year, rather than tulips, which need annual replacement.

Japanese flowering crab apple, *Malus floribunda,* is found growing wild in the mountains of Kyushu. Hardy from zones 4 to 8, possibly even further north, the trees smother themselves each year in midspring with great numbers of red buds that open to fragrant, rosy-pink flowers, which fade to white before they fall like so much confetti. Seen most frequently as a spreading bush, Japanese flowering crab apple can also be developed into a small or medium-sized tree about 30 feet tall, with a rounded or flattened head. This variable species is thought by some to be a hybrid of unknown parentage. The small, red-blushed yellow crab apples are modestly decorative for only a short period of time and need little clean-up, as the ½-inch-diameter fruits are a particular favorite with many species of birds. Reasonably resistant to disease, *M. floribunda* was regarded by Arie den Boer, an early authority on crab apples, as one of the oldest of all known ornamental crab apples, extremely floriferous, dependable, and marvelously beautiful.

Picturesque tea crab, *Malus hupehensis,* is a fine choice for specimen use. Reported as spontaneously occurring in Kyushu's Higo province, the small tree is native to China and northern India. Where adequate space permits, trees soon take on an irregular, widely spreading, vaselike form, reaching 16 feet tall and half again as wide. Deep pink buds open to fragrant, blush-pink flowers that fade to white just before petals drop. One drawback of the tea crab is its habit of flowering heavily only in alternate years, the result of heavy set of red-blushed, greenish yellow fruit. Resistant to most diseases, tea crab is sometimes affected by fire blight and is hardy from zones 4 to 8.

Sargent crab apple, *Malus sargentii*, is native to the mountains of Hokkaido, Honshu, Shikoku, and Kyushu, as well as Korea. Common and variable in the wild, it is useful in zones 4 to 8. A dwarf, spreading, shrublike crab apple, it branches out at the base without any attempt to form a central trunk or leader, growing about 6½ feet tall, perfectly sized for use with a playhouse. Deliciously fragrant, pure-white flowers unfold from pale pink buds, covering the little tree in a cloud of blossoms rather late in the season. Flowering is heaviest in alternate years, as is the production

of half-inch, deep red, glossy fruits. The fruits remain on the shrub until late in the winter unless eaten by birds. One important trait of *M. sargentii* is its resistance to apple scab and fire blight.

Toringo crab apple, *Malus sieboldii* is a rare native of Honshu suitable in zones 4 to 8. Growing 12 to 15 feet tall, it could be categorized as a large shrub or a small tree depending on the scale of your garden. Immature, year-old trees bear some resemblance to sargent crab apple, but toringo crab apple grows more rapidly and does not branch until the second year. Disease-resistant, toringo crab apple is one of the last to bloom; its blush-pink buds open to small, somewhat star-shaped white flowers in mid- to late spring. Eagerly eaten by several species of birds, the small, round, red or brownish yellow fruits, less than half an inch in diameter, are borne every year. A yellow-fruited form also exists, which some authorities want to place into a separate species, *M. toringo*.

Named for Maximowicz's Japanese assistant, Tschonoski Sugawa, tschonoski crab apple, *Malus tschonoskii,* is uncommon in the trade, and rare in the wild. This species was first brought to the United States by Charles S. Sargent, who collected seed in Nikko for the Arnold Arboretum. A large, upright, pyramidal tree that grows to 40 feet tall, tschonoski crab apple has the most striking foliage that can be imagined. Young shoots and their leaves are covered

These cycads in Kobe's Soraku-en Garden create
an elegant balance, softening the stones and
tightly pruned azaleas.

The patterned leaves of *Sasa veitchii*
create a handsome design against the
brown culms of a *Miscanthus* grass cultivar at winter's end.

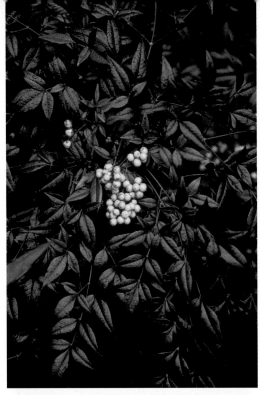

In a North Carolina garden, fruits of *Nandina domestica* 'Alba' have a lovely soft-ivory glow in the gray drizzle of a February afternoon.

Reflected in a pool, these Kurume azaleas create a marvelous May scene at the field research station of the Tokyo University Botanic Garden in Nikko.

Utsunomiya-shi's Ekoji Temple
garden, designed by Furuhashi
Yoshio. Moss-covered mounds are
enhanced with *Rhododendron
yakushimanum*'s flowers and the
vivid fuchsia blooms of *Bletilla
striata*.

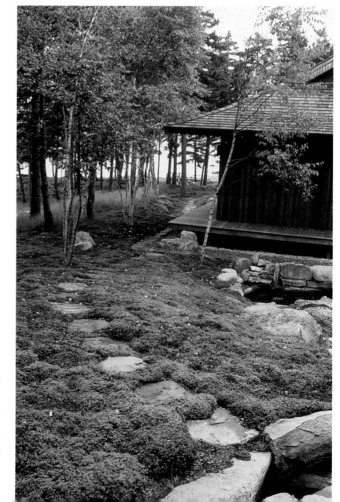

Along Maine's rocky coast Patrick
Chasse has used moss, *Polytrichum
commune,* as a soft, elegant, low-
maintenance ground cover.
PHOTO BY PATRICK CHASSE

A massed planting of epimedium creates a charming, shade-tolerant ground cover.

The delicate white flowers and bronze new growth of *Epimedium* x *youngianum* 'Niveum' repay a closer look.

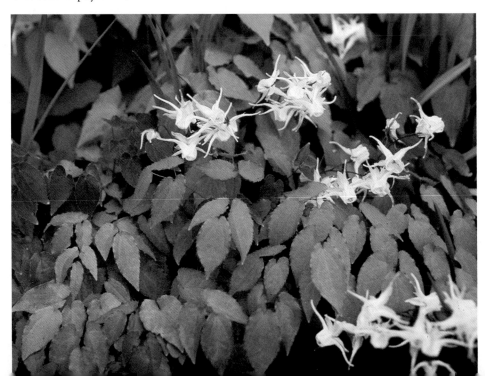

with a dense, felty, silvery-white pubescence that gradually wears off the upper surface. When autumn conditions are appropriate (warm sunny days and cool nights) the leaves turn vivid combinations of yellow, orange, crimson, and purple. A modest number of white flowers are followed by greenish yellow fruits 1 inch in diameter, also covered with a woolly pubescence when young, and turning reddish purple as they mature. Although perhaps outclassed by other crab apples for flower and fruit, the foliage of this species is superb.

FLOWERING CHERRIES

Among the early plants brought by the Japanese from China during the sixth or seventh century, about the same time as Buddhism, were several flowering cherries, mume apricot, flowering peach, the chrysanthemum, and the peony. Once introduced, these plants became naturalized citizens of their new home. Over the centuries many of them became thoroughly assimilated into the culture, acquiring distinctively Japanese associations.

Flowering cherries are highly prized for their attractive flowers; some trees also have handsome bark and/or good autumn color. I confess that my own preference is for single-flowered cherries. Seen growing wild in Japan, the delicacy and grace of pendulous boughs wreathed with single pink flowers dipping to the surface of a lake were the antithesis of gawky double-flowered garden cultivars. Often seen as top-grafted standards with a barrel-like trunk crowned by a Medusa of branches, these double-flowered varieties tend to lose branches to die-back at maturity, creating an even further malformed appearance.

In Japan ornamental cherry trees are planted individually, grouped along avenues, or massed by the thousands and tens of thousands. In general double-flowered forms, blooming somewhat later than the singles, are grown as solitary specimens. Single-flowered trees line avenues or are grouped in scattered groves in public gardens. Generally a single species will be used, even in massive plantings at "Flower-viewing Sites," where a single wild species of cherry, planted in tens of thousands, provides an enchanted landscape. At Arashiyama drifts of hill cherry or Japanese mountain cherry, *Prunus serrulata* var. *spontanea,* are planted, skillfully intermixed with pines for a dark backdrop.

In our gardens the intermingled planting of cherries and pines on a more intimate scale offers an attractive combination with extended seasonal interest. Very often white pines are used as boundary trees to screen out the neighbors. With one or a few cherries in an irregular, secondary row you gain the benefit of a backdrop for their spring flowers, the contrast of deciduous autumn foliage against evergreen conifer needles, and the polished bark of the cherries, perchance with snow piled on the branches as a winter scene. Though somewhat shallow-rooted, cherries still are hospitable to the underplanting of medium-sized shrubs, perennials, and bulbs. Earlier this century Collingwood "Cherry" Ingram, the noted English expert on these lovely trees, underplanted the cherry trees in his garden, Benden, with rhododendrons, azaleas, *Corylopsis pauciflora,* witchhazel, andromeda, and other shrubs.

Although it seldom attains heights of more than 30 feet in gardens, in the wild Japanese mountain cherry is a stately forest tree, occasionally reaching 65 feet tall. Care must be taken to select a suitable site, one with moist but well-drained soil. The species and its cultivars are suitable for gardens in zones 6 to 8. Dark brown bark is handsomely marked with horizontal striations. Pink flowers, an inch or so in diameter, appear in April together with the leaves. Numerous cultivars are available today: 'Amanogawa' (meaning "milky way" or "celestial river") is a narrow, columnar tree up to 20 feet tall with fragrant, pale pink, single to semidouble fragrant flowers in early May. 'Benden' is also narrowly upright with copper-bronze leaves in spring, vivid red foliage in autumn, and single, purplish pink flowers in April. 'Kwanzan' has large, unscented, fully double, bright cyclamen-pink flowers almost 2½ inches across and stiffly ascending branches when young, spreading in

maturity to form a wide-crowned 40-foot-tall tree. 'Kojima' (= 'Mt. Fuji') is a small tree with horizontally spreading, sometimes pendulous, branches with very large, fragrant, single white flowers in early April before the leaves appear.

Japanese mountain cherry is firmly embedded in Japanese legend. In the fourteenth century the reigning emperor, Go-Daigo, was seized by his enemies. His captors decided to take him south into exile on Kyushu. Knowing the route by which they would travel, Kojima, his loyal lieutenant who had escaped capture, took a different, more circuitous route. His plan was to reach an inn where the emperor and his escort would stop for the night, and at which site grew a very famous cherry tree. Knowing the emperor's passion for cherry blossoms, Kojima tore a strip of dark chestnut-brown bark from the trunk and on its smooth surface wrote a message of encouragement to his master. This story is a popular motif for paintings.

Sargent cherry, *Prunus sargentii,* very much resembles *P. serrulata*. A fine forest tree up to 50 or 60 feet tall in the wild, it grows as far south as the Yamanashi department in central Honshu but in such southerly regions is essentially a mountain species that grows at elevations above 2,500 feet. In northern areas—Hokkaido and Sakhalin—it grows at considerably lower levels. Quite cold tolerant, *P. sargentii* has been reported to withstand -23° Fahrenheit without injury. It grows well in zones 5 through 9, and even survives in the warmer portions of zone 4 but does not flower there reliably. Opening in April or May, the flowers, up to 1½ inches in diameter, are a blush pink. The foliage is among the first to change color in autumn; its leaves often turn bright orange and crimson before the end of September. In winter the glossy bark is clearly revealed; that of mature trees is a rich madder brown.

Autumn flowering cherry, *P. subhirtella* var. *autumnalis* blooms intermittently during mild periods from November to April in England and in the southeastern United States. Although hardy in zone 6, winter flowering depends on milder-than-usual weather. Winter flowers are sessile, held tight to the branches. Stems lengthen in spring, and flower clusters hang from the branches. Hard frost kills any open flowers but more follow in succession. A story, dating to the opening years of the fifth century, tells how one fine November day the emperor and his courtiers were merrymaking on the grounds of his palace near Kyoto. The emperor could not believe his eyes when a single cherry petal came floating down into his cup of sake. Was he drunk? He ordered his retainers to search until they found the tree from whence came the petal. And in a nearby suburb was discovered autumn flowering cherry.

Higan cherry, *Prunus subhirtella,* has many other common names, among them winter flowering cherry, spring cherry, and rosebud cherry. The numerous forms include variable flower color from nearly pure white to deepest rose pink; flower size ranging from less than 1 inch to about 1½ inches in diameter, and either single or double in form; and branches ascending, arched, or completely pendulous. The broad-crowned tree with cascading slender branches creates a graceful image, accentuated by autumn, winter, or spring flowers. Hardy from zones 6 to 8, with careful placement this species can be extended into the warmer portions of zone 5, and the cooler regions of zone 9.

Yoshino cherry, *Prunus* x *yedoensis,* is a plant of garden origin, a hybrid of *P. subhirtella* and *P. speciosa*. Popular, floriferous, and widely planted on river banks and in parks in Japan, it is hardy, quick growing, and short-lived. This species (together with Japanese mountain cherry) is the ornamental Japanese cherry planted in Potomac Park, around the Tidal Basin in Washington, D.C. A single specimen, given room to grow, becomes a wide-spreading tree 40 or 50 feet tall, usually half that size in gardens. Blossoming in March, myriad fragrant flowers more than 1 inch across open pale pink and then fade to white. 'Akebono' is a selection with translucent pale pink flowers. *Prunus* x *sieboldii* is likewise a hybrid, this time of *P. speciosa* and *P. apetala*. It is an old introduction, and grows slowly to maturity as a small tree. Very beautiful when "in blow," it covers itself with countless semidouble fragrant pink blossoms, each nearly 2 inches in diameter.

Fuji cherry, *Prunus incisa,* is a purely Japanese species from the mountainous regions of south central Honshu, especially plentiful on the southern and eastern slopes of Fujiyama from 1,800 feet upward. It has a spartan constitution, as might be gathered from its subalpine habitat, and seems untroubled by late frosts. Though in the wild it makes a small, bushlike, round-topped tree about 8 feet tall, in cultivation it often grows much larger. Summer pruning can downsize it. Fuji cherry's purplish-brown bark and graceful branches have a subtle appeal, and its modest size is more suitable for today's smaller gardens. The flowers are what make it worth growing—white or pinkish in bud, nearly always pure white when fully open (late March on the Kanto plain to May at higher elevations), with red calyces that give them a lovely rosy blush when viewed from a distance. 'February Pink' has light pink flowers and is in bloom by February, thus in regions where spring frosts are still occurring buds will be damaged. 'Praecox' blooms even earlier, opening pale pink flowers in January. 'Moerheimii' is a small, dome-shaped, wide-spreading, weeping form with pink-budded flowers opening in late March to blush-white flowers.

Fuji cherry was introduced to America in 1915 by E. H. Wilson, who was very fond of it, but then everyone associated with ornamental cherries seems to like it: Arthur Johnson, in his slim book *Rhododendrons, Azaleas, Magnolias, Camellias & Ornamental Cherries*, felt that fuji cherry could be unreservedly recommended for small gardens. And Dr. John Creech referred to it as a small flowering cherry for the future in an article published in *American Horticulturist* in April 1993. "Cherry" Ingram extolled fuji cherry's virtues: it grows well in sun or shade, pruned or unpruned, even clipped into a hedge. He produced 'Okame', a hybrid between *P. incisa* and *P. campanulata,* which in 1988 received the Styer Award from the Pennsylvania Horticultural Society. 'Okame' has a neat, tidy habit, making an upright tree about 30 feet tall that bears numerous delicate, small, carmine-pink flowers accentuated with red calyces in March.

Oriental bush cherry, *Prunus japonica,* was described by Thunberg in his *Flora Japonica* of 1784. Cultivated in Japan but native to China, it is a slender-twigged, small shrub about 5 feet tall with pinkish white flowers produced together with the foliage in April. Very hardy, it can be grown from zones 3 to 6, but may suffer damage in some years in the warmer portions of its range where mild periods in late winter trigger early growth that is then snubbed by frost. Abundant small white flowers are followed by tart red cherries. Fruiting is best in alternate years, and even then requires two different clones for cross-pollination.

Introduced to America from Japan a century ago, miyama cherry, *Prunus maximowiczii,* is a modest-sized tree that grows about 24 feet tall. It has pleasing, creamy-white flowers that open rather late in spring, but it is even more useful for its autumn foliage color, which turns vivid scarlet before falling, at least in the thickets and forests of central Honshu northward to Sakhalin, as well as those of the Korean mainland, Manchuria, Sakhalin, and Ussuri, where it is native. In England the usual autumn colors are tawny orange or dull, rusty red. Color is richer in New England than in the southeastern United States.

Japanese alpine cherry, or nipponese cherry, *Prunus nipponica,* is a shrub or small tree from the high mountains of Hokkaido and central and northern Honshu. It reaches altitudes of 7,500 feet in the warmer portions of its range and grows up to 16 feet tall with ascending, spreading branches and a very short trunk. Where there is heavy winter snowfall the trunk is even shorter. New shoots, brownish in color, turn grayish in their first autumn, weathering away in their second and third year so that mature growth has a handsome, polished chestnut-brown bark. Pink flowers open from May to July, depending on local conditions. Quite showy in bloom, it is equally attractive in autumn when the leaves turn yellow

to orange. Suitable in zones 6 to 8, this species is worth searching for.

FLOWERING APRICOT

Ume, or the Japanese apricot, *Prunus mume,* is said to be indigenous to the mountains of Kyushu. However, as a much-planted Chinese species, with numerous cultivars popularly grown in gardens, it is also just as likely to have been naturalized. A pretty little shrub or small, 20-foot-tall tree, *P. mume* is early flowering and subject to frost damage, but otherwise hardy to -5° Fahrenheit. It is best grown in zones 8 and 9, or in sheltered gardens in zone 7. The scented flowers are borne freely and, in milder climates or where some shelter from the frost can be provided, the tree is an asset to the small garden. Japanese gardeners have developed whites and pinks, singles and doubles; there are now more than 250 cultivars in all.

One year an early visit to Longwood Gardens in Kennett Square, Pennsylvania, delighted me with blooming, snow-covered Japanese apricot. Trees with pink flowers were showier, as white flowers blended indistinguishably with the snow that still clung to the branches. I remember January visits to the University of North Carolina Arboretum in Raleigh, seeing Japanese apricot in full bloom in the still wintry landscape. In Japan the small fruits, inedible when raw, are salted and pickled, with red shiso leaves included for coloring.

These pickles have been made for centuries and they last for centuries too! When two-hundred-year-old pottery jars were unearthed, the pickled plums they contained were found to be still edible. Together with rice, pickled plums are a lunchbox standard, and are considered good for one's health.

STEWARTIA

Blooming in summer, Japanese stewartia, *Stewartia pseudocamellia,* makes a welcome addition to the garden. Native to the mountains of Honshu, Shikoku, and Kyushu, this elegant small tree is useful in zones 6 to 8. Fat, shimmery buds form in early summer, unfolding in mid- to late summer to white, camellia-like flowers more than 2 inches wide, centered with a boss of golden stamens. Flowers open over a month or so, providing a long display period. Plant small, container-grown specimens at the edge of a woodland in light shade with a soil high in organic matter, moist but well drained. The natural form is orderly, and pruning is unnecessary. Branches have a charming, graceful arch, and as the tree ages it develops an exfoliating bark. Older reddish brown bark flakes off in irregular patches to reveal paler yellowish brown bark beneath. Fall color is pleasing. Reputed to reach 65 feet tall, stewartia is very slow growing. In twenty years mine has reached 16 feet or so, tall enough to enjoy from a second-story window.

JAPANESE SNOWBELL

Japanese snowbell, *Styrax japonicum,* is native and very common to thickets and open woods in the hills and mountains of Hokkaido, Honshu, Shikoku, and Kyushu. It can also be found in the wild in Korea, China, Formosa, and the Philippines. Hardy from zones 5 to 8, it might be planted in zone 9 gardens where summers are moderate. *Styrax japonicum* is a multi-branched, small tree that grows to about 30 feet. Its glossy, dark green, sharply pointed leaves, pale green underneath, create a fine textured canopy. White, somewhat scented, pendulous flowers, like broad, shallow bells, open in late May and early June, clearly visible beneath the foliage canopy. To better appreciate the flowers, position a bench beneath the tree. Japanese snowbell grows best with fertile, moist, but well-drained soil and partial shade.

A fifty-year-old specimen at the University of California Botanical Garden in Berkeley is 18 feet tall, with a well-developed trunk and canopy. Growing on a damp, lightly shaded mossy bank with some overstory protection, it is a good, mature specimen tree. There is scattered die-back, Elaine Sedlack reports, which she attributes to homesickness. Garden writer George Valchar has Japanese snowbell in his New Canaan, Connecticut, garden, where it happily self-sows. The tap-rooted seedlings must be transplanted while still rather small.

CONIFERS

Slow-growing conifers are not necessarily dwarf; many mature to a size that obscures entire houses, let alone livingroom windows. Make sure the tree you choose is suitable for local growing conditions and that there is sufficient room for your selection to mature. Plant evergreens individually as specimen trees, or group several to form an excellent year-round screen on a heroic scale, or as a backdrop for flowering trees in spring, and autumn foliage at year's end. One or many, conifers provide winter interest to the landscape, but consider your options carefully before you plant.

FIR

Japanese fir, *Abies firma,* is the only fir from Japan that is useful in the American South, thriving from zones 6 to 9. Found in the hills and mountains of Honshu, Shikoku, and Kyushu, it is perhaps the tallest, most impressive Japanese fir, reaching a height of 130 feet in the wild, but typically only half that height in cultivation. Horizontally spreading branches form an oval or flattened, rounded crown, making a stately specimen. The dark gray bark is rough and scaly; stiff, tough needles are dark green above, paler on the underside. With such dignified appearance and stately proportions, Japanese fir is most suited to large gardens and public parks. It should be sited where it receives protection from late spring frosts that can damage new growth. Ample moisture in summer is also important. Ernest Wilson mentions the Japanese fir as commonly planted on temple grounds and in parks throughout its natural range in Japan. Von Siebold first properly described Japanese fir, and thus got to name it. Dr. George Hall introduced it to the United States in 1862.

Dake-momi means mountain fir, an appropriate name for Nikko fir, *Abies homolepis,* native to the mountains of Honshu, Shikoku, and Kyushu. It grows at elevations that make its useful range zones 5 to 6. Discovered by von Siebold, who saw it growing in gardens in Osaka and Nagasaki, Nikko fir was first introduced to Europe by John Gould Veitch in 1861. Taller in the wild, in cultivation Nikko fir slowly reaches 65 feet tall. The tree forms a regular, conical crown with stout branches densely clothed with stiff dark green needles about 1 inch in length. Four-inch-long cones are held upright on the branches; they are purplish (sometimes green) when young, turning brown when mature. Bark is gray and scaly. Nikko fir will tolerate, even thrive in shade when young, which may help it establish in warmer regions.

Veitch fir, *Abies veitchii,* is a handsome, graceful tree for colder climates, zones 3 to 5, perhaps extending to zone 6 in cool, somewhat moist sites. In the mountains of Honshu and Shikoku, Veitch fir makes a narrow, tapering, pyramidal tree with very numerous short, slender branches. In more open situations it is shorter and the branches are longer. The smallest of the Japanese firs, Veitch fir grows 50 to 80 feet tall. With its high, narrowly conical crown and its short, horizontally spreading branches to the ground, it resembles a stylized Christmas tree. The branches have ringed folds near the base, and both branches and trunk have gray, smooth bark. The needles are glossy and deep green; the cones are bluish purple, occasionally green, turning brown as they mature.

Japanese Plum Yew

Japanese plum yew, *Cephalotaxus harringtonia,* is a small tree scarcely over 30 feet high. Native to the forest understory of the mountains from Kyushu to northern Honshu, Japanese plum yew grows in moist, somewhat shaded conditions. At higher elevations it grows in heavily shaded deep ravines, sheltered under taller conifers. It also grows wild in Korea and northern China. Although not especially popular in Japan, *C. harringtonia* is a welcome addition to American landscapes, useful for its good looks and its ability to thrive in heavy shade. Japanese plum yew is often seen as a shrubby, rounded plant that eventually grows 4 to 8 feet tall and wide; these shrub forms are discussed in the next chapter.

False Cypress

Hinoki false cypress, *Chamaecyparis obtusa,* is native to the mountains of Honshu, Shikoku, and Kyushu. Useful in zones 5 to 8, it is grown extensively as an ornamental both here and in Japan. Sacred to Shintoists, hinoki false cypress is often planted in temple courtyards. It is also used for reforestation because the timber is highly valued for interior woodwork on houses, for framing temples, and for its lustrous surface, which also takes lacquer remarkably well. It has multiple garden uses, depending on the cultivar selected. The species itself or taller clones can be used individually as specimens or grouped for screening purposes. Those cultivars of intermediate or moderate height might be used as foundation plantings or mixed with perennials in the herbaceous border, while the smallest cultivars are suitable for the rock garden. Susceptible to mite infestations in regions with dry, hot summers, hinoki false cypress accepts average conditions but is most satisfied when given a moist site in regions with high humidity. In the wild, hinoki delights in cool rocky slopes and prefers a northerly aspect. Scale-like, dark glossy green foliage is attractive year-round; the cinnamon-brown shredding bark on older specimens exfoliates in spring and adds additional interest. Growing up to 130 feet high, this tree has a dense, wide crown, acutely conical toward the top. Overall, its appearance is graceful, with pendulous branch tips, and branchlets flattened in an even plane and clothed with moderately thick, dark green needles. Selected cultivars are discussed in the next chapter.

Sawara false cypress, *Chamaecyparis pisifera,* is as frequently and widely planted as hinoki false cypress. Native to the mountains of Honshu and Kyushu, in North American gardens its useful range is zones 5 to 8. Brought to Europe by von Siebold in 1860, it was introduced to the United States by Dr. Hall in 1862. The tree reaches 160 feet in height, with a narrowly conical crown and smooth, reddish brown bark that exfoliates in thin strips. Typically, the species has dark green or bluish green foliage, with cultivars falling into three distinctly different foliage types. Timber utilization is similar to that of hinoki false cypress lumber. Selected cultivars are discussed in the next chapter.

JAPANESE CEDAR

Japanese cedar, *Cryptomeria japonica,* is found in the mountains and hills of Honshu, Shikoku, and Kyushu. Suitable from zones 6 to 9, this tree with its beautiful conical form grows equally well in Connecticut and at the University of California-Berkeley Botanical Garden. An elegant, 80-foot-tall evergreen with short, glossy needles in plumy, spiraling clusters on long whiplike branches, Japanese cedar makes a fine specimen. In winter needles

turn a burnished bronze. Gray, faded, old needles often persist, giving a shabby appearance. In milder climates, siting the trees in a wind-swept, perhaps coastal, site allows wind and rain to knock the old needles off. The columnar trunks are covered with peeling cinnamon-red bark. Japanese cedar takes a long time to outgrow its place in the garden; twenty-five-year-old trees are usually less than 25 feet tall.

Popular and useful, Japanese cedar has been cultivated in parks and gardens, extensively grown for timber, and logged for so long that spontaneous native populations are rare. Planted since ancient times, imposing avenues and groves of this majestic tree provide much of the charm of many famous temple gardens in Japan. Trees known to have been planted in parks and on temple grounds five and six centuries ago attest to its longevity. Timber is used in building houses and is especially valued for making sake tubs. Particularly fine-grained, unusually colored, or oddly marked wood is used for screens, doors, ceilings, and ornamental house fittings. In ancient times the forests on Yakushima were logged for temple columns and pillars, with timber from this area commanding a higher price than that logged elsewhere. Kaempfer was the first Westerner to discover this tree in Japan.

A wonderful specimen that Elaine Sedlack says evokes constant comment and questions from visitors to the University of

California Botanical Garden in Berkeley is *Cryptomeria japonica* var. *elegans*. Planted in 1945 it has, over time, layered itself to produce a grove of leaning trunks, all with stunning, burnished coppery-wine color in autumn. Most common of the hundreds of cultivars that exist, this has soft, slender juvenile needles and bronze-red to purple winter foliage, often with a bowed or curved trunk up to 65 feet tall. The original Western introduction was by von Siebold, who sent plants from Japan to Buitenzorg around 1826.

LARCH

Japanese larch, *Larix kaempferi* (= *L. leptolepis*), is native to the mountains of Honshu. In gardens it is used for naturalizing, in mass plantings, or as a specimen, and is practical in zones 4 to 6. A large tree with a massive trunk and heavy, rather widely spaced, horizontal branches, Japanese larch can grow to 100 feet. Its open appearance is somewhat minimized by the gracefully drooping branchlets. Japanese larch is an apparent conundrum, a deciduous evergreen. In spring tight clusters of pale green needles provide a lacy effect against the dark reddish brown bark, maturing to dark green in summer. When autumn arrives, the needles change to a rich red or to shades of yellow before dropping. Often planted for timber in Japan, the wood is very durable and is used for mine props, railroad ties, tele-graph poles, and ship-building.

First mentioned by Kaempfer, the Japanese larch was thought by Thunberg to be the same as the European larch, but it was later recognized as a distinct species and named for Kaempfer. In the wild, full-size trees grow on volcanic soils at elevations of 1,625 to 7,475 feet on the south side of Mt. Fuji. Dwarfed by the local growing conditions, trees continued up to 9,425 feet as shrubs. Gerd Krussmann, author of the *Manual of Cultivated Conifers,* writes that, given well-drained soil with ample moisture, *Larix kaempferi* is superior to any other larch in cultivation.

SPRUCE

Sakhalin spruce, *Picea glenhii,* has a handsome reddish new growth appearing rather late in spring that matures to bright green above, dull green beneath. The Japanese name, *aka-yezo-matsu,* means "red Yezo pine." The Sakhalin spruce is very hardy and is found in cold marshy ground and bogs on Hokkaido and also in mountainous regions of Honshu and Sakhalin. Ernest Wilson saw some specimens all growing on moist rocky slopes; they were easily recognized even at some distance by the characteristic chocolate-brown bark that readily distinguishes Sakhalin spruce from other spruces. These lofty trees grow 85 to 130 feet tall, with a stout trunk ranging from 10 to 15 feet in girth and a narrowly conical crown.

First identified by von Siebold from a cultivated plant in Tokyo, Yedo spruce, *Picea jezoensis,* ranges over much of northeastern Asia: in Hokkaido and also northeastern Manchuria, eastern Siberia, northern Korea, Sakhalin, and the Kurile Islands. Growing 100 feet tall, it is similar in habit to Norway spruce, *P. abies,* with a conical crown, horizontal branches, and drooping, pendulous branchlets. The brown bark turns purplish as the tree matures, flaking off in round plates.

Tiger-tail spruce, *Picea torano* (= *P. polita),* grows plentifully on volcanic soils of recent formation, and is found in the mountains on Honshu's central districts, Shikoku, and Kyushu. A moderately sized tree growing 20 to 80 feet tall, sometimes higher, tiger-tail spruce is densely branched in a nearly horizontal or ascending pattern. Clothed with stiff, very prickly, extremely sharp-tipped, shiny, bright yellowish green needles, the Japanese common name *bara-momi* (tiger-tail) refers to the pendulous, tail-like branches on very old trees. Rough grayish-brown bark flakes off in patches. First discovered by von Siebold, tiger-tail spruce was introduced into England by John Gould Veitch in 1861, and into the United States by Dr. George Hall the following year.

PINE

Common and variable, Japanese red pine, *Pinus densiflora,* is found in the hills and low mountains of Hokkaido's southern districts, Honshu, Shikoku, and Kyushu. Hardy in zones 5 to 7, it is most attractive in maturity when it assumes a graceful, picturesque habit. Somewhat slow-growing, the wait for *P. densiflora* is worthwhile, especially as the tree is pest-free and needs little care. The somewhat sparse, slender needles, 3 to 4 inches long, vary in color from olive green to a brighter bluish green. The tree always appears well clothed, as needles persist for three years. Discovered by Thunberg, Japanese red pine was introduced into the Leiden Botanic Garden by von Siebold in 1854. John Gould Veitch sent seed to England in 1861, and the following year Dr. George R. Hall gave seeds to Parsons Brothers Nursery on Long Island. By 1916 fifty-year-old specimens on the Hall estate had grown 50 to 60 feet tall. One unusual selection is dragon's eye pine, 'Oculus-draconis', whose green needles have two golden-yellow bands. Another elegant cultivar is the Tanyosho pine, 'Umbraculifera', multistemmed and shrubby in appearance, with its many branches held in a vaselike pattern, creating a flattened, umbrella-like canopy. This cultivar is even more slow-growing than the type, eventually reaching a height of 10 to 15 feet. The bark provides an additional attractive feature; the trunk and larger branches are a distinctive, warm orange-red color especially handsome against snow. Japanese red pine is known to hybridize with *P. thunbergii.*

Japanese white pine, *Pinus parviflora,* is a mountain species, growing at elevations of 8,125 feet on Honshu, Shikoku, and Kyushu. Hardy in zones 5 to 9, this slow-growing tree eventually reaches 65 feet tall, making it a striking specimen even at an early age. Its branches are strongly horizontal and set in distinct layers. The grayish black, scaly bark remains smooth for some years, eventually becoming brittle and exfoliating in thin, small flakes to reveal the reddish brown undersurface. Common in Japanese gardens, Japanese white pine is ordinarily clipped and trained, even as bonsai. 'Variegata' is a cultivar with partially yellow speckled or edged needles, observed in Japan before 1890. Ernest Wilson saw Japanese white pine growing among other conifers, such as hinoki false cypress and Japanese fir, and deciduous trees, including stewartia and magnolia, with a shrub undergrowth of rhododendron, skimmia, and Japanese andromeda. This rich plant community reinforces our understanding of the diversity of evergreen trees and shrubs native to Japan.

Historically, Japanese black pine, *Pinus thunbergii,* has been more widely planted in Japan than any other tree except cryptomeria. Such frequent cultivation from the earliest days of Japanese history led Ernest Wilson to think it impossible to determine the tree's original range. A maritime species, probably at one time it was widely distributed along the coastal regions of Japan. Owhi, in his *Flora of Japan,* considers it to be a common native of the seashore and lowlands of Honshu, Shikoku, and Kyushu, and also of South Korea. In forests, sheltered from wind, the trees grow with a nearly straight trunk, spreading branches, and an oval or flattened crown. Although growing 65 feet tall or higher in such sites, *P. thunbergii* rarely attains more than 30 to 35 feet in gardens. The picturesque crooked trunk and ponderous sprawling branches endear the black pine to the Japanese, who find its broadly pyramidal, often irregular open form gives the tree a special character. Blackish gray, fissured bark and horizontal or often somewhat pendulous branches add to its visual appeal. Tolerance to salt spray and strong winds make it popular for coastal sites, and Japanese black pine is widely used on Long Island and elsewhere along the Atlantic Coast. It needs good drainage, doing poorly where the soil remains wet or is periodically flooded. Japanese black pine is a familiar subject of woodblock prints, scroll paintings, and embroidery. The great highways of the Tokkaido, from Kyoto to Tokyo, and the Oshu-kaido, from Tokyo to Aomori, were lined with rows of this pine. Like red pine, the black pine was discovered by Thunberg and introduced into Holland by von Siebold in 1855. John Gould Veitch sent it to England in 1861.

Dwarf stone pine, or dwarf Siberian pine shrub, *Pinus pumila,* are discussed in chapter 4.

Some Japanese pines will tolerate California conditions, Elaine Sedlack tells me. Japanese black pine grows the fastest and is most vigorous. Japanese red pine grows more slowly, but is healthy where drainage is adequate. Japanese white pine actually grows better in the San Francisco Bay Area than it does farther inland, where summers are hotter.

PODOCARPUS

Another yewlike plant (more popular in Japan than plum yew), yew podocarp or bigleaf podocarp, *Podocarpus macrophyllus*, occurs naturally along the coastal regions of southern Kyushu, Shikoku, western Honshu (approximately as far as Tokyo), and Ryukyu. Growing 50 feet tall, yew podocarp thrives in zones 8 and 9, and in protected locations in zone 7. The straight trunk is clothed in gray, shallowly fissured, shredding bark. The wood is very rot-resistant, and is in great demand for furniture. The plant is dioecious, and females have rather inconspicuous greenish or purplish pea-sized fruit held in a fleshy purple receptacle, similar to yew fruit in its red receptacle. Plants have rather stout branches and somewhat yewlike, glossy, very dark green foliage. The needles are considerably larger than those of yew, up to 6 inches long and rather leathery. In Japan yew podocarp

is often clipped in a precise manner, trained in cloud-pruned forms (dense foliage masses floating on bare stems). Unpalatable to deer, it was planted on temple grounds where deer parks were a feature. Thus commonly found in shrine and temple gardens, yew podocarp has also been planted in cemeteries and used as a hedge plant and for topiary in gardens. It is also practical as a windscreen along beaches because of its tolerance of salty spray and sea winds. Ernest Wilson saw yew podocarp growing wild at the base of an active volcano in Osumi province, Kyushu, in a mixed forest of oaks and conifers with an undergrowth of aucuba and skimmia, suggesting garden use of the tree in a mixed planting. Yew podocarp was introduced to Holland by von Siebold in 1830. It received better distribution later via the nursery catalog of the L. Boehmer Co., Yokohama, which operated between 1882 and 1908. Dr. George Hall brought it to the United States from Japan in March 1862.

UMBRELLA PINE

Japanese umbrella pine, *Sciadopitys verticillata,* looks almost artificial with its conical form, precise tiers of whorled branches, and large, plump, glossy dark green needles radiating on the branches like spokes on a wheel. Often planted in Japanese gardens, the species is native to the mountains of west-central Honshu, Shikoku, and Kyushu. Hardy from zones 6 to 8, it needs protection from winter sun scald and desiccating winds in zone 6, and grows only in regions with moderate summer conditions in zone 8. Umbrella pine stays shrubby for years. In cultivation it grows very slowly, eventually maturing to a narrow, conical, "Christmas tree" 65 to 95 feet tall, making an unusual accent in the garden. In spring 1995 I saw a 5-foot specimen at a local Connecticut nursery priced at $450.

Umbrella pine has so formal an appearance that it is best in a cultivated setting. Given a suitable site, trees need little or no maintenance, being free of serious pests or diseases. It is easy to grow in Berkeley, reports Elaine Sedlack, preferring light shade but tolerant of full sun (with some yellowing) if moisture is adequate. Discovered by Thunberg in 1775–76, umbrella pine was first introduced by the Dutch to Java. 'Aurea' is a form with golden-yellow needles selected in Japan prior to 1889. 'Pendula' has weeping branches. A very old specimen, no doubt from the time when the site was home to Jozoji Temple, stands in Tokyo's Shiba Park.

YEW

Japanese yew, *Taxus cuspidata,* is a tree or a shrub depending on whether you select the species or cultivars. Generally cultivated in Japan as a hedge plant, yew may also be used for topiary, as a tree or shrub, or as a closely sheared low bush. In its native range—the mountains of Hokkaido, central and north-western Honshu, Shikoku, and Kyushu— the species grows as a tree 65 feet or higher. Yew can be used as a specimen, a screen, a hedge, or as foundation planting in zones 4 to 7. It is tolerant of sun or shade, although protection from winter sun scald and drying winds is a good idea in colder areas, just as midday shade is helpful in regions with hot, dry summers. Well-drained soils are best, as excess moisture can be fatal, especially for new transplants. Dry sites should also be avoided. Plants accept considerable shearing and clipping, rendering the Japanese yew an excellent choice for formal hedges and topiary; dark green, thickly clustered, somewhat succulent needles also make a very effective screen, with one big *if.* If deer are in the area, constant protection in the form of fencing, netting, or spraying with repellents is a necessity, particularly in winter. Though highly poisonous to domestic livestock, yew is apparently one of the preferred foods of white-tailed deer. In cold winter weather, needle color often deepens to an almost blackish green. Female plants have soft, fleshy, scarlet-red berries, actually arils, wrapped around a highly poisonous seed. The fruits are quite showy, and attract any number of birds that eat the fruit without ill effect. The reddish brown, very hard, tough, durable wood is rot-resistant and long-lasting in wet soil, thus highly valued in Japan for house pilings and building foundations, as well as for cabinet work, carving, and, formerly, for bows.

Discovered by Thunberg and formally described by von Siebold, Japanese yew was introduced to England by Robert Fortune between 1854 and 1856. It has never been as popular there as in the United States, where it is favored in place of the less hardy English yew, *Taxus baccata*. Dr. George R. Hall introduced Japanese yew to America in 1862, giving material to Parsons Brothers Nursery of Flushing, Long Island.

Shrub forms of the Japanese yew are described in the next chapter.

JAPANESE HEMLOCK

North Japanese hemlock, *Tsuga diversifolia,* is a tree that grows to 80 feet tall in its native range on the high mountains of Honshu, Shikoku, and Kyushu, where it is rather common. In gardens it more often grows quite slowly and compactly to 30 feet, and is attractive for its short needles that completely encircle the twigs, radiating in all directions and thus displaying their pale underside. Best grown in gardens in zones 5 to 7, it tolerates summer heat poorly. 'Gotelli' is a dwarf form.

BROADLEAVED EVERGREEN TREES

As a generalization, broadleaved evergreen trees are less cold-hardy than deciduous trees or conifers. Welcome additions to gardens in zones 7 through 9, they are largely unsuitable in colder regions.

CAMELLIA

Sasanqua camellia, *Camellia sasanqua,* and common camellia, *Camellia japonica,* are familiar to southern gardeners. Like other, less well-known Japanese natives such as stewartia, cleyera, ternstroemia, and eurya, and our native *Franklinia alatamaha,* camellias are also in the Tea family. Sasanqua camellia is found in abundance near the seashores of Honshu, Shikoku, and Kyushu, and also in Korea and Ryukyu. Common camellia is found in thickets and grassy slopes in the mountains of Kyushu.

Both camellias may be grown outdoors in zones 7 to 9, and, where climate permits, are easy to cultivate, needing only light woodland conditions, a humus-rich soil, and adequate moisture. Because they are shallow-rooted, camellias are quickly injured by drought. Both species grow 7 to 12 feet tall, and 5 to 7 feet wide. There are some differences in form: sasanquas have a denser appearance, most with single pink or white flowers, 1½ to 2½ inches in diameter, opening over a two- or three-month period in late autumn. They are grown in the Southeast as a natural or clipped hedge, as an accent or specimen plant, and in informal borders. Common camellias have a looser, more open look, larger leaves and larger, showier, single or double blossoms from late autumn until spring. Blooms

come in red to white, and flowers are sometimes striped or blotched. Common camellias are used in background plantings, as
individual specimens, sometimes even as
espalier.

An early November stroll through the
gardens of the Atlanta Botanical Garden
took me to a woodland planting of camellias, their dark, polished, evergreen leaves
and elegant flowers an abrupt delight in the
empty autumn woods. I've also seen a sizeable camellia outdoors on the bay side of
Long Island, growing in a sheltered corner
of a house. At Planting Fields Arboretum,
also on Long Island, there is an entire
glasshouse for camellias, with mature trees
growing in ground beds. They can also be
grown in sizeable pots. In zones 5 and 6
camellias can be kept outdoors in a shady
place for the summer, then moved to a cool
greenhouse for the winter. It is the exquisite
flowers that move gardeners to such horticultural efforts. The blooms are perfect in
form, but they lack any fragrance. There
are more than 2,000 registered cultivars of
common camellia, and over 300 sasanquas,
far too many to even begin to list. Roslyn
Nursery, in Dix Hills, Long Island, offers
several camellias hardy to zone 6. As you
would surmise, these flower in late fall or
early spring, and are hybrids with a hardier
Chinese species.

Snow camellia, *C. japonica* ssp. *rusticana,*
is a charming subspecies, smaller growing
and with smaller, flat, single, snow-white
flowers with a central golden boss of stamens. Native to the thickets and thin woods
of mountain slopes on the Japan Sea side of
central and northwestern Honshu, this
camellia is spring-flowering, from April to
June, and is of interest to a camellia afi-
cionado to extend the season of bloom.

CLEYERA AND TERNSTROEMIA

Japanese cleyera, *Cleyera japonica,* is native
to Shikoku, the central and western districts
of Honshu, and Kyushu, and also to Korea,
Ryukyu, Formosa, and China. It grows as a
large shrub or small tree that eventually
reaches 30 feet in height, although in cultivation, expect Japanese cleyera to reach only
8 to 10 feet high and 5 to 6 feet wide. It has
handsome dark green, glossy, leathery,
camellia-like evergreen leaves evenly spaced
along the green-barked branches. In early
summer, deliciously fragrant, pendant, bell-
like white flowers more than ½ inch across,
appear in the leaf axils. These turn yellowish
as they age, and are followed by red fruit
that turn black as they mature. Japanese
cleyera is rather tender and is most suitable
to zones 8 and 9. Experimentally minded
gardeners might try it in the warmer portions of zone 7 in a protected microclimate.
It prefers half shade and a fertile, moist soil.
Tolerant of city conditions and heavy shade,
cleyera is useful for patio planting or as a
specimen, as well as for screening. Although
it does not require pruning, it can be clipped
or pruned rather heavily, allowing its use as

a hedge even in constricted quarters. At the Atlanta Botanical Garden where wet summers promote its rapid growth, cleyera is being cultivated as a combination hedge and screen. 'Variegata' is a less vigorous selection with thinner, bright green leaves marked with yellow and rose-pink toward the edges.

Since ancient times cleyera has been used in Shinto rituals, its branches offered on household altars. My friend Furuhashi Yoshio told me that a branch of cleyera with *nusa* (a white paper sometimes made of hemp fiber) is an object of worship; the soul of the god dwells within. Where cleyera, a plant of the warm southern districts of Japan, cannot grow, *Eurya japonica* is used as a surrogate, but it is not considered as beautiful.

Cleyera has a close look-alike, Japanese ternstroemia, *Ternstroemia gymnanthera,* with which it is often confused in the nursery trade. There are small differences: ternstroemia's leaves bunch at the tips of the shoots, and its fruits ripen from green to yellow, splitting open at maturity to reveal bright red seeds. Frequently, however, plants do not set fruit. The deliciously fragrant white flowers are less than 1 inch in diameter. Ternstroemia is found in the wild near seashores in Honshu's Tokaido district and westward, on Shikoku and Kyushu, and also in southern Korea, Ryukyu, Formosa, China, India, and Borneo. Readily transplanted, ternstroemia grows well in partial shade. It needs a sheltered site in any but the mildest regions.

LOQUAT

It is a contrary aspect of human nature to want what we can't have. My brother, who lives in Davis, California, wants to grow the lilacs he remembers from our Brooklyn childhood. I am enthralled by all the unfamiliar plants that thrive in the mild California climate. On walks through his neighborhood I particularly enjoy passing by a yard where loquat, or Japanese plum, *Eriobotrya japonica,* is growing. Native to Honshu's western district, Shikoku, Kyushu, and also China, loquat is much planted for its fruit, which is also the reason I like to stroll by the tree in Davis in late spring. Round to pear-shaped, not quite 2 inches in diameter, and yellow, the fruit has an aromatic, tart-sweet flavor. It is easily bruised and ships poorly, and therefore must be enjoyed locally. Only hardy in zones 8 and 9, loquat is a small tree growing about 25 feet tall. Stout branches are covered with a wonderful coarse, downy, golden fuzz when young. Deep green, sawtooth-edged leaves are as much as 10 or 12 inches long and have a brown woolly undercoat. Small, creamy white, fragrant flowers appear in large, woolly clusters in November or December. Good drainage is important, but otherwise the tree is not fussy about soil. Loquat is susceptible to fire blight, which can be a serious problem in some areas. I have found that seed germinates readily, and several can be grown in a large pot as a container ornamental in colder regions.

EURYA

Eurya japonica is a large evergreen shrub or small tree that is variable, and very common to the thickets and thin woods of Honshu, Shikoku, Kyushu, and elsewhere in Asia. Glossy, handsome, dark green, nearly 2½-inch-long leaves provide year-round interest, turning deep burgundy in winter where the site is sunny. 'Winter Wine' is lower-growing and wider-spreading, with more reliable winter color. 'Variegata' has leaves with a creamy white edging. Eurya's greenish white flowers and black fruits are not especially showy. Like cleyera, it is useful in zones 8 and 9.

JAPANESE ANISETREE

Japanese anisetree, *Illicium anisatum,* is native to the thickets and forests of Shikoku, Honshu's Kanto district and westward, and Kyushu, as well as to Ryukyu, Formosa, and China. Growing 8 to 12 feet tall and spreading nearly as wide, Japanese anisetree may be used en masse in Western gardens for screening, or as a large-scale foundation plant. In Japan this common small tree is frequently planted in temple gardens and Buddhist cemeteries. It does well in sun or part shade in zones 7 to 9. Its evergreen, leathery, olive-green, smooth leaves are up to 4 inches long and have a pleasing, spicy fragrance when crushed. The pale yellow-white, 1-inch flowers appear in July, and are likewise fragrant. This plant falls into the small tree/large shrub category, with much depending on the scale of your garden and the other plants growing there. Japanese anisetree is lovely in combination with Japanese plum yew or yew podocarp.

CHAPTER FOUR

Shrubs

If, to use a common analogy once more, trees are the framework of the garden, then shrubs could be considered the furniture. They come in a variety of styles—upright, mounded, or creeping; evergreen or deciduous; with thin, open growth or dense enough to serve as a screen; adorned with beautiful flowers and fruit or not. Some shrubs may fill the role of trees in a small garden; others can be grown in a container. The majority are large enough to create a significant display, and yet not require excessive space. Pruning can control size and shape in either a formal or informal manner. The ideal is to balance spring bloom, summer display, autumn foliage, and winter effect to create a garden that is interesting throughout the year. While each category of plants contains possibilities for different seasons, shrubs are particularly useful in this regard, and many of the excellent shrubs we already welcome to our gardens are of Japanese origin.

SHRUBS FOR THE SPRING GARDEN

Azaleas and Rhododendrons

There are so many excellent azaleas and rhododendrons of Japanese origin that an entire book could be written about them. Deciduous or evergreen, varying from small to large shrubs, sometimes even growing as small trees, the species themselves have created a foundation upon which hybridizing and selection is based. All azaleas fall within the genus *Rhododendron,* although in popular terms we often separate them according to leaf and flower size. These woodland shrubs have a fine fibrous root system, and need a loose, open, acid soil that is rich in organic matter. A surface mulch of shredded leaves or pine straw helps maintain the cool moist root-run they prefer. For most species, high dappled shade is ideal. They can be grown in an informal, naturalistic manner. Some, especially the small-leaved, evergreen azaleas, lend themselves to formal shearing. Elaine Sedlack at the University of California Botanic Garden in Berkeley has clipped a large planting of 'Christmas Cheer' azaleas so all the flowers appear in a single plane, producing a neon-bright sheet of crimson 12 feet across in spring.

Earliest to bloom is Korean rhododendron, *Rhododendron mucronulatum,* a deciduous species native to Honshu and the northern districts of Kyushu, as well as to Korea and China. In early spring (mid-April in cooler regions, late January in milder areas) clusters of 3 to 6 rosy purple flowers appear on the tips of the still-leafless branches. As the color of its flowers is close to magenta, planting Korean rhododendron near forsythia can result in a strident association. 'Cornell Pink' is a cultivar with rosy pink flowers, a color somewhat easier to combine with that of other early flowers. The foliage of this deciduous rhododendron provides a second season of interest, turning a pinkish-bronze or yellow before dropping in autumn. The more sunlight the shrub receives, the more intense the fall color. Growing from 3 to 6 feet tall, this species is hardy from zones 5 to 7, with a little stretch either way to protected sites in the warmer portions of zone 4, and shaded areas with moderate summer temperatures in zone 8. Because it flowers so early, don't plant this shrub in frost pockets in colder regions to avoid damage to the unfolding flowers.

Evergreen azaleas, native to Japan and popular there as garden and container plants, are well liked in our gardens too. I think these azaleas are misused, often wretchedly clipped into geometric forms in foundation plantings. Azaleas can yellow and become sickly in regions with alkaline soils, and they are often devoured by deer. Still we continue to plant them. But where they are grown with an understanding of their basic needs, evergreen azaleas create a wonderful understory to the deciduous woodland garden or any lightly shaded site. They provide two seasons of interest: exquisite flowers in spring and evergreen foliage in winter. As companion plants to small trees such as flowering dogwood or Japanese maple, evergreen azaleas can create an elegant garden requiring little maintenance. Informal plantings in combination with spring bulbs and shade-tolerant perennials such as primroses, woodland phlox, epimedium, hosta, and astilbe make an equally attractive design.

SATSUKI, SATSUKI HYBRIDS, AND HIRADO AZALEAS

In Japan, satsuki azaleas were developed during the Edo period (1615–1867) as a low-growing, late-blooming range of hybrids of *Rhododendron indicum*. Satsuki means "fifth month," which in the lunar calendar in use in Japan until 1873 would correspond to June. Satsuki bloom in late spring, with large flowers often unstable in color with striped or flecked blossoms. Carl Pehr Thunberg, writing in his *Travels* in late May of 1776, noted at Odowara, "*Azalea indica* stood in almost every yard and plot, near the houses, in its best attire, ineffably resplendent with flowers of different colours." That these were cherished plants in Japan is indicated by the fact that there were 168 garden forms recorded as early as 1692. The different clones of 'Gunpo' (or 'Gumpo' as it is frequently given) belong here. Some of these azaleas were introduced to Europe in the eigh-

teenth and nineteenth centuries, forming the basis of the Belgian conservatory, or forcing, azaleas.

In the United States, the term *satsuki hybrids* is applied to a group of fifty-three cultivars, all with Japanese names, acquired by Benjamin Y. Morrison of the U.S. Plant Introduction Station in 1938 and 1939 from the Chugai Nursery in Kobe. These hybrids are more tender than the species, and are at their best as garden plants in the southeastern states and the Pacific Northwest. In the northern states they must be enjoyed as potted plants, protected in a cool greenhouse over the winter.

Dr. John Creech of the United States Department of Agriculture Plant Introduction Service, on a collecting expedition in 1961, visited Hirado Island and obtained those we now call Hirado azaleas. His further acquisitions in 1976 include forty-eight cultivars of the Miyama Krishima azaleas. All of these, plus the Kurume and satsuki azaleas, were in cultivation in the Edo period. This was the period of seclusion, when samurai lived in a time of peace. Their skills included not only training in weaponry but also in the social arts of poetry, calligraphy, painting, and ornamental horticulture. Feudal nobility—the daimyos and shoguns—developed an intense interest in the cultivation of chrysanthemums, Japanese iris, peonies, and azaleas.

Azaleas were divided by the Japanese into two groups: *tsutsuji,* May blooming and with brilliantly colored flowers, represented by the Kurume and Hirado azaleas; and *satsuki,* which flower in early summer and include large-flowered bonsai types and garden varieties with dense evergreen foliage that frequently turns a purple color in winter. In Japanese gardens satsuki are often sheared into dense mounds. *Matsushima* satsuki azaleas are variable, striped selections. Plants may have pure white, solid red, or pale red flowers, red flowers striped white, or light red flowers striped with darker red, all on one plant. Matsushima can also refer to a specific clone of that name, 'Matsushima'. One extremely variable satsuki clone, 'Shokko', is even more variable, and a single plant may have white flowers splashed, spotted, and streaked with red, as well as solid colored red, pale red, and white flowers. This cultivar is said to be four or five hundred

years old, which would place it at the beginning of azalea cultivation.

Rarely thriving north of the warmer portions of zone 7 except in sheltered sites, both tsutsuji and satsuki take after their tender parent, the Indian azalea, *Rhododendron indicum,* which is native to southern Japan. Evergreen, with deep green, somewhat lustrous leaves and large (2 to 3 inches in diameter) rose-red to scarlet flowers in mid-June on a 3-foot shrub, Indian azalea has been a parent to many hybrids.

GLEN DALE AZALEAS
The Glen Dale hybrids, and there are more than 400 of them, were developed at the Plant Introduction Station in Glen Dale, Maryland, by Benjamin Y. Morrison. Breeding began sometime prior to 1935, and lasted for twenty years. Three species—*Rhododendron indicum, R. kaempferi, R. mucronatum*—and the Kurume hybrids were the beginning. The result was the creation of azaleas suitable for garden cultivation in the mid-Atlantic states. Growth habit varies from upright to spreading, on low, medium, or tall shrubs. Flowers, up to 4 inches across, may be single, semidouble, or double, and striped, flecked, or in some other manner variegated. The Glen Dale hybrids are hardy from the warmer portions of zone 6 to zone 9.

Snow Azalea

Perhaps you might see a plant offered under the name 'Indica Alba'. The handsome dark green, hairy-leaved plant smothers itself in spring with pure white, single flowers. This is not, however, one of the indica hybrids, but rather, a related species, *Rhododendron mucronatum,* commonly called the snow azalea. I have found this to be respectably hardy in my Connecticut (zone 6) garden, and it is reported to do well in Boston with winter protection. In a severe winter it will be somewhat deciduous, but flowers will bloom unharmed in late April or early May. Old plants will reach 4, or even 5 feet tall in a loose, open habit, growing even wider than high. (It is easy to confuse this species by name with *R. mucronulatum,* but the two plants are distinctively different.)

Mollis Azaleas

Sometime in the 1870s, the Dutch firm of Anthony Koster and Sons began hybridizing *Rhododendron japonicum* with *R. molle,* a tender Chinese species. Separately, but simultaneously, Anthony Waterer of Knap Hill, England, was making the same crosses. The results were the Mollis hybrids, *R. x kosteranum,* which have the hardiness of the Japanese species. Further crosses by Waterer of the Mollis hybrids with other hybrid groups produced the Knap Hill hybrids. With as many as 20 or 30 flowers in a cluster, colors range from pure white to pale pink, rose, yellow, bright orange, and red. Some are delightfully fragrant. These are among the most popular deciduous azaleas, and a decided improvement on the Japanese azalea, *R. japonicum,* native from the southwestern district of Hokkaido southward to Honshu, Shikoku, and Kyushu. Although in late spring the species has 2 to 8 golden yellow, orange, or vermillion red flowers, each up to 2 inches across, they have a rank, unpleasant odor.

As might be expected from such a convoluted parentage, hardiness in the Mollis and Knap Hill clones is variable; some can grow in zone 5, flowering in early June. This variable hardiness comes from another species, *R. obtusum,* native to Hokkaido.

Kurume Azaleas

Rhododendron obtusum is itself probably of hybrid origin. Widely cultivated in Japan where it is a garden plant of considerable antiquity, its different cultivars—called Kurume azaleas—may be evergreen, semievergreen, or even deciduous. Most forms are hardy from zones 7 through 9, with a few suitable in zone 6. Flowering in mid-May, bloom color varies from a warm orange-red to a clear, vibrant red to purple. E. H. Wilson saw these as nursery plants in the Tokyo area in 1914 and brought only herbarium specimens home to the Arnold Arboretum. But he ordered an assortment of Kurume azaleas, which were sent to John S. Ames of Massachusetts, arriving in

1917. Such was the excitement they engendered that Wilson returned to Japan in 1918, to make a special visit to Kurume, center for the development and sale of these azaleas. At the nursery of Kijiro Akashi he selected the fifty best from among the 250 different varieties being grown there. The "Wilson Fifty" vary greatly in size and hardiness, and were important in the development of the Glen Dale hybrids.

The Kurume hybrids we grow today originated from cultivated forms of *R. obtusum* and naturally occurring crosses in wild populations of *R. kaempferi* and *R. kiusianum* growing on Mount Kirashima near the city of Kurume. In Japan, selection of these hybrids in the wild populations began in the nineteenth century. The Japanese cultivars selected by E. H. Wilson were distributed in the United States, England, and Holland. These original Kurume azaleas were very compact in growth, reaching about 30 inches tall. Since their introduction into the United States, seedlings have produced plants that mature at 8 feet. Most are evergreen and produce prodigious numbers of small flowers early, or no later than midseason. 'Hinodegiri' with early, small, carmine-red flowers, and 'Hino Crimson', which blooms later and has somewhat deeper red flowers, are vivid examples. I find that, unless shaded from strong sunlight, the flowers quickly fade, scorch, and turn brown. Their color must be carefully matched to the flowers of surrounding plants blooming at the same time. Early blooming 'Blaauw's Pink', with its vivid salmon-pink flowers, can be difficult to partner. One combination that has worked well for me is 'Hinodegiri' planted under a paperbark maple, *Acer griseum*. The russet and copper tones of the maple's unfolding new leaves and the cinnamon of its flaking bark are pleasantly enhanced by the azalea's flowers. My favorite of the readily available cultivars is 'Hinomayo' with spotted, delicate pink flowers. Young plants are somewhat leggy and rather upright in growth, developing a more rounded form at maturity, when they will reach 5 to 6 feet.

Kaempferi Azaleas

When Professor Sargent of the Arnold Arboretum in Boston returned home in 1892 after his stay in Japan, it could only be expected that some plant material found its way to the United States with him. One of his introductions was torch azalea, *Rhododendron kaempferi,* sown from seed he brought home. In time the resulting plants were set out on the wooded hillsides of the arboretum grounds, where today they create a vivid springtime display. Perhaps the most widely distributed azalea in Japan, torch azalea is found on sunny slopes in the hills and mountains from Hokkaido to Honshu, Shikoku, and Kyushu. It blooms in April or May (depending on climate) and earns its name with flowers varying in color from flaming brick red to salmon red to a softer deep salmon rose. As with other red-flowered azaleas, some shade is advisable, especially at midday, to avoid fading. This is a tall species, growing 9 feet high, or more. Deciduous, it is more tolerant of cold conditions than *R. obtusum,* growing well in zone 6 and even in protected sites in the warmer parts of zone 5.

About 1920 a Dutch nurseryman developed the Kaempferi hybrids, crossing *R. kaempferi* with *R.* 'Malvatica'. Other cultivars were crossed with second- and third-generation plants, resulting in an eclectic group. Hardier than Kurume azaleas and with larger flowers, the color range of these kaempferi hybrids is red to rose to white.

Joseph Gable, a nurseryman from Stewartstown, Pennsylvania, tried a different cross, that of *R. kaempferi* with *R. poukhanensis.* He selected seedlings for hardiness and then recrossed them onto *R. mucronatum,* some of the hardier Kurumes, and others. The intent was to produce very hardy evergreen azaleas. Flowers on his Gable hybrids, consisting of about 70 different clones, range from white to orange-red to rhodamine violet (a brilliant bluish red). Flowers are single or semidouble, with flower clusters up to nearly 3 inches across. The shrubs are so smothered in flowers when in bloom that the leaves cannot be seen. 'Rosebud', a slow-growing, low,

dense, spreading cultivar with double, hose-in-hose, rose-pink flowers is an absolute gem, and another of his clones, 'Stewartstonian', with bright, clear red flowers is still a basic nursery azalea.

RHODODENDRONS FOR THE ROCK GARDEN
A dainty, often creeping, evergreen shrub, *Rhododendron keiskei* grows 1 to 3 feet tall. Native to rocky wooded slopes in the mountains of Honshu, Shikoku, and Kyushu, it blooms in April or May, with inch-wide, funnel-like, greenish yellow flowers. Hardiest of all the yellow-flowered species, it is useful in zones 6 and 7, and in zone 5 with winter protection. Selected cultivars include 'Ebino', a free-flowering dwarf form with clear, pale lemon-yellow flowers; pale-yellow-flowered 'La Rocaille', which can grow 8 feet high and wide in forty years; 'Dr. Nick', a dense, compact, 3-foot-tall mounding shrub with large yellow flowers; and 'Yaku Fairy', a very dwarf form with large, lemon-yellow flowers.

Dainty, low-growing or prostrate, *Rhododendron kiusianum* from the high mountains of Kyushu is also suitable for a rock garden. With dense twiggy growth, small, deciduous leaves, and small rose-purple flowers, this species is perfectly in scale with the choicest of alpines.

YAKUSHIMA RHODODENDRON
Rhododendron yakushimanum, sometimes

referred to as *R. metternichii* var. *yakushimanum,* is long-lived at the University of California Botanical Garden in Berkeley, provided it is kept mulched and fed. This surprises me, for it comes from high, wind-swept mountains on Yakushima at elevations of 3,900 to 5,800 feet. Yakushima rhododendron is a very attractive, elegant species. It grows 3 to 3½ feet tall, spreading wider, with 3-inch-long, lustrous, dark green leaves heavily felted with pale brown hairs (called indumentum) on the underside. New shoots are covered with a silver fuzz in spring. The flower buds are a deep cherry pink, opening to pale apple-blossom pink flowers that later fade to white. The mingled colors of blooms at different stages offer a most attractive appearance. Layering is a simple means of propagation; in fact the bottommost branches will often root on their own where they are in contact with the soil. When well developed, the branch can be cut between the rooted portion and the main plant, thus providing a new shrub for another site in the garden. To do this yourself, lightly wound the underside of the branch and hold it in good contact with the soil. You can pin the branch to the ground with "hairpins" made from a wire coat hanger, or, even more simply, by placing a rock on top of the branch.

There are a number of cultivars available. 'Ken Janeck' is larger than the species, with very heavy indumentum and large pink flowers. 'Kochiro Wada', with smaller, convex, deep green leaves and heavy indumentum, was selected by a Japanese nurseryman of the same name, for its tidy, dome-shaped habit, its white-haired branches, and its pink buds that open to white flowers. 'Mist Maiden', one of the earliest selections, is still quite fine, with large apple-blossom pink flowers fading to white. 'Yaku Angel' has long narrow leaves and begins flowering while young, with a generous display of white blooms. Deep-pink-flowered 'Yaku Prince' is larger than low-growing, compact, floriferous 'Yaku Princess', which has pink buds that open to pure white flowers.

Flowering Quince

Flowering quince or japonica, *Chaenomeles speciosa,* is a Chinese shrub much grown in Japan and with numerous cultivars of garden origin. Japanese quince, *Chaenomeles japonica,* is a small shrub growing 1 to 3 feet tall with scarlet, crimson, or orange-red flowers in April or May, native to the mountains of Honshu and Shikoku. Aromatic, golden yellow, applelike fruits, a few inches in diameter, they add autumn interest and may be made into preserves with a better flavor than those from the larger fruits of the Chinese species. So fragrant are the fruits that a few kept in a bowl will perfume a whole room.

The first European to discover this

shrub was Thunberg, who found it in the Hakone mountains. Japanese quince, hardy in zones 4 to 9, is useful at the front of the border to face down taller shrubs. It is subject to apple scab, which often results in complete defoliation by late summer. Spray with a fungicide in spring, repeating at 7- to 10-day intervals as necessary. Equally important, rake up and dispose of fallen leaves in autumn to prevent the spores of the disease from wintering over. Dr. John Creech notes that there is a true prostrate dwarf from the Kirashima mountains of Kyushu, which sounds intriguing for the rock garden. *Chaenomeles japonica* var. *alpina* is a dwarf suckering shrub generally not exceeding 18 inches tall with brick- or orange-red flowers and foliage displaying reddish to bronze tints. There is also a rare, white-flowered counterpart, *C. japonica* f. *alba*.

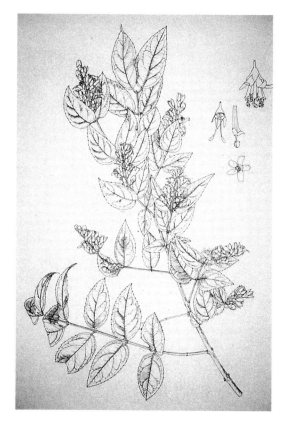

Deutzia crenata

Deutzia

Slender deutzia, *Deutzia gracilis,* is found in the mountains of Shikoku, Honshu's Kanto district and westward, and Kyushu. Growing 3 to 4 feet tall and spreading 4 feet wide, slender deutzia produces numerous upright clusters of pure white flowers in spring and early summer. Some pruning, every third year at a minimum, is necessary to remove dead wood and maintain the graceful rounded form. Useful in zones 5 to 8, deutzia can serve as an informal low hedge. Some have noted that deutzia are highly effective flowering shrubs with no other virtue than those of their flowers. 'Nikko' was collected in Japan by Dr. John Creech. Although often sold as a cultivar of *D. gracilis,* it is actually a selection of *D. crenata*. With profuse double white flowers, slender arching branches, and a low, spreading habit, 'Nikko' is a charming dwarf shrub for the lightly shaded garden. I have planted it with silver-variegated, yellow-flowered *Lamiastrum* 'Hermann's

Pride' and *Campanula carpatica* for a delightful spring combination.

Deutzia crenata is native to Hokkaido, Honshu, Shikoku, and Kyushu, where it is common and variable. It is often confused with *D. scabra*. Both grow 6 to 10 feet tall and spread 4 to 8 feet wide, in zones 6 to 8. In 1861 the British plant collector Robert Fortune sent a double, pink-flowered form, 'Plena' (= 'Rosea Plena'), found growing in a Yokohama temple courtyard, home to England. There are several cultivars, many of which were developed by the French nursery of Lemoine late in the nineteenth century.

FORSYTHIA

That golden herald of spring, *Forsythia suspensa,* is another Chinese shrub so long admired and cultivated in Japan that it was taken as a native by early European visitors. Thunberg vacillated when describing it, calling it first *Ligustrum suspensum,* and then *Syringa suspensa*. In fact, the plant has nothing to do with privet or lilac. More than two hundred years ago in 1786, Vahl, a Danish botanist, named it for William Forsyth, chief gardener of the Chelsea Physic Garden (then known as the Apothecaries Garden) in London. There is actually a Japanese species, *F. japonica,* a rare native of the Honshu mountains that is not generally available.

JAPANESE HOLLY-GRAPE

Japanese holly-grape, *Mahonia japonica,* is, like forsythia, another instance of a Chinese plant that passes for Japanese. Introduced long ago, this popular garden shrub has outstanding evergreen foliage, and attractive flowers and fruit. The pinnately compound leaves, from 12 to nearly 20 inches long, have 9 to 15 stiff, glossy, dark bluish green hollylike leaflets that are a paler yellow-green on the underside. In March or April the plants display long drooping clusters of yellow flowers, followed by bluish black grapelike fruits covered with a whitish bloom in summer. Hardy only in milder climates (zones 7 and 8), Japanese holly-grape grows best in light to moderate shade on sites that do not dry out. Maturing at 5 to 7 feet tall, *M. japonica* is suitable for individual use as a specimen, or in groups.

SPIREA

Japanese spirea, *Spirea japonica,* is rather common and very variable in the mountains of Hokkaido, Honshu, Shikoku, and Kyushu, and also in Korea and China to the Himalayas. In the West, we more often grow its hybrid offspring, *Spirea* x *bumalda,* which is quite cold-tolerant to zone 4, even zone 3 with winter die-back to be expected. It is also tolerant of mild climates, and is suitable to zone 9. Growing up to 3 feet tall, the hybrid has flat clusters of rosy pink to rich crimson flowers in early to midsummer, with some scattered bloom afterward. There are several selections: 'Anthony Waterer' is an "oldie but goodie" just over a century old, with deep carmine-pink flowers from June through August, and dark green, sometimes variegated, leaves. 'Goldflame' has coppery orange-brown new growth in spring, fading to golden yellow, and turning copper-orange again in autumn. Its pink flowers pose a rather startling contrast in late spring. I like to use 'Lime Mound' in herbaceous borders, where its small size and attractive leaf color fit nicely with many perennials. It has coral-red new growth that fades to a cool lemon-yellow or chartreuse, then turns orange-red in autumn. 'Shiburi' (= 'Shirobana') has clusters of pink flowers alternating with white. If pruning is necessary, thin out old shoots in late winter or early spring. Crisp-leaf spirea is considered by some as *S.* x *bumalda* var. *bullata,* while other taxonomists give it specific rank. Unknown in the wild, it is almost certainly of garden origin. A dainty dwarf, it is charming for a somewhat dry site in a rock garden, with somber, dark green, crinkled leaves and small flat clusters of rusty red flowers.

Spirea nipponica is marvelous in late May or June when the outwardly arching branches are wreathed in white flowers handsomely displayed against the dark leaves. It is native to the mountains of Honshu's Kinki district, and eastward.

Prune after flowering to keep it shapely, removing old growth at the base. 'Snowmound' is a free-flowering shrub with dark green leaves. The cultivar name reflects the masses of pure white flowers that clothe the shrub in May.

SHRUBS FOR SUMMER INTEREST

HARLEQUIN GLORY BOWER

Harlequin glory bower, *Clerodendrum trichotomum,* is an unusual deciduous shrub with interesting flowers in late summer and beautiful fruit. It can be grown as a multi-stemmed shrub to about 6 feet tall or, with more difficulty as it tends to sucker freely, trained to a single trunk and used as a standard. Common on Hokkaido, Honshu, Shikoku, and Kyushu, it is also found in Korea, Manchuria, China, Ryukyu, Formosa, and the Philippines. Since harlequin glory bower flowers in August on new wood, it can still be useful in colder areas where it is cut to the ground by cold winter temperatures. The suggested range is from the warmer portion of zone 6 through zone 8. I grow it in a mixed border, where it flowers together with 'Sans Souci', a rose-red lily; the vertical lavender wands of liatris; and the rose-pink daisies of prairie coneflower, *Echinacea purpurea*. Harlequin glory bower's numerous small flowers, held in long-lasting rosy red calyces, look like little white stars or snowflakes. They are followed by bright, metallic-blue berries, equally attractive against the calyces as the berries age to blue-black. The catalpa-like foliage has a bold, coarse texture, and a rather musky odor like peanutbutter if bruised or crushed.

HYDRANGEA

Hydrangeas are native to North America and Asia, with nine species in Japan. These are perhaps the most familiar of the summer-blooming shrubs of Japanese origin. One, *Hydrangea anomala* ssp. *petiolaris,* is a vine, and will be discussed in chapter 7. Among the others are some of the most beautiful flowering shrubs for our gardens. In general they prefer a soil high in organic matter, moist but well-drained—that mystical, mythical perfection so often prescribed by garden books. Hydrangeas wilt in summer sun if the soil is insufficiently moist. One alternative is to plant them in woodland or at woodland's edge, where midday shade offers some protection. The species that bloom in early summer flower on shoots that grew the previous year. Pruning is more to tidy up weak or scraggly growth, which is removed at the base, and to remove last year's spent flowers. Timing is important; pruning should be done in spring as the buds swell, to allow the old stems to provide a modicum of winter protection by trapping snow. I find winter bud damage, and the limp, shabby,

blackened appearance of frost-killed leaves in autumn, to be hydrangea's only drawbacks.

Hydrangea macrophylla var. *normalis,* also known as bigleaf, lacecap, or florist hydrangea, is found in sunny coastal places along the shores of Honshu. Usually it is the hortensia type, var. *macrophylla,* that is most often cultivated in gardens and is also familiar as a potted plant sold at Easter. Hortensia-type hydrangeas have only showy, sterile flowers, resulting in a large, globular, mophead. Hardy from zones 6 to 9, bigleaf hydrangeas need a sheltered, shady site in regions with hot summers. In cold winter regions choose a protected site, for if stems are killed back, flowers will be absent that year. Vigorous new growth shoots from the roots in spring. One year, out of sheer frustration, I dug up three hydrangeas, stuck them into large pots, and wintered them in a sort of walk-in cold frame I have. They flowered quite nicely after I planted them back in the garden in spring.

Hydrangeas grow best in at least moderately acidic conditions. Flower color shifts with the pH of the soil: clear blue flowers occur in acid soils around pH 5.5 with iron and aluminum; pink colors develop where the pH is above 6.0, and are actually a sort of chlorotic effect. Remember that the inherent color of the cultivar also has an influence, and one that is naturally blue will turn a muddy pink or magenta in alkaline soils; the obverse is also true. There are numerous cultivars. 'Ayesha' has unusual gray-lilac flowers. 'Domotoi' has double flowers that can be either pale blue or pink, depending on pH, although it grows better in acid soil. 'Europa' has deep pink florets on a tall, vigorous shrub. 'Holstein' has pink-purple flowers. 'Mandschurica' is somewhat more cold-hardy than most cultivars, and also offers pink or blue flowers. 'Nikko Blue' has mid- to deep-blue flowers, depending on pH. 'Otaksa' has a compact habit and blue flowers. 'Pia' (= 'Piamina') is a dainty miniature under 2 feet tall with pink flowers. 'Preziosa' has pink to blue-purple flowers—depending on pH again—on 3- to 4-foot-tall plants.

Lacecap hydrangea, var. *normalis,* is a seaside plant from the coastal regions of Honshu that is sometimes grown by the Japanese in their gardens. It has large, sterile flowers on the outside of the flattened cluster, while small, fertile flowers make up the majority. Lacecaps are sometimes hardier than the mop-heads (prettier and more graceful too, in my opinion). 'Blaumiese' has large trusses of indigo to deep blue flowers. 'Bluebird' is smaller, with rich blue flowers. 'Blue Billow' was raised from seed collected in Korea by Dr. Richard Lighty of the Mount Cuba Center in Delaware, and is hardy to below-zero temperatures. 'Blue Wave' prefers lightly shaded conditions. Compact-growing 'Lanarth White' tolerates less than ideal conditions such as wind-swept and poor

soil, and has unusual flower heads: blue fertile flowers interspersed with white sterile ones. 'Lilacina' has pink-purple to lilac flowers. 'Mariesii' is an old, rather hardy variety with large flat corymbs of rosy pink flowers. 'Mariesii Variegata' has white-margined leaves and soft blue flowers. It prefers lightly shaded conditions.

Hydrangea paniculata is a familiar, commonplace shrub of suburban yards, typically labeled as "P.G." (*paniculata grandiflora*), or peegee hydrangea. Its solid conical trusses of mostly sterile flowers give the appearance of an about-to-melt ice cream cone. The graceful arch of their natural form is pleasing, but often these shrubs are pruned into standards, which suddenly erupt from a lawn for no apparent reason. They can be used with taste and dignity as in one garden I visited. Several standards had been regularly spaced against a brick wall, and enclosed in clipped, curved hedges of boxwood to create a pleasing formal display. Each parterre also had a seasonal display: white tulips in spring, white pansies in winter, and appropriate annuals in summer.

Common and variable, found on sunny slopes and open woods in the mountains of Hokkaido, Honshu, Shikoku, and Kyushu, *Hydrangea paniculata* is also native to the southern Kuriles, Sakhalin, and China. With greater cold-hardiness than hortensia or lacecap hydrangeas, it can be grown from zone 4 to 8. Growing 8 to 20 feet tall, it spreads 6 to 8 feet with a wide, arching form at maturity. It is tolerant of light shade, but is most floriferous in full sun, and accepts both seaside and city conditions. Blooming in late July or August, its white flower clusters persist through winter. As they age, they assume tints of pink and apple green, fading to tannish brown. There are several cultivars, of which the most familiar, 'Grandiflora', is a sterile flowered form with very large panicles. 'Praecox' blooms earlier, in June, while 'Tardiva' is late-blooming, flowering in August or September.

Hydrangea involucrata is a fairly loose, open shrub growing 4 to 6 feet tall with faintly pink-blushed or very pale blue flower clusters in August or September. Native to sunny, rocky sites or lightly shaded, open woodlands in the mountains of northern and central Honshu, Shikoku, and Kyushu, it is not as cold-tolerant as *H. paniculata*. Usually it is the sterile, somewhat deeper pink, billowy, double-flowered 'Hortensis' that is cultivated, in part for its showiness, but also because it seems hardier.

KERRIA

Kerria, *Kerria japonica,* is an old-fashioned, deciduous shrub whose double-flowered form, 'Pleniflora' (= 'Flora Pleno'), has been in cultivation since 1805. Both double- and single-flowered forms were first described by Kaempfer in his *Flora Japonica* of 1784.

Common in the mountains of Hokkaido, Honshu, Shikoku, and Kyushu, the useful range for this shrub is zones 5 to 9. Growing 4 to 6 feet tall with a similar spread, its suckering habit often develops a small assembly of whiplike, upright, slender, green-barked stems. Their winter appearance, especially in a snowy landscape, is charming. Kerria grows in sun or shade, but I find the orange-yellow flowers hold their color best in shade. 'Plena''s fully double pompons of flowers on arching branches begin in late May, with scattered repeat bloom into summer. The single-flowered form, reminiscent of a little yellow wild rose, fits nicely into the naturalistic woodland garden. Perhaps my favorite is 'Picta', with white-edged leaves and single flowers. This often reverts to more vigorous plain green-leaved shoots that must be removed lest they replace the variegated portion.

JAPANESE TREE LILAC

Japanese tree lilac, *Syringa reticulata,* can be considered as either a very large shrub or a small tree, depending on the scale of your garden. In Japan it is native to the mountains of Hokkaido, Honshu, Shikoku, and Kyushu, and is hardy in zones 3 to 7. In the cooler portion of its range, Japanese tree lilac matures at 25 or 30 feet tall, with a low, domed crown. Heart-shaped, dark green leaves, 3 to 6 inches long, provide a coarse texture. The purplish brown bark

In May a luxurious profusion of wisteria
flowers roofs over a stone-pillared arbor
at Utsunomiya-shi's city park.

Its bold foliage and bright orange daisies make ligularia a handsome plant for
sunny sites with moist soil.

The cheerful yellow flowers of ephemeral *Adonis amurensis* brighten woodland gardens in late February. PHOTO BY FURUHASHI YOSHIO

Eranthis pinnatifida is Japan's rare, white-flowered counterpart to a European
harbinger of spring, the yellow winter aconite. PHOTO BY NIHEI TAKEO

At the field research station of the Tokyo University Botanic Garden in Nikko, scattered white flowers of *Anemone flaccida* brighten the forest floor in May.

A closer look at a single flower in the author's garden reveals its exquisite details.

Like gleaming white goblets, the May flowers of *Paeonia obovata* var. *alba* lend their radiance to the author's woodland garden.

Boldly rising on stout stems in the author's woodland garden, the soft mauve-lavender flowers of *Glaucidium palmatum* appear in May.

exfoliates, offering a shaggy appearance similar to some flowering cherries. In June and July ample clusters of creamy-white, fragrant flowers appear, their musky scent a bit like that of privet, its close relative. 'Ivory Silk' is a sturdy, compact, more cold-tolerant Canadian selection with cherry-pink-tinted bark.

SHRUBS FOR AUTUMN INTEREST

Striking foliage color and fruiting effect are the foremost qualities provided by autumn shrubs. Autumn foliage can be even more vivid than the most colorful of flowers. Showy fruits provide a different, equally attractive display.

BEAUTYBERRY

Callicarpa dichotoma is well named beautyberry. Though small, the clusters of small berries are an unusual, light purple color, even more striking against the bare branches after leaf drop. The pale pink flowers in early summer are inconspicuous, partially hidden by the leaves. The shrub itself is somewhat loose and leggy, growing about 6 feet tall and somewhat wider. Regular pruning will help keep a graceful form, or, alternatively, mixing it with other shrubs will help disguise its lanky form. Native to portions of Honshu, Shikoku,

and Kyushu, and also to Korea, Ryukyu, Formosa, and China, it may suffer die-back in cold winter areas. It is most suitable in the warmer portions of zone 5 through zone 8. As with many other fruiting shrubs, planting a couple of different clones, or cross-fertile species that flower at the same time, will result in a heavier fruit set than if only one is used.

Japanese beautyberry, *Callicarpa japonica,* is a somewhat larger shrub with deeper purple fruits. It is more cold-tolerant and rarely exhibits winter die-back, as might be expected from its natural range in the southern districts of Hokkaido, Honshu, Shikoku, Ryukyu, Formosa, China, and Manchuria. There is even an attractive white-berried form, 'Leucocarpa'. Rather humdrum through the spring and summer, beautyberry is a showstopper when in fruit. Elaine Stedlack told me that, though beautyberry is relatively unknown in the Bay Area, it is easy to grow and sets nice displays of fruit. Consider underplanting it with masses of a lavender fall-blooming crocus such as *Crocus speciosus* to accentuate the autumn impact. It is most appropriate for a rustic, naturalistic, informal garden.

JAPANESE CLETHRA

Our native summersweet, *Clethra alnifolia,* is a welcome addition to moist or wet soils, and is tolerant of moderately shaded sites. In time it spreads to form a large clump, making summersweet suitable for screening, or massing along a pond or stream. Its Japanese counterpart, *C. barbinervis,* has a more stately, graceful manner of growth and is more appropriate for specimen use. Taller, more treelike, Japanese clethra also blooms in mid- to late summer, with white, many-flowered panicles, but I find the reliable, rich orange-red autumn foliage, and the cinnamon-brown peeling bark reasons enough for its use. The gracefully trailing, horizontally nodding flower clusters are a bonus, especially since they have little fragrance.

Common and very variable on the hills and mountains of Hokkaido, Honshu, Shikoku, and Kyushu, Japanese clethra is also indigenous to Korea's Quelpaert Island. It is reliably hardy in zone 5, and also grows well in Berkeley's mild climate, dependably producing deep fall color. Japanese clethra often develops several trunks and remains a large shrub for years before gaining the stature of a tree.

Viburnum

Japanese bush cranberry or linden viburnum, *Viburnum dilatatum,* is a deciduous shrub growing 6 to 9 feet tall, sometimes a little higher, and spreading 6 to 8 feet wide. The somewhat hairy, medium green, coarse leaves turn russet red in autumn, and small, numerous, white flowers in flattened clusters 3 to 5 inches across, create a fine display in late spring. But it is the sumptuous display of scarlet fruit from early to midautumn for which Japanese bush cranberry is usually chosen. Native to thickets in hills and lower mountain elevations, this shrub is hardy in zones 5 to 8. There are several forms and cultivars among which to choose. The form *xanthocarpum* has yellow fruit. 'Catskill' is a dwarf form with more compact growth and leaves that turn orange-yellow to red, against which the dark red fruit is quite striking. 'Erie', also dwarf, has foliage that turns yellow, orange, and red in autumn, with profuse, striking pale pink fruit maturing to a warm coral red. Dense-growing 'Iroquois' has outsized leaves over 6 inches long that turn orange-red in autumn, and abundant production of long-lasting, glossy, scarlet-red fruit. Japanese bush cranberry is a good shrub for naturalizing by planting in groups and masses in light shade or full sun, where flower and fruit production is better. An evergreen background sets off autumn fruit and foliage color even better.

Japanese snowball bush or doublefile viburnum, *Viburnum plicatum,* is a familiar shrub. Oddly enough, it was the sterile, double-flowered form that was described first, thus making it the species type. The shrub is hardy in zones 6 to 8. Its snowball-like clusters of flowers drip unevenly off the branches, but since they are all sterile, *V. plicatum* has no fruiting interest.

I prefer *Viburnum plicatum* f. *tomentosum* (= *V. tomentosum*), whose fertile and sterile flowers are set together in each clus-ter, like lacecap hydrangeas. This form is the wild type, native to thickets in the mountains of Honshu, Shikoku, and Kyushu, and also to Formosa and China. Fertile flowers in the center of each cluster are followed by coral-red fruits that mature to black. Its tiered horizontal branching pattern, laced with white flowers in April after the leaves appear, creates an elegant display. Adaptable to conditions ranging from sun to partial shade, from moderately moist to rather wet, this is a superb choice for the shady garden. Low branches that sweep the ground often root with soil con-tact. These will then form a leader and can be severed from the parent plant to use elsewhere in the garden. Somewhat hardier than the straight species, this form and many of its cultivars can be grown in zone 5. 'Lanarth' is compact, with pro-nounced horizontal branching, light green leaves, and large flowers; 'Mariesii' also has large flower clusters, and symmetrical, strongly tiered horizontal branching, but it rarely sets fruit; 'Newport' is a dwarf that grows to 3 feet high, with good burgundy-red autumn leaf color. Several cultivars have pinkish flowers: 'Pink Beauty''s bloom white, aging to a rouged flush; 'Rosacea' has mingled pink and white flowers; while 'Roseum' has white flowers aging to deep pink. Apart from novelty, I'm not sure how the pink flowers are an improvement—since I grow doublefile

viburnum in heavy shade, I prefer the way white flowers stand out and create a more striking effect. A mature shrub at the end of a path serves as a beacon, enticing me to sit on the bench before it—as if gardeners had time to sit!

With barely a toehold on Tsushima Island in Japan, Korean spice viburnum, *Viburnum carlesii,* has the door to many gardens opened for it by the intensely clovelike fragrance of its flowers in April and May. This species is more cold-tolerant than you might think, and is suitable from zones 4 to 8. Rounded clusters of flow-ers—pink in bud, opening to white—appear as the leaves just begin to unfold. The leaves expand to 2 to 4 inches long, and are soft gray-green in color and some-what velvety to the touch. 'Compactum' has dark green leaves, profuse clusters of white flowers, and a tighter habit, remain-ing below 5 feet high for many years. The species has been used as a parent for sever-al interspecific hybrids: *V.* x *carlcephalum* is the result of a cross with *V. macrocephalum* (a Chinese species); it has large, dense flower clusters with the fragrance and cold-hardiness of the Korean spice vibur-num. 'Cayuga', a second-generation back-cross with great numbers of small flower clusters, grows about 6½ feet tall, with greater resistance to powdery mildew and leaf spot.

EVERGREEN SHRUBS
FOR WINTER INTEREST

An all-evergreen garden is a static one, with little change from spring's awakening to summer's maturation, autumn's ripeness and winter's rest. When a shrub has both spring and winter interest, I have chosen to focus on the latter. For example, *Leucothoe keiskei, Mahonia japonica,* and *Pieris japonica* have attractive flowers in the garden's awakening season, but, as broadleaved evergreens, also endow interest when the garden sleeps in winter. It is the balance of bare deciduous branches and evergreen foliage, both needled conifers and broadleaved shrubs, that adds liveliness to the sleeping landscape; those persistently evergreen trees and shrubs set off the different growth habits, textures, and bark colors present in the garden, adding visual appeal for the house-bound winter gardener.

ARDISIA

Ardisia crenata has a wealth of common names—coral ardisia, coralberry, spiceberry, Christmas berry—from which you might correctly deduce that this shrub has handsome, long-lasting red berries. Found in the low mountain forests of Shikoku, Kyushu, and southern and western Honshu, as well as in Ryukyu, Formosa, Korea, China, and India, this is a tender shrub hardy only in zone 9. Growing 6½

feet tall, the upright, mostly unbranched stems are clothed in whorls of leathery evergreen leaves, 3 or more inches long. Though coralberry spreads underground, sending up shoots as it goes, it does not make a dense mass. Coralberry is better naturalized in partial shade, with several shrubs massed in an informal, irregular display, than isolated and grown individually for specimen use. In summer small pink or white flowers appear in clusters at the tips of branches, followed by extremely showy, long-lasting clusters of ½-inch diameter coral-red to scarlet berries. 'Alba' is a cultivar with white berries.

AUCUBA

Spotted laurel, Japanese laurel, or Japanese aucuba, *Aucuba japonica,* has two personalities. In mild winter regions it is as ubiquitous a shrub as is apt to be found, prosaic and boring to "sophisticated" gardeners. Where winters are cold enough to cut branches to the ground, it is grown as a herbaceous perennial or as a house plant. It is common in the lowland and mountain forests of Shikoku, western Honshu, and Kyushu. With their fondness for unusual and unique forms, the Japanese have selected many cultivars. Hardy as a shrub in zones 7 to 9, spotted laurel grows 4 to 5 feet tall, spreading 3 to 4 feet wide. Where I garden in Connecticut (zone 6) it has survived several winters. When there is consistent snow cover, or when I remember to heap oak leaves over it, it survives above ground. Otherwise it retreats to its roots, but comes up again in spring.

Tolerant of heavy shade, spotted laurel will grow in the darkest corners. Its elliptic to narrowly oval, glossy, leathery, evergreen leaves are 3 to 8 inches long. The extent of their variegation is astonishing: 'Bicolor' has large teeth along the margin, with a central yellow spot on green; 'Crotonoides' is a female with leaves mottled in golden yellow; 'Crotonifolia' is a female with leaves finely speckled with white and gold; more subtle, 'Fructo-alba' has sparsely blotched leaves spotted pale green and gold, and whitish fruit; 'Gold Dust' is a popular old female cultivar with gold speckled leaves and red fruit; 'Longifolia' (= 'Salicifolia') is a female with bright green, unmarked, willowlike leaves; the dark green leaves of 'Picturata' (= 'Aureo-maculata') have a large central golden-yellow blotch; 'Variegata' (= 'Maculata'), also called gold dust plant, has dark green leaves speckled and blotched in bright golden yellow; while 'Viridis' (= 'Concolor') has unmarked dark green leaves.

Knowing whether a clone is male or female is vital if fruiting is important to your garden scheme. Aucuba is dioecious, which means each individual shrub is either male or female. The first clone introduced to European gardens was a spotted-leaved female brought to England from Japan in 1783 by John Graeffer. Lacking a male to pollinate her, the plant never produced an autumnal display of red berries; that is, until Robert Fortune discovered the male form of *Aucuba japonica* in the Yokohama garden of George Hall in 1861. The plain green-leaved male was sent to a nursery in Surrey, and subsequently a fruiting plant was exhibited in Kensington in 1864. It caused a sensation, and within a couple of years male plants were sold (priced by the leaf) or rented out "to stud" by ambitious nurserymen. After several decades, the excitement died down and small potted fruiting plants were readily available, ready to go out in the garden. Typically, female spotted laurels have showy, attractive, bright coral-red or scarlet-red berries. Forma *luteocarpa* has yellow berries, while f. *leucocarpa* and 'Fructo-alba' have white fruit.

Aucuba japonica var. *borealis,* native to Hokkaido and the Japan Sea side of Honshu, was introduced by Dr. John Creech in 1955. A decumbent form growing barely a foot high, the prostrate branches survive the cold winters under heavy snow cover. Plants in the Asian Valley display garden of the National Arboretum in Washington, D.C., make a nice, dense, low-growing exhibit.

JAPANESE PLUM YEW
Historically, Japanese plum yew, *Cephalotaxus harringtonia,* has been a popular

garden shrub in the Southeast, where it is preferred for its superior heat tolerance to Japanese yew, *Taxus cuspidata*. Japanese plum yew is steadily gaining favor in the Northeast since it is not browsed by deer; they have been found to be completely untouched adjacent to an entirely denuded Japanese yew. Needles are longer than those of a true yew—1 or 2 inches long—and rich green and very glossy above, on outspread to somewhat nodding branches.

Known only in cultivation, a form first grown in Japan is 'Fastigiata', introduced to the West by von Siebold in 1830. This handsome shrub has especially dark green needles and an upright, columnar form, particularly when young, growing 3 feet tall and only 12 to 18 inches wide. Long, rodlike branches are held steeply upright, scarcely branched and identifiable by needles in tidy, complete whorls around the branchlets. After twelve to fifteen years plants form a more rounded mound, 8 feet tall by 5 or 6 feet wide. The needles turn olive green when grown in full sun in southeastern gardens. 'Fastigiata' is an excellent accent in a shade garden, and especially useful in containers. In colder regions where snow or ice might damage them, tie the branches, especially those of young trees, with a spiral of monofilament fishing line from top to bottom. This is especially important on young plants. Also avoid exposed, windy situations. Otherwise Japanese plum yew is hardy from zones 5 to 9.

'Duke Gardens' is a cultivar originating in the Sarah P. Duke Gardens in Durham, North Carolina. A sport (a spontaneously occurring mutation from the regular form) of 'Fastigiata', it forms a dense, sun-tolerant, dark green mound 3 to 5 feet tall and almost as wide. 'Fritz Huber' is a relatively low-growing, compact form of 'Fastigiata' that slowly reaches 2 feet tall with an equal or greater spread, and develops a vaselike outline with branches arching slightly from the center.

There are two golden variegated forms of Japanese plum yew. 'Fastigiata Aurea' has golden margins on the needles and grows a bit more slowly. 'Korean Gold', also a fastigiate form, has new growth that is entirely golden yellow in spring, chartreuse in midsummer, and green by winter. This selection of a Korean plant is cultivated in Japan as golden Korean podocarpus.

Additionally, there are truly prostrate forms growing 1 to 4 feet high and spreading from 2 to 20 feet wide, or more. These are usually confused in the trade with a number of low spreading clones incorrectly sold as 'Prostrata'. The true form is a low, spreading, sport of 'Fastigiata' with glossy, very dark green needles on slightly arching, gracefully drooping branches. It originated at Hilliers Nursery in England where a 30-year-old plant was only 30 inches high and a little over 8 feet wide. A magnificent specimen growing at the

Brooklyn Botanic Gardens shows that the form eventually reaches 2 to 4 feet tall, and can spread 20 to 30 feet wide.

Hinoki False Cypress

You can choose from a number of cultivars of hinoki, *Chamaecyparis obtusa,* depending on the situation. There are selections of moderate height with golden, bluish gray, or silver-white needles. Others have a more open appearance and fernlike foliage. There are also slow-growing dwarf forms with a coral-like contorted texture. There are even very dwarf forms tiny enough for rock gardens.

Tall to medium in height, upright, of normal vigor, green-needled 'Gracilis' has a conical, more compact overall appearance than that of the species (described earlier in chapter 3). First imported from Japan around 1862 by von Siebold, 'Gracilis' grows 15 feet tall with outspread branches. The branchlets form an irregular, scallop-shell pattern, clothed with short, dense, somewhat glossy needles. At about the same time von Siebold introduced 'Lycopodiodes', which is more of a dwarf in form (remember, "dwarf" is a relative term when we talk about trees). This cultivar grows 8 feet high and over 6 feet wide, and it has a shrubby appearance with a somewhat open, rounded form. Irregular ascending branches have thick twigs tipped with cockscomb-like clustered branchlets that are covered with dark bluish green needles. 'Lycopodiodes Aurea', also introduced to Europe more than a century ago, is a dwarf form as well, but is slower growing, reaching scarcely over 3 feet high with light yellow needles. 'Tetragona Aurea' was introduced even earlier, around 1870. Dwarf, seldom more than 6½ feet tall, it is usually upright, with ascending or outspread branches. The short, irregularly arranged branches are covered with densely imbricated (overlapping) needles in four tidy rows, ranging in color from glossy golden yellow to a more bronze yellow. 'Nana Aurea' is another dwarf, conical form that grows to 6½ feet tall. First imported from Japan in the mid-nineteenth century, it has horizontally spreading branches, and golden yellow and partly whitish yellow branchlets.

Another plant imported at about the same time, 'Pygmaea' is a broadly globose dwarf form. Grafted forms grow about 5 feet tall and as wide; as an own-rooted (not grafted) plant it reaches scarcely 2 feet tall but much wider, with spreading branches, fan-shaped twigs, and bright green needles that turn somewhat brownish in fall and winter. 'Filiformis' has a conical habit, accentuated by long, thin branches that droop at the tip. It was found in a Tokyo garden by Maximowicz about 1865. 'Kanamahiba' is a dwarf form with thickish, cockscomb-like clustered branches that are contorted at the tips. Introduced from Japan around 1900, it now and then reverts to the original form, so these growths must be pruned out.

Sawara, *Chamaecyparis pisifera,* is extensively planted in Japan as an ornamental. Introduced from Japan by Robert Fortune in 1861, 'Argenteovariegata' grows 30 feet tall, with branchlets that are somewhat variegated with white on the tips, and are very attractive in new spring growth. Fortune also introduced 'Aurea', with golden-yellow branchlets and needles that green in shade.

Plants in the plumosa group have foliage that falls between the typical, ordinary (scalelike in this instance) sort and the soft juvenile needles of the squarrosa group (squarrose means rough, with projecting scales). Foliage also does not hug the branches so closely. 'Plumosa' itself has a conical habit, growing 30 to 60 feet tall, with outspread branches. 'Plumosa Argentea' is somewhat slender, with small white branch tips that turn green in their second year. Overall, the needles are dark green. 'Plumosa Aurea' has golden-yellow foliage on the branch tips that are especially vivid in early summer. 'Plumosa Flavescens' is a dwarf form, conical or globose to about 3 feet, with yellow-white branchlets and needles that generally green up in fall.

Chamaecyparis in the filifera group (*filiform* means very long, thin, and threadlike, and is usually applied to leaves) have a fine, stringy texture produced by thin, pendant branches covered with tightly adpressed (lying flat and close to the stem), scalelike foliage. The squarrosa group has juvenile, softer, needlelike foliage, spreading widely from the twigs and branches to produce a velvety, mossy appearance. 'Squarrosa', introduced by von Siebold in 1843, grows 30 to 60 feet tall, with a broad, openly conical crown. It is densely twiggy with spreading branches that nod at the tips. The needle color is a good silvery gray. 'Squarrosa Argentea' grows 6½ feet tall and has needles that are more conspicuously silver-gray.

JAPANESE FAN PALM

Sago palm, or Japanese fan palm, *Cycas revoluta,* is an interesting living fossil, found only near the seashore of Kyushu and Ryukyu. Hardy in zones 8 and 9, it may seem rather odd to recommend such a tender plant for winter interest, but its fountainlike appearance, so useful in foundation plantings, or when massed, or even as a specimen for gardeners in the South, is apt to be overshadowed by showier flowering shrubs in spring and summer. Winter allows sago palm a more prominent place.

Sago palm is too primitive a plant to have flowers. On male plants the golden-haired conelike sporophyll cluster is about 18 inches long, and appears in the center of the plant surrounded by a fountain of fernlike foliage. On young plants the rich dark green, glossy, pinnate leaves range from 18 inches to more than 3 feet long, double that length on old plants. Sago palm grows 6½ feet tall. Unusual dwarf, cristate, or variegated clones are unlikely to be available outside Japan.

JAPANESE FATSIA

Japanese fatsia, or glossy-leaved paper plant, *Fatsia japonica,* is an evergreen shrub, sometimes reaching over 9 feet tall, with palmate foliage. (Its relative, rice-paper plant, *Tetrapanax papyrifera,* is a Taiwanese, possibly Chinese plant.) Fatsia is easy to transplant, and tolerant of pruning, air pollution, and wind. It prefers shade and a moist site but grows well even in a sunny site, and is hardy in zones 8 and 9, and, with protection, in zone 7. Since fatsia grows wild in woods near the sea on the Pacific side of Honshu, Shikoku, and Kyushu, as well as in Ryukyu and South Korea, a sheltered, wind-protected site is best, to shield the leaves from damage. The plant was discovered by Thunberg, and originally as *Aralia*. Introduced to England in 1838, it was at first grown as a conservatory plant. The large, glossy, 7- to 9-lobed evergreen leaves are reminiscent of those on castor bean, and can reach 14 inches long and wide, with a coarse texture. Fatsia is attractive as an espalier or in a large container. It is especially handsome with a finer-textured plant, such as holly fern, as ground cover. Fatsia tolerates deep shade, crowded urban settings, and salt spray, but since wind damages the leaves, a seaside site would be problematical. Prune in early spring to remove winter-damaged foliage, to encourage new growth, and to control size; otherwise the plant will form a straggly small tree. Since foliage is fatsia's most attractive feature, encourage good growth with light fertilization in spring and again in summer.

There are several cultivars of Japanese fatsia: 'Aurea' has gold, variegated leaves; 'Marginata' has deeply lobed, gray-green leaves with off-white margins; 'Moseri' is a vigorous, more compact cultivar with especially large leaves; and 'Variegata' displays wide creamy-yellow margins and leaf tips. 'Moseri' is one parent of an intergeneric hybrid with Irish ivy, *Hedera hibernica*. X *Fatshedera lizei* has shiny, 5-lobed, evergreen leaves two-thirds the size of Japanese fatsia, a more vining habit, and has about the same hardiness range. It is useful as an espalier.

JAPANESE HOLLY

Japanese holly, or box-leaved holly, *Ilex crenata*, is a workhorse evergreen for zones 6 to 9. It can be sheared as a hedge or grown as a specimen. There are even dwarf selections suitable for the rock garden. Native to thickets and wet places in the lowlands and mountains of Hokkaido, Honshu, Shikoku, and Kyushu, this shrub is often planted in Japanese gardens, especially as a hedge. They are good substitutes for boxwood where that shrub becomes winter-damaged. Japanese hollies can be left alone as an informal hedge or sheared into a precise formal outline. Though the type grows as a small tree 15 feet high, there are more modest shrub-sized cultivars in the 4- to 8-foot range, smaller moundlike selections growing 3 feet tall, and even smaller, tiny dwarfs, suitable for the rock garden. Eventual size plays an important roll in cultivar selection. Japanese holly is most successful in full sun in the colder portion of its range but partial shade is acceptable; in southeastern and southern gardens, shade is necessary. Moist, fertile soils with adequate drainage are best. In colder regions, protect plants from drying winter winds.

For specimen use or as a tall hedge where screening is wanted, consider 'Buxifolia', 'Latifolia' (= 'Fortunei'), or 'Sentinel'. If more moderate size will serve, then you might choose 'Compacta' or 'Highlander'. Perhaps you need foundation plants and intend to still look out the windows several years from now. 'Convexa', 'Hetzi', or 'Microphylla' would be suitable selections. There are accent or edging cultivars of Japanese holly, good for the front of a planting bed or even as a ground cover. These include the popular 'Helleri', 'Kingsville', 'Repandens', and 'Stokesii'. Several minute, slow-growing cultivars are suitable for the rock garden or their specialized miniature landscape containers called trough gardens. Racing along with the speedy growth rate of 2 inches a year, 'Dwarf Pagoda', 'Elfin', 'Green Cushion', and 'Muffit' are expensive, collectors' plants.

JUNIPER

Chinese juniper, *Juniperus chinensis,* is a garden mainstay, variable from trees growing 65 feet tall to ground cover plants only 18 inches high. With appropriate selection, there are cultivars useful as specimens and for screening, mass plantings, foundation planting, or ground cover. Found near the seashore on Honshu, Shikoku, and Kyushu, as well as in China and Mongolia, this widely variable conifer is a favorite of Japanese gardeners. It is popular in North American gardens as well, and thrives in zones 4 to 9. Chinese junipers usually display both needlelike juvenile foliage and scalelike mature foliage on the same plant. Selected cultivars may show predominantly one or the other. Color can vary from bluish green or bright green to softer yellowish or olive-green, or even white variegated needles. This shrub is dioecious. Female plants produce attractive clusters of ¼-inch fruits, covered with a bluish white bloom. A number of cultivars exist, some more widely available than others. Treelike 'Aurea', a male clone, has dull yellow foliage. 'Columnaris' is a handsome, dark green, tall, narrow clone growing 30 feet tall or more, and only 7 to 8 feet wide. It is wonderful for screening. 'Columnaris Glauca' (= 'Blue Column') has bright bluish green, dense, juvenile foliage. Female 'Kaizuka' (= 'Torulosa', Hollywood juniper) grows 10 to 12 feet tall with a 6- to 8-foot spread. The somewhat twisted, loosely upright branches of this cultivar produce a roughly spiraled, conical form useful as a formal accent.

Some plants often listed in nursery catalogs as cultivars of *J. chinensis,* are classed by the *RHS Index of Garden Plants* as hybrids of Chinese juniper with *J. sabina,* which should be categorized as *J.* x *media.* These include the popular 10- to 14-foot-tall and similarly wide silvery blue-green 'Hetzi', and all the Pfitzer junipers, such as the gracefully arching 'Pfitzeriana', which grows 5 to 7 feet tall and 8 to 10 feet wide; 'Pfitzeriana Aurea', which has soft golden-yellow branch tips that turn yellowish green by autumn and winter. Dense and prickly needled, silvery blue 'Pfitzeriana Glauca' turns purplish blue in winter, as does smaller, 3½-foot-tall, 6½- to 10-foot wide 'Pfitzeriana Compacta' (= 'Nick's Compact').

Other junipers are discussed as ground covers in chapter 5.

LEUCOTHOE
Leucothoe keiskei is a miniature charmer, a lilliputian counterpart of the familiar American species, drooping leucothoe, *L. fontanesiana* (= *L. catesbaei*). It is native to shaded wet rocky cliffs in the mountains of Honshu's Kanto, Tokaido, and Kinki dis-

tricts, and prefers a moist but well-drained soil and a shaded site. There its thick, lustrous, dark green leaves clothe stems that arch 8 to 10 inches above the ground. With some sun the leaves turn a rich plum-red in winter. In spring, white bell-like flowers (similar to those of a blueberry) trail at the tip of each of last year's branches. Its dainty size and wide spread make it suitable for a large, shaded rock garden setting, in a woodland edging beside a path, or as a ground cover. It is also one of the few shrubs that seem unpalatable to deer and other browsing animals.

PRIVET
Japanese privet, or wax-leaf privet, *Ligustrum japonicum,* is a very adaptable shrub, tolerating drought, heat, cold, and even salt spray in coastal settings. It can be used for a loose, informal unclipped hedge; a sheared, trained, formal hedge; as topiary; or in a background planting. It is found in the woods and thickets of hills and lowlands on Shikoku, central and western Honshu, and Kyushu, and also in Korea. This 6- to 10-foot-tall, 5- to 6-foot-wide evergreen shrub is hardy in zones 7 to 9. Deep green, leathery leaves have a waxy luster and, provide neat attire that is especially attractive in winter. The upright clusters of small white flowers, fragrant or pungent depending on your sense of smell, appear in late summer. There are several interesting cultivars. 'Fraseri' has yellow to

chartreuse new growth that turns green as it matures, 'Jack Frost' has glossy green leaves with a narrow creamy-white edge. 'Silver Star' is a compact, upright, slow-growing form with dark green leaves edged in cream, with a silver tint. 'Variegatum' has leaves edged and flecked with white. Taller but otherwise very similar, Chinese privet, *L. lucidum,* can be distinguished by the sunken veins on the underside of the leaves. Curlyleaf ligustrum, *L. japonicum* 'Rotundifolium', grows only 4 feet tall and spreads 3 feet wide, with a dense arrangement of round or broadly oval leaves that grow in an unusual curling or twisted habit. A rigidly upright shrub known only as a cultivated plant, 'Rotundifolium' is interesting in a patio or courtyard garden, perhaps as a container plant.

Border privet, *Ligustrum obtusifolium,* is a much-branched, twiggy, 10-foot-tall deciduous shrub, very common in thickets and sparse open woodland in the hills and lowlands of Hokkaido, Honshu, Shikoku, and Kyushu, as well as Ryukyu and Korea. Hardy from zones 4 to 8, this shrub is a popular choice for hedges. In areas where autumn weather brings sunny days and cool nights, the medium to deep green, glossy leaves take on a purple hue before dropping. Regel privet, *L. obtusifolium* var. *regelianum,* is often considered more desirable for informal, unpruned hedges since it has a graceful arching form when young,

maturing to a blocky form. At 6½ feet tall, plants are also more compact.

California privet, *Ligustrum ovalifolium,* is a semievergreen or deciduous shrub, depending on where it is grown. Its useful range is zones 6 to 9; it is more evergreen in the warmer portion. In colder regions it is susceptible to winter damage, exacerbated by pruning late in the season or the use of fertilizers high in nitrogen after midsummer. California privet grows 14 feet tall and is frequently used as a hedge or screen. There are a number of cultivars available: 'Albomarginatum' has white-edged leaves; 'Argenteum' has leaves with silvery margins; 'Aureum' (= 'Aureo-marginata') has leaves with a broad yellow edge; 'Lemon and Lime' is similar, with pale green leaves edged in yellow; 'Variegatum' has leaves flecked with pale yellow. Of garden origin, ibolium privet, *L.* x *ibolium,* is a hardier hybrid of California privet and border privet. It grows well even in zone 5. 'Variegatum' has soft creamy edges to the leaves.

HEAVENLY BAMBOO
Heavenly bamboo, *Nandina domestica,* is very popular in Japan. It is planted at the base of large trees, near large stones, by a water container or a building, or as a hedge. It has become a familiar occupant of southern and southeastern gardens in the United States. The leaves are more densely clustered toward the top of unbranched or

sparsely branched bamboolike stems, which can grow 6 feet tall or more. The compound, narrow, evergreen foliage creates an attractive display year-round. In spring new growth is bronze-copper to red, maturing to green in summer, and then turning red-purple to bright red in autumn if grown in sunny sites. Large clusters of bright red berries in 12-inch terminal clusters (sometimes white, rarely pale violet-purple) add autumn and winter interest. Heavenly bamboo is native to mountain ravines and valleys in the warmer central and southern districts of Japan, as well as central China and India. It grows well in zones 7 to 9, and in zone 6 in a sheltered, protected site. Regular pruning, with yearly removal of older stems, will help maintain a more attractive form.

There are a number of cultivars available. 'Umpqua Chief' grows 5 to 6 feet tall, with narrow leaves first spotted red in autumn, then turning completely red in winter. 'Moyer's Red' grows 6 to 8 feet tall and has good winter color. 'Umpqua Princess' is smaller, growing 3 to 4 feet tall, with narrow leaves producing a fine, see-through texture. 'Nana Purpurea' is bushy, grows 4 feet tall, and has year-round rich crimson-purple color in sunny sites. 'Compacta' grows 4 to 5 feet tall, with lacy foliage and excellent fall color. Some heavenly bamboo are dwarf: 'Harbor Dwarf' has somewhat puckered leaves and grows only 18 inches tall in zone 6 (2 to 3 feet tall in milder regions), sometimes dying back

to the ground in winter; 'Pygmaea' also grows a dainty 18 inches tall but unfortunately fruits poorly; 'Fire Power' grows just 2 feet high and wide with incandescent, glowing red winter color. The leaves and young stems of 'Variegata' are variegated deliciously with white, cream, and candy pink. 'Alba' has ivory-white fruits.

JAPANESE ANDROMEDA

Very popular for foundation plantings, Japanese andromeda, *Pieris japonica,* is another deer-proof shrub, a fact noted in historical records concerning the deer park at Nara in Japan. The evergreen leaves are not so thick and waxy as those of leucothoe, and unfortunately are prone to attack by lace bugs, which spoil the foliage's appearance. When necessary, new growth—richly colored bronze, bright red, or chartreuse—should be treated with the appropriate chemical solution (either foliar spray or soil drench systemic) after it matures. Flower buds form in late summer or early autumn, and their trailing tassels are attractive against the evergreen leaves, adding additional winter interest. The dense clusters of waxy white flowers open in April or May. Though native to the sunny hillsides of Honshu, Shikoku, and Kyushu, Japanese andromeda is best planted in a lightly shaded site, or at least protected from strong sun and harsh winds in winter.

There are a respectable number of cultivars available, usually selected for depth of color of the new shoots or flower buds. 'Bisbee Dwarf' is a compact miniature with tiny, dark green, glossy leaves and pink flowers. Slowly growing 18 inches tall, 'Pygmaea' is sparse flowering and has very small narrow leaves. 'Variegata' has leaves with a thin, crisp, creamy-white margin, pink-flushed when young; while slower growing, it is not dwarf. Selected forms with white flowers include 'Mountain Fire' and 'Valley Fire' (both with a showy display of white flowers against vivid red new foliage.) 'Whitecaps' and 'White Cascade' have long-lasting flower clusters. 'Christmas Cheer' blooms early with pink to deep pink flowers. 'Dorothy Wycoff' has a compact habit and dark pink to red flowers, while profusely blooming 'Flamingo' has deep rose-red flowers. 'Valley Rose' has pastel pink flowers.

DWARF STONE PINE

Dwarf stone pine, *Pinus pumila,* can best be described as a creeping, more or less prostrate shrub. It has no trunk, but its main branches, 30 to 50 feet long, form a dense tangled mass 1 to 8 feet high. It grows in the coldest, most exposed areas near the snow line in alpine regions of Hokkaido and the northern districts of Honshu, as well as in eastern Siberia and Kamchatka. Ernest Wilson, the noted American plant collector, found dwarf stone pine on mountain peaks on Hokkaido, along with rhodo-

dendron, willows, and alpine plants. In Sakhalin he found it growing at sea level on sand dunes, and in meadows with shore juniper, salt spray rose, crowberry, and the scrubby growth of fir and larch. Dwarf stone pine is exceedingly cold-hardy—useful from zone 2 to the cooler portions of zone 7. Harsher conditions produce lower growing plants, as it is the environment that dwarfs this species. Under good conditions it can grow up to 8 feet tall with a far-reaching spread.

JAPANESE SKIMMIA

Japanese skimmia, *Skimmia japonica* ssp. *japonica,* is a rather common, low-growing, suckering, evergreen shrub native to the mountain forests of Honshu's Kanto districts and westward, Shikoku, and Kyushu. This plant was first described by Kaempfer in 1712. The deep green, leathery leaves are 3 to 5 inches long, resulting in a coarse texture. This low, rounded, mounding shrub grows 4 feet tall, and spreads 3 feet wide, making it a good choice for foundation planting or in the foreground of a mixed shrub border. Japanese skimmia is dioecious: male plants have larger, more fragrant white flowers in spring, while in autumn female plants bear 3-inch-wide clusters of bright scarlet berries that persist right through winter. Male plants were first introduced to Kew in 1838, and they did not attract much attention. Von Siebold suggested it could be grown in cool greenhouses together with camellias, which have beautiful but scentless flowers. I think von Siebold's suggestion an excellent one, and if camellias were hardy in my garden, I'd plant skimmia as companions for fragrance, fruit, and foliage. Skimmia is best in regions with moderate summer temperatures; it is recommended for zones 7 and 8. However, I know gardeners with sheltered sites along the Long Island Sound in zone 6 who grow skimmia quite well. It wants shade or partial shade, and woodland conditions of loose, open soil rich in organic matter, and moist but well-drained. A few cultivars are available: 'Nymans' is a freely fruiting female clone with large red berries. 'Rubella' is a male clone with bright red leaves in winter, especially the upper ones, and deeply colored red flower buds in winter. Its flowers are very fragrant in spring.

JAPANESE YEW

Japanese yew, *Taxus cuspidata,* is so familiar it needs little introduction. The species itself is discussed in chapter 3. Yew is an excellent choice for clipped hedges, topiary, foundation plantings, or as an evergreen accent plant, but only in deer-proof gardens. Yew appears to be the preferred item in Bambi's salad bar. Dwarf cultivars such as slow-growing 'Densa', a broad, very flat-topped female clone reaching 2 to 3 feet tall and spreading 6 feet wide, can be used as a formally clipped landscape accent. Dainty

'Minima' is a very dwarf upright clone slowly growing 12 inches high and at home in the rock garden. 'Nana' grows 2 to 3 tall and has a wider spread; 'Prostrata' is similar, growing 3 feet tall. Both are suitable for foundation plantings. *T. cuspidata* var. *nana* is a low-growing dwarf shrub from the mountains on the Japan Sea side of Honshu that is frequently grown in Japanese gardens.

Many selected hybrids of intermediate yew, *T.* x *media* (*T. cuspidata* x *T. baccata*) are important shrubs for hedges, screening, or foundation plantings. These include: the nonfruiting male 'Brownii', cold-hardy to zone 4 and ultimately growing 5 to 6 feet tall and spreading 8 to 12 feet wide; 'Hatfieldii', also male, less cold-hardy, useful only to zone 6 (5 with protection), and having a broadly pyramidal form when mature; female, fruiting 'Hicksii', with columnar habit, is common in many "builder's special" shrub collections, a good plant when used with some discernment as an upright, accent coniferous shrub.

WINDMILL PALM

Windmill palm, or hemp palm, *Trachycarpus fortunei,* could be placed with trees, as each plant has a straight, simple trunk. On the other hand, although it can reach 15 to 35 feet tall with a 10- to 15-foot spread, it mostly grows only 9 to 12 feet tall, certainly on the scale of a shrub. Windmill palm is also more likely to be used as a shrublike specimen rather than a shade-giving tree. Limited to Kyushu's southern district, windmill palm is widely planted in central and southern Japan, where it is used to create a tropical effect. (The *RHS Index of Garden Plants* states it is "probably" from northern Burma and central and eastern China, naturalized in China and Japan.) It can only be grown outdoors in gardens in zones 8 and 9. For best display, use it on its own, individually, or in a small grove, but not mixed with other shrubs and trees. Windmill palm can be used as a container plant as well as in the garden, to provide a strong upright accent softened by the foliage. The species name commemorates Robert Fortune.

Windmill palm's straight trunk is covered with dark brown to black hairlike fibers, the remains of old leaf stalks. Leaves cluster at the top of each trunk, each leaf 20 to 30 inches across, made up of fanlike segments radiating in an almost complete circle and drooping at the tip. It is dioecious; female plants bear large clusters of bluish black to indigo fruits, which are covered with a whitish bloom when they mature in autumn. A lightly shady site protected from the wind is best. Amend the soil with organic matter, maintain moderate fertility, and make sure there is good drainage. Provide ample water, especially when the plants are young.

CHAPTER FIVE

Vines and Ground Covers

VINES

J ust as with trees, shrubs, and perennials, the diversity of vining plants found in Japan is remarkable. This is to be expected, for many climbing plants occupy the forest's edge where they can utilize neighboring trees to clamber up into the sunshine, and much of Japan was once richly wooded. Some vines, such as wisteria and clematis, are familiar and popular inhabitants of our gardens. Others, such as actinidia and akebia, are less well-known. Rarely are vines employed to the same extent as woody plants, which is unfortunate. Whether grown for the beauty of their flowers, their attractive foliage, or simply as a living roof on an arbor, vines have a distinctive quality and unique appeal.

Vining plants may be annual, dying after a single season's growth. Others are perennial, and still others (such as the popular and familiar clematis and wisteria) have persistent woody stems that remain throughout the year. How they climb is specific to each plant, rather than the type of vine. Some twine, winding their vining stem or specialized tendrils around a support. In the wild this support would most often be an adjacent shrub or tree, while in gardens a pole, trellis, or wire might also be used. Others cling by means of aerial rootlets or specialized holdfasts that attach the vine to tree trunks, rock walls, fences, or buildings.

Whichever mechanism the plant employs, support must be provided from an early age. If you intend a tree or shrub to be the support, realize that the ground closest to the trunk or most heavily shaded by branches is inclined to be dry. Plant the vine out beyond the drip line and use a bamboo cane or some other guide to lead it in the desired direction. Use care to match the vigor of the vine to its living prop, as some twining vines become powerful enough to strangle and kill their host. Similarly, clinging vines can pull down a poorly mounted trellis, and wisteria can pop shingles or even gutters off a roof. Vines employing holdfasts can be a problem if the fence or pergola to which they cling needs periodic painting. Sometimes it is better to grow the vine on a separate wire trellis that can be carefully unhooked from the main structure and swung out at an angle while the work is done, to be reattached after the paint or stain is dry.

ACTINIDIA, OR HARDY KIWI

Actinidia, or hardy kiwi, *Actinidia kolomikta,* is a midsize twining vine that can reach 15 feet up a trellis. The leaves of the male plant are most attractive, maturing from spring's bronze new growth to a broad heart-shape handsomely splashed with shades of pink. These blotches later turn a creamy white suffused with pink. Female plants are less noticeably variegated. For some reason cats regard actinidia with the same rapture as they do catnip. Young plants especially must be protected against their feline enthusiasm. Give the plants a sunny site and moderately fertile, neutral to acid soil. Actinidia is hardy to zone 5. It is usually found climbing on trees at forest edges and along roadsides of northern Japan, as well as the southern Kuriles, Sakhalin, Amur, and Manchuria. Actinidia arrived in the United States in 1961, when Dr. John Creech collected cuttings from a highly colored male plant at Shikotosuko, Hokkaido.

AKEBIA

Fiveleaf akebia, *Akebia quinata,* is an example of Western botanists incorporating the Japanese name into the plant's Latin name. This deciduous woody climber has a neat, fine-textured quality provided by the dark green, palmately compound leaves. Turning purplish green, they persist well into winter, and the vine is semievergreen in the milder portions of its range of zones 4 through 9. Commonly found in thickets of the hills and mountains of Honshu, Shikoku, and Kyushu, as well as in Korea and China, it grows rapidly, twining on any suitable vertical support such as a chain-link fence or trellis. With a height of 30 to 40 feet and an indeterminate spread, pruning may be necessary to keep the vine under control. Fiveleaf akebia prefers a sunny site, with average moisture and a neutral to acid soil. The inconspicuous flowers, hidden by the leaves, are deliciously fragrant.

PORCELAIN BERRY VINE

Some caution should be shown in planting porcelain berry vine, *Ampelopsis brevipedunculata,* as there have been reports of it escaping from cultivation and becoming a pest. It spreads by means of seed, and it is just these handsome fruits that give it the name of porcelain berry. A vigorous vine that is woody at its base, porcelain berry attaches itself by means of twining tendrils, climbing a trellis, fence, shed, or tree to 15 feet or higher. The vine itself does not twine. Often it is slow to establish when first planted and is a good example of the horticultural adage, "The first year it sleeps, the second year it creeps, the third year it leaps." The 3- to 5-lobed, bright green leaves are handsome enough, but it is the berries for which the vine is grown. Their color shifts through turquoise, lilac, green, and blue. Sometimes a single cluster will include all these colors. Porcelain berry vine is very common in hillside thickets on Hokkaido, Honshu, Shikoku, and Kyushu, as well as in Korea, China, Manchuria, Ussuri, and the southern Kuriles. Somewhat slower growing, more tender, and with smaller leaves, is the cultivar 'Elegans'. Its white-and-pink variegated leaves make it an elegant specimen, but it is less useful as a screening plant.

CLEMATIS

In England clematis has been called the queen of vines. Magnificent flowers and charming silky-haired puffballs of seed are reason enough to grow several different kinds. The vines clamber by means of leaf petioles that twine around tree branches or a wire trellis with equal ease. I love the look of clematis winding through conifers such as tall yews or junipers. In England I've seen them mingled with climbing roses to extend the season of bloom. Remember that the thin woody stems are easily damaged; you must provide a secure means of leading the vine to its support. A bamboo cane serves this purpose well.

Clematis florida is a Chinese plant long cultivated in Japan as an ornamental. Several cultivars are known: 'Alba Plena', with fully double flowers, has stamens that are transformed into a tight, symmetrical, central mass of greenish white petal-like structures. The main flush of bloom occurs in June, with young growth continuing to flower into October. 'Alba Plena' has a long history of cultivation in Japan, from whence it was introduced to Europe in the nineteenth century. 'Sieboldii' (= 'Bicolor'), introduced from Japan in 1837, is also double, with a narrow, petal-like transformation of the stamens forming an anemone-type center. The stamenoides first unfold a light greenish purple, maturing to deep purple, and provide a handsome, shaggy contrast to the creamy white sepals. Both cultivars are somewhat tender and need the mild winter conditions of zone 7 and warmer.

'Sieboldii' can be grown as a container plant, set out on a terrace in summer and brought into a cool greenhouse in winter.

Clematis fusca is found in grassy places on Hokkaido, and also in eastern Siberia, Kamchatka, Sakhalin, and the Kuriles. In July this clematis has distinctive, urn-shaped purple flowers, thickly covered with dark brown hairs. It grows best with a hard pruning early in spring, and is hardy to zone 5. There are reports of a dwarf variety from Hokkaido, possibly a subspecies, that grows only 18 to 24 inches high. This type does not climb, and it flowers about a month earlier.

Clematis japonica grows in thickets on the mountains of Honshu and Kyushu. In May or June flowers appear on the previous year's growth, opening into glossy, fleshy-petaled, campanula-like bells that are a rich purplish red color like highly polished mahogany. 'Gokonosho' is that rarity, a variegated clematis, its leaves singularly splashed and mottled with creamy white, each one different. Somewhat difficult in cultivation, 'Gokonosho' also tends to revert. The more vigorous plain green shoots must be assiduously removed whenever they appear.

Clematis patens flowers in May or June, bearing large creamy white to pale bluish purple flowers 4 to 6 inches in diameter. The species is found in Honshu, Shikoku, and Kyushu, as well as in China. More often, selected cultivars are grown rather than the wild species. 'Fortunei' has double, milky white flowers 5 inches across that turn pink as they age; 'Standishii' has slightly larger, pale lilac double flowers that are lilac-rose in the center. Both are hardy to zone 6.

Sweet autumn clematis, *Clematis terniflora* (= *C. maximowicziana*, *C. paniculata*), is a very common autumn-blooming species from Hokkaido, Honshu, Shikoku, and Kyushu, and also Korea and China. In September and October it produces numerous bittersweetly scented white flowers, 1 to 1½ inches across, which display handsomely against the dark green leaves. They are followed by seeds in persistent, fluffy, grayish white pompons. Although deciduous, sweet autumn clematis retains some foliage in southern regions. The tangled stems can grow 15 to 30 feet long with an indeterminate spread that can completely hide a chain-link fence. This species is quite cold-hardy and is useful over a broad range from zones 4 to 9. Blooming as it does on new growth in autumn, any necessary pruning for rejuvenation or to control growth should be done in spring. Left alone, the vine forms a top-heavy tangle with sparse growth at the lower portion.

EUONYMUS
Euonymus fortunei var. *radicans* is a common and variable leathery leaved evergreen climber found nearly as often creep-

ing along the ground. It is indigenous to the woods and thickets of low mountains on Hokkaido, Honshu, Shikoku, and Kyushu, as well as to Korea, China, and Ryukyu. Hardiness varies among the cultivars commonly grown. In general they are effective from zones 5 through 7, with some selections useful in zone 4. Scale insects are often a problem, especially in zones 8 and 9. Deer also frequently cause severe damage. There are several readily available cultivars. Bigleaf wintercreeper, var. *vegeta*, is sometimes offered as 'Vegeta'; it grows either as a loose open shrub or a climber, and has abundant, attractive fruit and rounded medium green foliage. It is quite cold-hardy to zone 4. Several shrubby, scandent cultivars for zone 5 and higher include 'Emerald Gaity', which grows to 5 feet tall and has white variegated foliage; 'Emerald 'n Gold', which is slightly lower-growing with yellow variegated leaves; and 'Golden Prince', which grows the lowest (to 2½ feet tall), and is yellow variegated until early summer, later turning mostly green.

CLIMBING FIG

Climbing fig, or creeping fig, *Ficus pumila,* is native to Shikoku, Honshu's Tokaido district and westward, and Kyushu, as well as to Ryukyu, Formosa, and China. Dr. John Creech collected this plant on Shikoku. Grown as a houseplant and often employed for indoor topiary, climbing fig

is also popular as a garden plant in zones 8 and 9. Aerial rootlets allow the 30-foot-long stems to cling to masonry walls, rapidly creating a solid, evergreen cloak. It prefers shade or partial shade and average moisture. Its 1-inch-long, rich dark green leaves have a fine texture. Mature fruiting branches grow outward from the relatively flat mass, with larger, coarser 2- to 4-inch-long leaves. Where possible these should be pruned out to keep the vine cover 1 inch thick, rather than the potential 16-inch-deep mass into which mature shoots can develop.

JAPANESE MORNING GLORY

Morning glory, *Ipomoea nil,* is a familiar annual vine with single-flowered cultivars such as 'Heavenly Blue' and 'Scarlet O'Hara'. In Japan morning glories can be as much a specialist's plant as are dahlias in the United States. Of garden origin, plants of imperial Japanese morning glory, *I.* x *imperialis,* differ in having larger, often fringed or fluted double flowers. Grown in pots and pruned continuously, much like chrysanthemums, these plants eventually produce very large, very bright, double flowers in a range of colors from white to pink, red, purple, and blue, variously striped and margined. The hard seed coat should be nicked with a small triangular file, then soaked overnight in tepid water before planting. I use a thermos bottle to keep the water from cooling. There is a wild perennial morning glory with bluish purple flowers, *I. indica,* which grows in the grass or seaside cliffs of the Ki peninsula, and on Izu island of Honshu in Japan, as well as in Ryukyu, southeastern Asia, and Australia. It is not grown in gardens.

Japanese Hops

Japanese hops, *Humulus japonicus,* is very common in thickets and along roadsides in the lowlands of much of Japan, and is also native to Ryukyu, Formosa, and China. A perennial climber, it is frequently used in gardens as a very rapidly growing annual with large maplelike, rough-haired leaves. 'Variegatus' is a more ornamental cultivar with attractive, creamy white, streaked and blotched leaves. It does grow true from seed; however, the variegation is inconstant, with some plants having more than others.

Climbing Hydrangea

Climbing hydrangea, *Hydrangea petiolaris,* is a wonderful deciduous vine for the shady garden in zones 5 to 8. Rather common in the mountain forests of Hokkaido, Honshu, Shikoku, and Kyushu, it is also native to Sakhalin, the southern Kuriles, and southern Korea. The aerial roots hold fast and allow the scandent shrub, stretching as much as 50 to 65 feet, to cling to wooden fences, masonry walls, and tree trunks. Obviously, as this growth is too vigorous for a small understory tree, give it a nice mature oak or something of similar

stature. The vine will not actually strangle the host tree, but it is easier to let it stretch for the sky than to have it flop around needing pruning. Leaves are tidy and a pleasant green; the bark is a soft beige that flakes and peels away. As the plant matures it produces side shoots that lend it a more three-dimensional character. In June or July (May in southern gardens), large, flat, lacecap flower clusters appear, with larger sterile flowers at the edges. Climbing hydrangea grows best in partial shade; heavy shade reduces flowering, which will, in any case, only occur on mature plants.

Scarlet Kadsura

Scarlet kadsura, *Kadsura japonica,* is an elegant evergreen vine of modest dimensions (8 to 12 feet high) native to Shikoku, Honshu's Kanto district and westward, and Kyushu, as well as to China and Formosa. It is hardy in zones 8 and 9, and will grow in zone 7 in sheltered gardens with additional protection. In zone 9 the leathery dark green leaves, 2 to 4 inches long, turn reddish in winter; vines are sometimes deciduous in zone 8. Scarlet kadsura prefers moist, well-drained soil high in organic matter in a partially shaded site. It will twine up a fence or trellis, or, if support is lacking, serve as a ground cover. It is worth growing for its handsome presentation of red berries displayed against glossy leaves, but scarlet kadsura is dioecious, and you must remember to plant the occasional male to ensure pollination. In autumn female plants will then sport pendulous clusters of scarlet fruit, each 1 inch across. The leaves of 'Variegata' have cream to yellow edges.

Boston Ivy

The origins of Boston ivy have nothing to do with Massachusetts. *Parthenocissus tricuspidata* is native to Hokkaido, Honshu, Shikoku, and Kyushu, where it is common, and often found in thickets and forests on hills and mountains. In Japan it is widely used for covering walls. Hardy in zones 4 to 8, there are several cultivars grown in gardens: 'Beverly Brooks' has small leaves with good scarlet autumn color; 'Minutifolia' has leaves an inch or two across; 'Lowii' has very small, sharply lobed leaves 1 inch across that give a more refined texture better suited to smaller-scale city gardens; 'Purpurea' has red leaves tinged with dark purple in summer; 'Veitchii' has small, puckered leaves that are dark purple when young, red-purple in autumn. When growing Boston ivy on buildings remember that you'll need to lean out the windows and trim it back because it covers windows just as well as walls. The North American species, Virginia creeper, *P. quinquefolia*, which has 5 leaflets, is sometimes grown in Japan, where it is known as *amerika-zuta*.

Schizophragma

Schizophragma hydrangeoides is rather common to the mountain woods and thickets of Hokkaido, Honshu, Shikoku, and Kyushu. It is very similar to climbing hydrangea, differing only in having more coarsely toothed leaves and sterile flowers with only one large white or ivory sepal rather than the hydrangea's several. Flowering is reduced in deep shade, so a site at the edge of woodland is best. I have some climbing a white oak in my garden. The first few years it grew very slowly, but is now bounding along to its mature height of 30 to 35 feet. Mature specimens so clothe their supporting trees that the trunks are completely concealed, which seems not to trouble the trees in the least. In Berkeley, Elaine Sedlack grows this vine on sequoias. Snails seem to like them, but not slugs.

Wisteria

One May I saw a breathtakingly exquisite display of wisteria in bloom on a stone-pillared trellis in Utsunomiya-shi City Park, softly radiant in the spring rain. The Japanese call *Wisteria floribunda* the plant of two seasons since, flowering when it does, it is considered to demonstrate the passage from spring to summer. Rather common in the wild, this Japanese endemic is found in thickets and forests on the mountains and hills of Honshu, Shikoku, and Kyushu. In late spring and early summer it bears 8- to 20-inch-long clusters of fragrant violet-blue flowers. The looping woody stems reach 25 to 35 feet or more, twining clockwise, and can damage trees. A sturdy pergola or arbor is the best support. A range of flower colors have been developed, especially in Japan. Some cultivars include white-flowered 'Alba' with dense, nearly 1-foot-long clusters; bluish violet 'Issai' with 1-foot-long racemes (an unbranched, elongated cluster) of slightly fragrant flowers; violet to reddish violet 'Kyushaki' with 26-inch racemes of mildly fragrant flowers; blue-violet 'Macrobotrys' with racemes 24- to 36-inch racemes of intensely fragrant flowers; rose-pink 'Rosea' with 18-inch racemes of very fragrant flowers; and violet, double-flowered 'Violacea Plena'. Wisteria often takes its time about flowering; named, grafted cultivars sometimes require as many as five or ten years. Seedling plants usually wait even longer to flower well. Using a fertilizer with a low-nitrogen, high-phosphorous-and-potash content may promote earlier flowering. Root-pruning an established plant by severing roots 18 inches from the trunk with a spade is also helpful.

Vines to Avoid

The following are absolute thugs. I include them here only to caution against their cultivation.

BITTERSWEET

There is a native North American bittersweet, *Celastrus scandens*. A rapidly scrambling plant, it twines up adjacent shrubs, trees, or poles to a height of about 14 to 18 feet. When driving down New England roads in autumn, odds are the vine you see decorating the landscape is the exotic, rather than the native species. Both are dioecious; female plants fruit on terminal clusters, producing handsome, deep yellow-jacketed, red-orange seed popular with flower arrangers. In Japan, Oriental bittersweet, *C. orbiculatus*, is common, found in thickets and grassy slopes in the lowlands and mountains of its natural range: Hokkaido, Honshu, Shikoku, and Kyushu, and the southern Kuriles, Korea, Manchuria, Sakhalin, China, and Ussuri. It fruits on short spurs in the leaf axils, producing not only much more seed than the native species, but also seed that seems to germinate more freely. If you do use Oriental bittersweet in flower arrangements, be careful to discard the seeds afterward where they will have no opportunity to germinate.

JAPANESE HONEYSUCKLE

Another rampageous species is Japanese honeysuckle, *Lonicera japonica*. Hardy from zones 5 to 9, this vine was originally touted as an attractive semi-evergreen to evergreen ground cover with intensely fragrant, long-blooming, white to yellow flowers, that was suitable for use in rough areas and as an erosion preventative on banks. It has become a menace, naturalized in the East and even more of a threat in the South. If you must have it, then grow the less vigorous cultivar 'Aureo-reticulata', whose smaller leaves are veined with golden yellow, giving it a netted appearance.

Kudzu

I have used thin, mature stems of kudzu in basketry, and a meal I enjoyed at the Utsunomiya-shi Grand Hotel concluded with a dessert of sweet noodles made of kudzu powder. More often the subject of bad jokes and silly postcards, kudzu, *Pueraria lobata,* a very common native of Hokkaido, Honshu, Shikoku, and Kyushu, as well as Korea and China, is an absolutely aggressive menace in the South. In his book *The World Was My Garden,* published in 1938, David Fairchild notes that the Soil Conservation Service introduced kudzu in the South to control gullying and soil erosion. The coarse, hairy, twining vine does swarm over utility poles, trees, and buildings, covering literally acres of land; I suspect that reports of it grabbing slow-moving tour buses and cattle are exaggerations.

GROUND COVERS

Any plant, herbaceous or shrubby, might be considered a ground cover where it is grown thickly enough to cover ground. Usually we reserve the term for plants with a reasonably rapid spread and sturdy disposition that permit its use in large areas. Ground covers come in many sizes, from vigorous, even coarse, rapidly spreading plants to more refined, dainty sprawlers. Plants with invasive tendencies may have more restrained relatives. The choice of ground cover will depend on the scale of the garden design and nearby plants. Appearance, ease of maintenance, and rate of spread are all characteristics that should be evaluated; evergreen foliage can be more important in the long term than a brief period of bloom.

Marlberry

Marlberry, or Japanese ardisia, *Ardisia japonica,* is native to forests on the hills and low mountains of Hokkaido's Okushiri Island, Honshu, Shikoku, and Kyushu, as well as Korea, China, and Formosa. It is hardy in zones 7 to 9, nominally hardier than the related coral ardisia, *A. crenta.* Marlberry is a procumbent shrub, growing only 10 to 16 inches tall. Reddish brown twigs are neatly dressed in glossy, evergreen, dark green leaves. The fruits are pinkish red in color. It makes a nice woodland ground cover, growing and spreading best in a moist, well-drained soil that is high in organic matter and reasonably fertile, mulched with chopped leaves or pine straw. There are several delightful-sounding cultivars: 'Hakuokan' has white and silver-green variegated leaves; 'Hinotsukasa' is slow growing with mostly cream-colored leaves;

'Ito Fukurin' has green-and-white variegated leaves; 'Matsu-shima' has waxy leaves with deeply toothed and frilled edges, and a creamy central blotch; 'Nishiki' (='Hokan Nishiki') has pink-and-gold variegated leaves. These variegated forms are less cold-hardy, suitable only for zones 8 and 9.

JAPANESE HOLLY FERN

Japanese holly fern, *Cyrtomium falcatum*, is a delightful ground cover for gardens in zones 8 and 9, which will be described in chapter 7.

BAMBOO

Running species of dwarf bamboo create attractive, graceful ground covers. Their aggressive nature also makes them difficult to control. The first few years' growth will be deceptive, as spring growth is influenced by the conditions of the preceding year, and the first two or three years will be spent settling in. Afterward, cablelike runners shoot along just below or at the soil surface with amazing speed and tenacity. These dwarf species are perhaps even more difficult to control than the large ones. In Massachusetts I was shown a shallow concrete ornamental pool that had been cracked, from outside, by the pressure of the bamboo. Be warned. Regular mowing around the edges will help restrain the culms. Planting bamboo on an island in a pond or lake is secure.

I like these dwarf bamboo in container plantings, set in quite large, rolled-rim clay pots, which are then used as an accent in the garden. In general their leaves are evergreen down to temperatures in the single digits. At lower temperatures the leaves scorch and drop, and even the culms may be killed back. Since all growth comes from the underground rhizomes, if they survive, spring growth will follow. There are a number of Japanese species, several of which are variegated, and many of which have alternative Latin names, causing confusion in the trade.

Dwarf fernleaf bamboo, *Pleioblastus argenteostriatus* (= *Arundinaria argenteostriata*), is a hardy, semidwarf bamboo that grows 2 to 3 feet tall. Unknown in the wild, the variegated phase has long been popular as a garden plant in Japan. It is particularly handsome as a container plant. It can be confused with dwarf whitestripe bamboo, *P. variegatus* (= *A. variegata*), a compact, low-growing, running bamboo with dark green leaves variously striped in creamy white. Sometimes on the same plant a few leaves are entirely white, others are mostly green, and the majority persistently variegated. Suitable for use as a ground cover or in containers, it is unknown in the wild. Also called dwarf fernleaf bamboo or pygmy bamboo, *P. pygmaeus* (= *A. pygmaea*), grows about 3 feet tall. Common in the hills of Shikoku and Kyushu, it is also found wild in Honshu's Suruga and westward. To add to the confusion, there is another dwarf fernleaf bamboo, *P. pygmaeus* var. *disticha,* formerly *A. disticha,* that is apparently an entirely different species. With sufficient space, this hardy, running, dwarf species (from 1½ to 2½ feet tall) with fine-textured, bright green leaves makes an excellent, rapidly spreading ground cover. *Pleioblastus auricoma* (= *A. viridistriata*, *Bambusa viridistriata*) has erect, slender culms that are an attractive dark purplish green, reaching 18 to 30 inches long. In spring the leaves, about 5 inches long and 1 inch wide, are variegated brilliant golden yellow and green, turning entirely green by midsummer. Color is best on new shoots; plants can be mown down late in winter to encourage fresh growth. New leaves have a very sensuous, velvety feel when pulled gently between the fingers.

Other species of dwarf bamboos that might be considered for use as ground cover include the extremely invasive *Pleioblastus gramineus* (= *Arundinaria graminea*). It is hardy in zone 7, but be careful to select the dwarfer clones as it can vary from 3 to 16 feet tall. *Pleioblastus humilis* (= *A. humilis*) is 2 to 3 foot tall, with very slender upright culms and medium green leaves up to 6 inches long and about ¾ inch wide. *Pleioblastus humilis* var. *pumilis* (= *Sasa pumila* or *A. pumila*) is even more compact, growing 1½ or 2 feet high, with somewhat arching culms and bright green leaves up to 6 inches long and ¾ inch wide.

Palmate bamboo, *Sasa palmata*, can be used as a tall, coarse ground cover, or as a dense, thickety low shrub, depending on the scale of your landscape. The culms, from 1½ to 4 feet long, lean over and then ascend upward, making an impenetrable mass of purple-streaked stems, annually extending their territorial boundaries by several feet. An aggressive, rampantly spreading plant, this bamboo will range far and wide unless securely contained. Loosely branched toward the top, the gleaming dark green leaves are quite large and broad, establishing a coarse, magnificent foliage texture for the garden. If grown as a container plant, the size will be somewhat reduced. Palmate bamboo can be grown from zone 5 southward, especially if there is snow cover for winter protection in the colder regions. One of the hardiest bamboos, its native range is Hokkaido, Honshu, Shikoku, Kyushu, and Sakhalin.

Kuma bamboo grass, *Sasa veitchii*, is lower-growing than the preceding species and less aggressive. Widely cultivated in Japanese gardens, much of its appeal is the dieback of its leaves in winter. Odd though this sounds, the leaf margins become conspicuously and attractively edged with a papery border of pale creamy beige winter-killed tissue. It is also suitable for use as a container plant. One of the hardier bamboos, kuma bamboo grass grows in zones 6 to 8. Its native range is Honshu's Chugoku district, Shikoku, and Kyushu.

EPIMEDIUM

Epimedium functions equally well as ground cover or in a small clump, accenting a tree trunk, a stump, a rock, or a curve in the path. Once established, plants can remain in the same place, untouched, for twenty years. If you want them to spread, dig plants up in late spring after the leaves are mature, separate the rhizomes, and replant in a larger space. Alternatively, the rhizomes can be divided in early autumn. Plant 12 to 15 inches apart for ground cover use. Different species occur in Japan, China, Europe, and North Africa. The Asian species prefer a cool, moderately moist, shaded site, and a soil high in organic matter. Their short, branching rhizomes creep along the soil surface of hillside forests. The compound leaves, often bronze colored when they first appear, turn green at maturity and remain evergreen through most of the winter. Maintenance is simple—in late winter or earliest spring, cut off all the old foliage before new growth appears.

Epimedium diphyllum is a dainty, graceful species making a mound of leaves only 8 to 12 inches tall and wide. It is native to the western district islands of Shikoku and Kyushu but is reasonably cold-hardy, to at least 5° Fahrenheit. It has come through colder winters in my garden, protected by snow cover. The exquisite white spurless flowers appear in April or May. *Epimedium grandiflorum* is a larger species, growing over a foot tall. It is native to the main island of Honshu, as well as the western district. It is hardy to about -4° Fahrenheit. The new leaves are pale beige-bronze, expanding to bright green, 2- to 3-inch-long spiny-edged leaflets in summer, and browning off in winter. Flower color is white to pale purple, with an elongated spur. There are a number of large-flowered cultivars available: deep pink 'Rose Queen', snowy 'White Queen', and dark violet 'Violaceum' are among the most popular. There is a hybrid, *E.* x *youngianum,* possibly occurring naturally in the wild, possibly of garden origin, that is a cross between *E. diphyllum* and *E. grandiflorum.* It forms small, 6- to 10-inch-high, dense upright mounds of foliage that are reddish bronze when the new leaves first appear in spring. Each leaf is divided into 9 leaflets, sharply serrated along the margin. In autumn the leaves turn a deep crimson-maroon. The most commonly offered cultivar is 'Niveum', with small, clear-white flowers; 'Roseum', with rose to lilac flowers, is sometimes available. They are hardy to 0° Fahrenheit. *Vancouveria hexandra* is a close North American relative of epimedium, native to the West Coast.

EUONYMUS

As noted earlier in this chapter, *Euonymous fortunei* var. *radicans* is often found in the wild creeping along the ground rather than clinging to tree trunks and rocks. Selections suitable for ground cover use include 'Colorata', also called purpleleaf wintercreeper, which has deep green leaves that turn a burgundy red-purple in winter and grows in zone 4. For zone 5 consider 'Gracillis' (= 'Argenteo-marginata,' 'Pictus,' 'Tricolor'), which has colorful variegation of white, creamy yellow, pink, or a mix thereof (pink seems strongest in cold weather). A delightful small charmer to clamber around the shady rock garden is 'Kewensis' (= 'Minimus') with dark green leaves about ¼ inch long.

Hosta

Any of the medium- to large-leaved hostas, planted so as to carpet the ground, can serve as a fine deciduous ground cover especially in a shady site. Those that are stoloniferous (producing horizontal underground runners at the base of the plant that produce new plants at their tips) make well-behaved, self-expanding ground cover from their creeping rhizomes. Stoloniferous *Hosta decorata* (= 'Thomas Hogg') has white-edged green leaves. Narrow, lance-leaved, green *H. lancifolia* has handsome purple flowers and is stoloniferous in loose, open soil. *Hosta longissima*, with long creeping rhizomes and slender grasslike leaves, needs ample moisture at all times. *Hosta sieboldiana* f. *kabitan* (= 'Kabitan') is a golden lanceolate-leaved, stoloniferous hosta. *Hosta tardiva* has rhizomatous roots and upright, slender dark green leaves, and flowers in autumn. Dwarf *H. pulchella* is good for a select site

in the rock garden; it has creeping rhizomes, leaves about 2 inches long, and relatively large flowers. 'Gold Edger' is a small golden-leafed hosta, increasing rapidly to create a thick, lush ground cover. 'Ground Master' has medium-sized blue foliage, handsome in a mass planting on a slope. Small, stoloniferous 'Neat Splash' has dark green leaves irregularly streaked and splashed with yellow. 'North Hills' is vigorous, medium to large in size, and quick-spreading. It has medium to dark green leaves with a clean, crisp, irregular, narrow white edge. Small, spreading 'Resonance' has furrowed, lanceolate, yellowish green leaves with deeper yellow variegation, and stoloniferous 'Wogon Gold' has lovely rounded golden leaves. Remember to protect plants from vermin large and small—both deer and slugs like to dine on the leaves.

Juniper

Shore juniper, *Juniperus conferta,* is native to the sandy sea coasts of Hokkaido, Honshu, Kyushu, and Sakhalin. Hardy from zones 6 to 9, this low-growing juniper is an excellent ground cover, exceptionally tolerant of salt spray. It is therefore useful not only in seashore gardens, but where ice removal in winter adds salt to roadside soil. Procumbent branches hug the ground, growing only 12 to 18 inches high and spreading 4 to 6 feet wide. Clothed in feathery, ½-inch-long, needlelike foliage, their color varies from bluish green to bright green. Best in full sun, shore juniper thrives in well drained, infertile sandy soil. A rapid spreader, this juniper is a good choice for sloping banks and sand dunes. Its trailing habit is also attractive in raised planters. Compact 'Blue Pacific' is a popular, heat-tolerant cultivar that has bluish green needles and grows 6 inches tall; dense, prostrate 'Emerald Sea' grows a foot tall with emerald-green foliage that turns yellowish green in winter; 'Luchensis' has grass-green needles; and 'Silver Mist' has bright silvery, bluish gray needles.

Japanese garden juniper, *Juniperus procumbens,* is found along Kyushu's seashores. Often grown as a ground cover in Japan, it is similarly used in our gardens in zones 5 to 9. Its low, mounding form has a deceptively soft appearance, but has a decidedly prickly feel when stroked. Growing 1 ½ to 2 feet tall, it spreads widely. One plant in my garden is 9 feet in diameter, and I periodically trim it back at the edges! Typically needle color is a soft green, although the 'Aurea' cultivar has gold-tipped needles. 'Bonin Isles', 'Nana', and 'Santa Rosa' are dwarfer, more compact forms with tighter growth habits.

Juniperus sargentii is found on the mountainous rocky cliffs and along the seashore of Hokkaido, Honshu, Shikoku, and Kyushu, and also in the southern Kuriles and Sakhalin. Useful over a wide range from zones 4 to 9, this cold-tolerant ground cover shrub grows 18 inches tall and spreads 10 feet or more. Short, deep to bright green, or bluish green needles clothe the branches, offering a refined, tidy appearance. Several cultivars are available: 'Compacta' has dark green juvenile foliage and a denser, more compact habit; 'Expansa Aureovariegata' has golden variegated foliage, grows 2 feet tall, and spreads 7 to 8 feet; 'Glauca' has bluish green needles; and 'Viridis' has light green needles.

Liriope

Creeping lilyturf, *Liriope spicata,* other species of lilyturf, and the closely related ophiopogon, *Ophiopogon jaburan,* can be used as ground covers or as accent perennials in zones 6 to 9. Evergreen, they all have good winter appearance and attractive autumn flowers. Creeping lilyturf has a suckering habit. Its deep green, narrow, straplike leaves grow about 10 inches long and ¼ inch wide, making a tidy ground cover useful for erosion prevention. In late summer upright spikes of small, tightly clustered lavender or pearl-white flowers appear, followed by blue-black berries. Once established, benign neglect is all the care that is necessary. If there is winter damage simply clip the plants back in early spring before new growth begins. *Liriope spicata* is found on Honshu, Shikoku, and Kyushu, and also in Ryukyu and China.

Liriope, or big blue lilyturf, *L. muscari,*

has dark green, arching clumps of leaves sometimes twice as long as *L. spicata*, and almost ¾ inch wide, giving it a bolder appearance. Native to the Kanto district and westward on Honshu, Shikoku, and Kyushu, it is also found wild on China, Formosa, and Ryukyu. Typically the dense spikes of tiny flowers are a deep, bright violet. Selections made for flower color and form include 'Big Blue', with large flower spikes and large leaves; strong-growing 'Majestic', with large, deep violet flower spikes and deep green leaves; and sun-sensitive 'Monroe White', with pure white flowers. Foliage selections include 'Variegata', striking both in and out of bloom, with golden-yellow striped leaves, and 'Silvery Sunproof' (= 'Ariake Janshige'), a somewhat more tender, white variegated form that becomes yellow variegated in heavy shade, and is properly placed in *L. exiliflora*, from Japan and China. Both *L. spicata* and *L. muscari* are hardy for me in zone 6, but the latter sometimes shows winter foliage damage unless covered with snow. Sound cultural technique suggests trimming them back in March, by hand for a small patch or with a lawnmower set to 1 or 2 inches high. Deer seem to fancy them, especially the variegated plants, sometimes yanking them out of the ground, roots and all. Lilyturf, *L. muscari,* is also appropriate as an accent plant, with autumn-blooming bulbs such as naked ladies, *Colchicum autumnale,* or, in mild winter regions, the Guernsey lily, *Nerine bowdenii.*

OPHIOPOGON

There are several species of ophiopogon in Japan. In appearance they are delicate cousins of liriope, with summer flowers and thin, fine, dark green, evergreen tufts of foliage.

Ophiopogon jaburan is a tufted, stoloniferous, evergreen, grasslike perennial, native to Honshu's western districts, Shikoku, and Kyushu. Drought-tolerant once established,

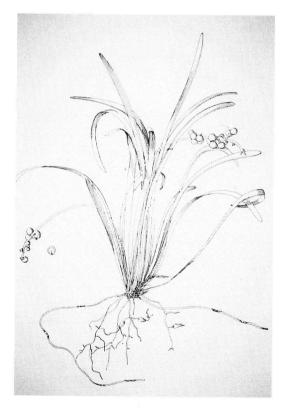

Liriope platyphylla

it makes an attractive ground cover requiring a minimum of care. Often a white variegated cultivar of garden origin is planted both in Japanese and American gardens. Growing 8 to 12 inches tall, *O. jaburan* 'Vittatus' (= 'Variegatus') has white flowers and symmetrically arranged, pale green leaves striped and edged in creamy white. It creates a cool, refreshing, bright effect in shaded areas. Highlight the foliage with white impatiens and white-leaved caladium, or use 'Vittatus' to edge a planting of white-flowered astilbes such as 'Bergkristall', 'Bridal Veil', or 'White Gloria'. They are equally pleasant in flower and a nice foliage contrast both before and after bloom.

Dwarf liriope, or mondo grass, *Ophiopogon japonicus,* is a dainty, fine-textured plant that is less robust than the preceding species. It grows only 6 to 10 inches tall, with leaves less than ¼ inch wide. Tolerant of drought and heavy shade, it is an ideal ground cover for dark, dry sites under trees or those permanently shaded by buildings. Left to its own devices (the benign neglect school of gardening), mondo grass has made lovely large patches of arching, almost trailing, foliage in my garden. Pale purple to nearly white flowers appear in July or August. Mondo grass is found in shaded places in the lowlands and foothills of Hokkaido, Honshu, Shikoku, and Kyushu, as well as in Korea and China, and is hardy from zones 6 to 9. It

has been suggested that this plant is not as hardy as liriope, both in the United States and in Great Britain, but I've not experienced any difficulties. There are several selections. 'Gyoku Ryu' and 'Kioto' grow only 2 to 3 inches tall; 'Kyoto Dwarf' is very similar; 'Nanus' (= 'Nana') slowly grows to 4 to 5 inches tall; 'Shiroshima Ryu' has dark green, 4- to 6-inch-high leaves neatly striped with white; 'Variegatus' also has green-and-white striped leaves; and 'Torafu' has 4-inch-tall leaves with horizontal yellow bands.

Ophiopogon planiscapus grows wild in the woods and thickets of the lowlands and foothills of Honshu, Shikoku, and Kyushu. The green-leaved form is rarely grown, with preference given to the exotic 'Nigrescens' (= 'Arabicus', 'Ebony Knight', 'Black Dragon'). Green new growth in spring matures to 6-inch-long, straplike, purple-black leaves that are evergreen. Pinkish violet summer flowers are followed by metallic, pealike, bluish black fruits in autumn. One year I used it in a container planting with dusty miller and violet-flowered impatiens for a very striking result. It is hardy in zones 6 to 9, but avoid an exposed site in colder areas.

Japanese Moneywort

If you like the looks of creeping jenny, *Lysmachia nummularia,* but it has taken over more than its allotted territory, the smaller, more restrained Japanese version,

The delicately fringed pink bells of *Shortia uniflora* make it one of Japan's most enchanting wild-flowers. PHOTO BY NIHEI TAKEO

Beautiful or bizarre—opinions vary—*Arisaema sikokianum*'s hooded flower is sure to invite comment from visitors to the garden.

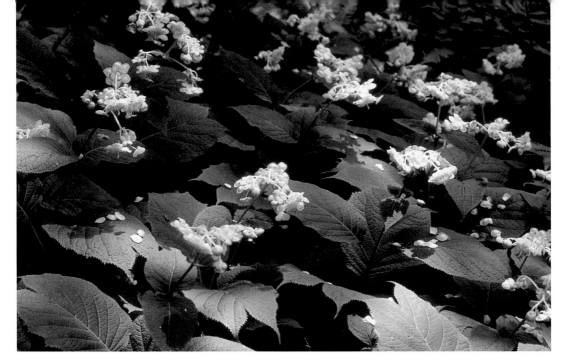

The forked tip of *Deinanthe bifida*'s leaf reminds me of a mermaid's tail, and its seafoam-like white flowers enhance the shady summer garden.

With elegantly striped, arching blades, *Hakonechloa macra* 'Aureola' is one of the few shade-tolerant grasses, and a welcome addition to the woodland garden.

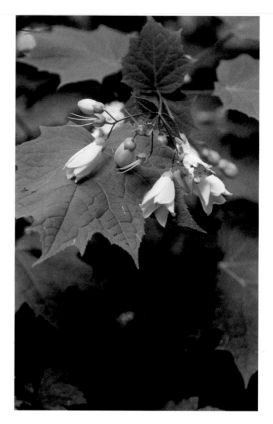

Like white wands, the flowers of *Cimicifuga japonica* var. *acerina* light up the autumn woods.

The pendant yellow bells of *Kirengesholma palmata* may be charmingly paired with cimicifuga, as they flower concurrently.

Fallen birch leaves signal autumn's arrival, and with it, the late blooms of *Hosta tardiflora* in the author's garden.

Like the antennae of some exotic shrimp, the stamens of red spider lily,
Lycoris radiata, adorn the showy flowers. Photo by Nihei Takeo

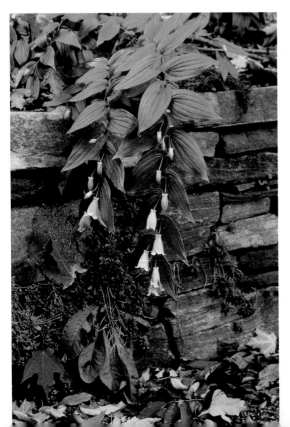

Dangling like a string of exotic yellow bells,
the flowers of *Tricyrtis macropoda* trail over a
wall in September.

L. japonica, might be just the thing. Native to thickets and roadsides in the lowlands and mountains of Hokkaido, Honshu, Shikoku, and Kyushu, and also to Ryukyu, Formosa, China, and Malaysia, it creeps along the ground making a mat of fresh green leaves. In early summer Japanese moneywort is spangled with small yellow flowers. Hardy to zone 4, it prefers moist to wet soil in light to moderately shaded sites.

JAPANESE DEAD NETTLE

Meehania urticifolia is rather similar in habit to creeping archangel, *Lamiastrum galeobdolon.* The upright stems flower in May, with spikes of 3- to 12-inch-long flowers that are bluish purple in color with dark purple spots on the lower lip. After blooming, the plants produce slightly arched runners that trail along the ground, rooting as they go. Found in the damp forests of mountains in Honshu, Shikoku, and Kyushu, as well as in Manchuria and Korea, Japanese dead nettle functions as a loose, rather open, deciduous ground cover. My plants seem to prefer a gentle slope to level ground, perhaps rambling more easily on the surface litter and humus-rich soil under the mature oak trees. There is a counterpart from the Appalachians, *M. cordata.*

Moss

If there is one ground cover Westerners associate with Japanese gardens, it would be moss. Kyoto, ancient capital of Japan, is noted for its moss gardens. In Roan-ji Temple's stone garden, Seki-tei, moss is the only plant in a rectangular walled courtyard of raked sand and fifteen stones. Haircap moss, *Polytrichum commune* (a circumpolar species very popular in Japan), clothes the base of the rocks, suggestive of forests on mountainous foothills.

Although we appreciate its quiet good looks, moss is one ground cover that Western gardeners rarely use. Attitudes may be changing, but the commercial availability of moss is rare. Not for us the ease of visiting Takeshimaya's garden department and purchasing a small flat for use with bonsai, let alone enough for landscape use. (The only nursery of which I am aware that sells mosses as named plants is We-Du Nurseries in Marion, North Carolina.) Patrick Chasse, a landscape architect and garden designer in Maine, does incorporate moss in his projects. He obtains haircap moss as sods, rescued from imperiled sites such as blueberry fields where moss is thought of as weeds, or pulpwood plantations routinely treated with herbicides.

One difficulty is that, while there are many different mosses, little information about them is available for the gardener. What has been written about mosses is often how to eliminate them rather than how to encourage them. Acid soil, around pH 5.0 to 5.5, is important, both to promote healthy moss and to discourage weeds. Traditional methods of acidifying soil use applications of finely powdered sulphur (flowers of sulphur), aluminum sulphate, or ferrous sulphate. Applied in spring or early summer, sulphur needs six to eight weeks to take effect, but the two sulfates produce results more promptly, in about two weeks. (Soil type—coarse or fine particles—also plays a role in how quickly the sulphur takes effect.) To lower pH from 7.0 (neutral) to 5.5, you will need 3½ pounds of sulphur per 100 square feet, 9 pounds of aluminum sulphate, or 16½ pounds of ferrous sulphate. Of the three, the last is my preference. There is often a correlation between pH and iron metabolism in plants. It seems to me that supplying iron in ferrous form with the sulphur is a better option than adding aluminum, which has been known to build up in soil with toxic results. To maintain acid conditions Stephen Morrell, curator of the John P. Hume Japanese Stroll Garden in Mill Neck, New York, applies a solution of 4 parts water and 1 part buttermilk. This is sprayed over the moss twice a year, in spring and fall, to maintain the *Hypnium* moss used there so beautifully. Such treatment is more practical for a relatively limited area. Reasonably high humidity, adequate water, and impoverished, rather infertile, quick-draining soils are also important.

Moss can be propagated. One spring I successfully tried the following technique: I prepared a flat by lining it with cotton cheesecloth, then filling it with an inch or so of a 50/50 mix of coarse sand and peat moss. (If you do not want to use peat moss, substitute composted sawdust.) This was watered with a 7:1 water:buttermilk solution. I covered the growing medium with a piece of cheesecloth a little larger than the flat, tucking the loose edges inside. I crumbled some pieces of moss that I had collected and dried for several days, and sprinkled the powdered bits evenly over the surface of the flat. I covered it with a third piece of cheesecloth, again tucking in the edges, and thoroughly but gently watered it, using a waterbreaker nozzle on the hose. I slipped a plastic drycleaner's bag over the flat (making sure the plastic did not touch the surface) and placed it in a shady site out of direct sunlight on the north side of a building. In a couple of months the moss had grown enough to be visible through the cheesecloth, and I slit the plastic in several places, removing it completely a few days later. Now I had to keep careful watch to prevent the moss from drying out. The growing medium had to remain damp but not soggy. Three months after planting, the moss was ready to move into the garden. I just lifted the sheet out of the flat, cheesecloth and all, leaving the remnants of the growing medium and liner layer behind.

Different mosses grow in different places, and it is important to match moss and site in your garden. Many prefer filtered light or midday and afternoon shade. Others, such as haircap moss, will grow and stay green in full sun, but lapse into partial dormancy in dry weather. Hard to tell apart, mosses are often distinguished by microscopic details. Gardeners will readily recognize short, dense, fine-piled, velvety, spreading mosses; hummocky silver-green mosses; and deep-piled, dark green haircap mosses.

Moss always looks best after a rain, when its color is intensified. The hose can always substitute if natural precipitation is lacking. Moss makes a perfect seed bed for rare, choice, and desirable plants such as shortia, trillium, and hepaticas, which will self-sow from your original planting into the moss. Unfortunately, so will unwanted plants, i.e., weeds; hand-weeding and habitat limitations (maintaining an acid pH and shallow soil) are the only maintenance methods and control. In autumn, rake fallen leaves off the moss as they can smother and kill it (although a few scarlet leaves from a Japanese maple, or a scattering of fragrant golden pine needles add to its autumnal beauty). Bamboo rakes are less hazardous to moss; I find springy metal leaf rakes often gouge and dig at its surface. If the moss is in an exposed location and snow cover is unreliable, a covering of pine boughs usually will bring it through the winter in better condition.

PACHYSANDRA

In Japan I did not see pachysandra or Japanese spurge, *Pachysandra terminalis,* used as a ground cover to the same ubiquitous extent that it has been applied in our country. Though this native of China and lowland and low-mountain forests on Hokkaido, Honshu, Shikoku, and Kyushu is frequently cultivated in gardens, it has not become a cliché element of corporate office parks, nor is it found as a tight encircling tutu around trees on suburban and city lawns. Useful in zones 5 to 7, plants grow poorly in regions with hot weather. Matted, creeping, white stolons speedily sneak their way into ever-expanding territory. Vigorous, fleshy, erect stems, 5 to 12 inches tall, produce loose carpets of foliage. Though plants often flower, they infrequently set white fruits. Quietly spreading to cover more than its fair share of a front walk, or vining up into azaleas with deleterious results, scandent pachysandra requires a vigilant eye and sharp clippers to keep it within bounds. (We seem to buy a flat or two, only to rip plants out by the bagful several years later.) That said, it is hard to think of a better evergreen carpet, especially on slopes and banks. One site I have seen, where the pachysandra spills down a slope, only to break at a rocky outcrop and then continue, is especially handsome with a dusting of winter snow. Only very vigorous perennials can compete. I have seen invasive *Anemone caroliniana* skillfully interplanted with pachysandra, where it produces its charming white buttercups and fresh green foliage against the pachysandra's more somber background. I have successfully used maidenhair fern, *Adiantum pedatum,* to add height and texture to a mass of pachysandra. 'Silver Edge' and 'Variegata' are two cultivars with white-edged leaves. They are less vigorous than the species, and lower growing. 'Green Carpet' has exceptionally dark green, glossy leaves. An American counterpart from the southern Appalachian mountains, Allegheny spurge, *P. procumbens,* has quietly silver-splotched, dull green leaves with a matte finish. It is fully evergreen in my zone 6 garden, and is hardy in zones 5 and 7.

CHAPTER SIX

Herbaceous Plants for the Sunny Perennial Border

Often, when asked where a plant comes from, gardeners are apt to respond with the name of the nursery where it was purchased, or the friend who shared it. Rarely do we pause to consider its country of origin. A disproportionate number of our most familiar perennials come from Japan. Reliable stalwarts like daylilies are a basic component of the Western flower garden. Others, such as patrinia, are relative newcomers. Japan has provided us with perennials for all seasons: epimedium in spring, balloon flower in summer, and ornamental grasses and chrysanthemums in autumn. What the plants in this chapter have in common is that all are herbaceous and all require at least six hours of full direct sunlight each day.

In spring the garden wakes, and frail, pale shoots emerge from the thawing soil. Unlike woodland perennials that often grow, flower, and return underground by midsummer, perennials in sunny sites tend to remain in growth through summer and early autumn. One must plan not only for the period of bloom, but also for the plants' appearance before and after flowering. How you combine herbaceous perennials is largely a matter of individual fancy, your personal aesthetic judgment. You may prefer subtle color schemes, while someone else favors vivid contrasts. Similarly, what you consider reasonable maintenance will depend on the time you are willing to devote and your inclination toward tidiness. Fortunately, there are perennials for all of us.

SPRING

Early-blooming perennials tend to be shorter than those that flower in summer and autumn. After all, at this time of year there are few competitors and little need to rise above them. Even low-growing early flowers can easily attract the attention of pollinating insects. The perennials that welcome spring should be planted near the front of the border, and grouped together for better effect.

COLUMBINE

Like dancing butterflies, the blossoms of columbines hover over the basal clump of foliage. Fan-leafed columbine, *Aquilegia flabellata,* has short-spurred, pale, creamy-white sepals and bluish purple or, rarely, white petals, forming a pleasingly plump flower held above glaucous, fan-shaped, and often overlapping leaves. The 12- to 18-inch-tall plants flower in April or May. Short-lived, columbines last three to five years, longer if drainage is good. They self-sow happily, and are also joyfully promiscuous with any other columbine that happens to be nearby. The next generation are all pretty, mind you, but not what you started out with unless you grow only one species. There are several dwarf forms that are described in chapter 8. Columbines have two insect pests: one, the leaf miner, tunnels between the upper and lower leaf surface, creating silver arabesques on the foliage. The damage is unsightly, but not deadly. The other is a minute green worm, larva of the columbine moth, which skeletonizes leaves from their edge. Bt, *Bacillus thuringensis,* is the most reliable and least toxic means of control.

Aquilegia buergeriana is taller, its flowering stems 12 to 24 inches high. The 1-inch-long nodding flowers have brownish purple to yellowish sepals, and dull purple petals that fade to yellow at their tip, with a slender erect spur. Native to Honshu, Shikoku, and Kyushu, it flowers from June to August. *Aquilegia oxysepala* was once thought to be a variety of the preceeding species. Slightly taller, it also has more attractive flowers, with claret to violet sepals and petals that pale to ivory, with a strongly hooked spur. It is a frequently found native of the mountains of Honshu, Shikoku, and Kyushu, as well as Korea, Manchuria, eastern Siberia, and northern China.

BLEEDING HEART

Owhi considers bleeding heart, *Dicentra spectabilis,* a native of China, Manchuria, and Korea that is cultivated in Japanese gardens. The *RHS Dictionary* lists bleeding heart as native to Siberia and Japan. In the West we know that it was introduced to England by Robert Fortune in 1847 from the Chinese island of Kushan. Bleeding heart quickly became, and today remains, one of the most popular spring-blooming plants for our gardens. Coarse, fleshy, thonglike roots send up arching stems up to 4 feet long with fernlike leaves. In spring the rosy-red, heart-shaped buds open to pink and white locketlike flowers. Plants yellow and go dormant in summer, especially when grown in full sun. Adequate moisture will slow but not prevent this untimely dormancy. Pure white-flowered 'Alba' (= 'Pantaloons'), with paler foliage, does not go dormant but insists on a moderately shaded site.

PEONY

Chinese peony, *Paeonia lactiflora*, is native to northern China, Korea, Manchuria, and eastern Siberia. In Japan it has been cultivated for such a long period, both for ornamental and medicinal purposes, that it is difficult to say with accuracy just when it was first grown there in gardens. The large white to rose or red-purple flowers, often double, bloom in May. They are depicted in scroll painting and embroidered on fabric.

This plant has it all: shoots attractively flushed with red as they appear in spring, superb flowers, and robust green summer foliage that often turns a rich orange-red in autumn before the plant goes dormant. Peonies are also very long-lived. My friend Helen Muller lives in the Westport, Connecticut, house that belonged to her parents. In the garden is a double pink peony with a paler center that was sent to her mother by a friend in Pennsylvania in the early 1920s; the plant has been in the garden for seventy years.

Such a truly perennial addition to the garden well repays thorough site preparation and attention to planting. October is the ideal time for planting bare-root peonies, though container-grown specimens can be planted in spring. Dig a large, deep hole in a sunny area with good drainage. Mix compost or leaf mold with top soil and superphosphate and muriate of potash fertilizers at the rate recommended on the bags. Be sure to mix the fertilizers well with the soil, and add a layer of unamended soil on top. (Chemical fertilizers are salts and can burn plant roots or leaves if they come into direct contact.) Backfill the hole two-thirds full. Then lightly firm the soil. The one fussy requirement that peonies have is planting depth—they will grow but not bloom if there is more than 1 to 2 inches of soil over their plump red growth buds. If the soil is not firmed before setting the roots, it is liable to settle and thus carry the peony crown too deep. Set the fleshy peony roots in the hole and, with a board across the opening, use a ruler to see how deep the crown actually is. Make any necessary adjustments upward or down, and then finish filling the hole, working soil in and around the heavy roots. Water when the hole is partially backfilled, and again when it is completely filled. The first winter it is a good idea to mulch newly planted peonies after the ground has frozen. Pine boughs are a good choice. In subsequent years peonies do not need mulching. They grow well in cold climates, and indeed have more problems in the Deep South from summer heat. There are numerous cultivars in colors ranging from white to palest pink to shell pink, rose, red, and maroon. Some have a single row of petals surrounding the golden boss of stamens, others have stamens transformed to colored, petal-like stamenoids, and still others, extravagantly fully double flowers. Some cultivars flower early in peony season, others somewhat later, thus extending the display. Although peonies need little maintenance after planting, the double-flowered cultivars do require staking, as their numerous petals act like blotting paper, soaking up rain. The flowers become so heavy that they fall over and trail their petals in the mud, often causing stems to bend and break.

There are two native Japanese species of peonies, which are described in chapter 7.

SUMMER

The summer is a time of exuberance and exhilaration in the garden. Warm temperatures and gentle breezes coax us outdoors to enjoy the bounty of flowers that are in bloom. Many summer perennials make good cut flowers, allowing us to bring the display indoors. Unlike spring's small floral treasures that demand close viewing, summer's taller blooms enable us to create colorful gardens that can be enjoyed from across the lawn or from a porch or terrace.

GIANT HYSSOP

Hyssop, *Agastache rugosa,* is native to grassy places along streams and in valleys in the mountains of Hokkaido, Honshu, Shikoku, and Kyushu, and also Korea, Manchuria, eastern Siberia, China, and Formosa. With fragrant leaves much like those of beebalm, hyssops were popular in herb gardens well before their general use in flower gardens. Plump, dense, terminal spikes of purple flowers appear from August to October on plants 15 to 40 inches tall. A member of the mint family, hyssop is not as invasive as are so many of its close relatives. Plants are thrifty and self-supporting in full sun and moist but well-drained fertile soil. A good bee plant, hyssop is also useful as a filler in the late summer and early autumn garden. It is especially effective in combination with the pinkish lavender to blue flowers then in bloom, such as *Aster* x *frikarti* 'Monch', Japanese anemones, and aconites.

CAMPANULA, OR BELLFLOWER

There is an absolute carillon of bellflowers for the garden, and as you might expect, some Japanese species are among the old favorites for the herbaceous border. Their bell-shaped flowers create a welcome contrast to the numerous daisies that also brighten the garden at this time.

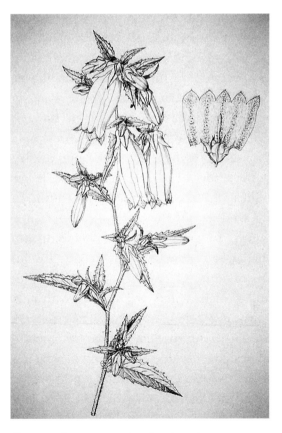

Campanula punctata var. *hondoensis*

If you thought that bellflowers were always blue or purplish blue, you're in for a welcome surprise. *Campanula punctata*'s large tubular flowers vary in color from waxy cream to shell pink to rose-pink, often deliciously speckled with crimson inside. The pendulous flowers, few in a terminal, spikelike arrangement, appear in June on stems 15 to 30 inches high. Hardy to zone 6, *C. punctata* dislikes colder zones or those with hot summers. It is a common plant found in the grassy meadows of the lowlands and low mountain slopes of Hokkaido, Honshu, Shikoku, and Kyushu. Named forms include 'Alba', with white or near white flowers; dwarf, white-flowered 'Nana Alba'; and 'Rosea', which is smaller in all its parts and has pale pink flowers. Somewhat invasive, the creeping rhizomes will form a carpet. Provide it with other vigorous perennials and ornamental grasses that likewise thrive in open, sunny situations with sandy, but not impoverished, soil.

While the typical form of clustered bellflower occurs in Eurasia, *Campanula glomerata* var. *dahurica* is found in the mountains of Kyushu, as well as in Korea, Manchuria, and eastern Siberia. Growing 18 to 30 inches tall, every stem is crowned in August and September with a dense terminal spike of about 10 blue-purple to deep purple flowers, each 1¼ inches long. Most likely, the forms you find at a nursery will be named selections of the Eurasian phase.

DIANTHUS

Whether called dianthus, pinks, or clove carnations, *Dianthus* have been popular in American, European, and Japanese gardens for their attractive flowers and tidy foliage. Sweet william, *Dianthus barbatus,* is frequently grown in Japan where it is called *amerika-nadeshiko* even though it is native to Europe. And we in turn admire and grow *D. superbus,* found in the mountains of Hokkaido, and central and northern Honshu, and also across Europe, Siberia, Manchuria, and Sakhalin. *D. superbus* has loosely clustered stems that first trail and then become more upright and branching, with sparse, linear, grassgreen leaves. Very fragrant pale lilac, soft pink, or white flowers, one to each branch, are deeply laciniate—finely, narrowly fringed—and feathery. Blooming from June to September, the flowers are charming at the front of a border. Late-blooming selections are included among Japan's classical seven flowers of autumn. Plants have a tendency to die out, but new ones are easily raised from cuttings. To keep plants more compact and tidy, cut them back hard after they finish flowering. There is a dwarf form suitable for the rock garden.

DAYLILY

The daylily is another stalwart perennial from Japan. Native from Europe to Siberia, the common tawny daylily, *Hemerocallis fulva,* brightens summer roadsides from New England westward to the Plains states with its warm brick-orange flowers. Plants that settle in and adapt to local conditions in this fashion are said to have naturalized: though they originate elsewhere they function as a native, reproducing and extending their range unaided. (Some naturalized plants, such as Oriental bittersweet, *Celastrus scandens,* can be real thugs, crowding out native species.)

Daylilies have attractive grasslike leaves that make an arching mound. A sturdy stem, or scape, forks above to display from a few to many flowers. The common name *daylily* refers to the fact that each flower opens for but a single day. While this may make it difficult to use them as cut flowers, several opening in sequence over a couple of weeks provide a suitably lasting display in the garden. The 6 segments of the flower unite at the base in an open lilylike form. In the wild species, flower color ranges from a warm, fulvous, rusty red to orange to shades of yellow and pale yellow. By far, the majority of daylilies sold at nurseries and garden centers are hybrids, with new cultivars offered each year. Their flowers are larger or smaller, ruffled or smooth, spiderlike or wide-petaled, and they have a wider color range including near-white, pink, melon, red, magenta, bicolors, and more.

Early development of hybrid daylilies was the work of Dr. A. B. Stout, director of laboratories at the New York Botanical Garden from 1911 to 1948. His technical research was in the sexual sterility of plants. The common tawny daylily is a sterile triploid, producing no seed. All the tawny daylilies you see growing wild along a suburban or country roadside are the result of asexual reproduction, in this case, increasing freely at the roots. Stout became interested in developing a wider color range for daylilies and in extending their season of bloom.

As native plants, twenty or so species of daylilies are found in Eurasia, with a half dozen indigenous to Japan. While the familiar single-flowered form of tawny daylily is not among these, a double-flowered form is mentioned in Owhi's *Flora of Japan,* and given the Latin epithet of *Hemerocallis fulva* var. *kwanso*. It is described as common in the hills and low mountains of Hokkaido, Honshu, Shikoku, and Kyushu.

Von Siebold introduced a variegated double-flowered tawny daylily, with elegantly white-striped leaves. It was described in England in the *Gardener's Chronicle and Agricultural Gazette* of 1864 as *Hemerocallis Kwanso foliis variegatis*. By the rules of botanical nomenclature, *Kwanso* can be applied only to the variegated-leaved, double-flowered form. The plant does, however, produce shoots that revert to all green. More chlorophyll means greater vigor, and if an alert gardener does not cut off the green shoots, the variegated portion will be over-

Hemerocallis fulva var. *kwanso*

whelmed. Frequently you see the green-leaved double-flowered form labeled as 'Kwanso', which is incorrect. I find the variegated form sufficiently beautiful to grow as a container plant for its elegant foliage alone.

I grow several other Japanese species. *Hemerocallis dumortieri* is one of the first daylilies to bloom, opening the season in May or early June in Connecticut, mid-April in North Carolina. The flowers are a clear cantaloupe-orange, with a rich brownish red stain on the buds that persists on the open flowers. The plants grow in dense, tight clumps less than 2 feet tall, with graceful leaves about 18 inches long and less than 1 inch wide. I wish the scape were a little longer because the flowers are partially concealed by the foliage. *H. dumortieri* was introduced by von Siebold, who sent plants to the Botanical Garden in Ghent over a century and a half ago. Native to the mountains of Hokkaido, and the central and northern districts of Honshu, as well as to eastern Siberia, Manchuria, and Korea, *H. dumortieri* is hardy to zone 4.

Hemerocallis middendorffi is very like *H. dumortieri* in appearance, with a low-growing habit and similar color, but with taller scapes that better display the flowers in May and early June. It is native to high mountain meadows in Hokkaido, and also to the Kuriles, Sakhalin, the Amur River region, Ussuri, Korea, Manchuria, and northern China. It is hardy to zone 5.

Lemon lily, *Hemerocallis lilioasphodelus* (= *H. flava*) has been a favorite of European gardeners for four centuries. As *Asphodelus luteus liliflorus,* it was mentioned by Matthias de Lobel and Penna in their *Historia* of 1570. Although it is native to Japan and Siberia, Leo Jellito and Wilhelm Schacht mention it as occasionally naturalized in moist meadows and woodland clearings in Europe. I collected mine from an abandoned garden, rescuing it from a thick tangle of poison ivy. Part of its appeal is the sweet, clean, citrus scent produced by the clear lemon-yellow flowers early in the season.

Dainty, grassy-leaved *Hemerocallis minor* is another of those "native or naturalized" plants, possibly introduced from China long ago. While some authorities consider it native only to northern China, Mongolia, eastern Siberia, and Korea, others include Japan. Arching, grasslike, dark green leaves are scarcely ½ inch wide and 15 to 18 inches long, creating a graceful mound above which the flowers are well displayed. The lemon-yellow, fragrant flowers appear in May and June. It would be charming along a little stream or, as I grow it, in the front of a perennial border. It is hardy to zone 4.

Modern daylily cultivars tend to peak in midsummer, no doubt influenced by national awards given at flower shows that are held in midsummer in the United States. There are some older cultivars introduced forty years ago, such as 'Autumn Minaret', 'Autumn King', and 'Chancellor', that do bloom late in the season, continuing to produce flowers until cut down by frost. *Hemerocallis littorea* is one of the plants Dr. John Creech saw on his trip to Japan in the fall of 1955. It was in bloom in November, near the seashore on a Shikoku cape. Its late period of bloom (August to October is given in the literature) has marvelous implications for the fall garden.

LIGULARIA

With leaves that droop at midday when grown in the open, ligularias clearly show their need for constantly moist to wet soils. Given sufficient water, they can be grown in full sun, but light midday shade is beneficial. There are numerous species of ligularia in Eurasia, seven in Japan, several of which have found their way into perennial borders. By far the most familiar of these is *Ligularia dentata*. A bold, attractive plant, it has large, dark green, heart-shaped leaves 12 inches long by 15 inches wide and toothed along the margin. Sturdy 15- to 40-inch-tall stems branch at the top, producing a nice display of large, raggedy, bright orange daisies in midsummer. 'Desdemona' and 'Othello' are two cultivars with an intense mahogany-red color on the underside of the leaves. Unfortunately slugs enjoy dining on new growth in spring, and the resulting damage is unsightly for the remainder of the growing season. A gardener's arsenal in the continuing slug wars includes handpicking, setting saucer-traps filled with beer, sprinkling the mollusks with salt, sprinkling diatomaceous earth (a light, friable siliceous material derived chiefly from diatom remains) around the plants, and using poisonous slug baits. Combine ligularia with other moisture-loving plants, such as astilbes, ferns, Japanese iris, and candelabra primroses. It is hardy to zone 4.

A ligularia with very different flowers, *Ligularia stenocephala* was described and named by Maximowicz. Native to wet places in the mountains of Honshu, Shikoku, and Kyushu, and also China and Formosa, it flowers in early summer. Its dark purple stems, growing 4½ feet tall, bear numerous orange-yellow daisies in a loose, open spike. The rounded, kidney- to heart-shaped leaves, nearly 10 inches across, are jaggedly toothed along their edges. This readily distinguishes it from *L. przewalskii*, with which it is frequently confused, as that species from northern China has deeply lobed leaves with a basically triangular outline. While *L. przewalskii* is hardy to zone 4, *L. stenocephala* is only hardy to zone 5.

A more compact ligularia, with possibilities for smaller gardens, is *Ligularia hodgsonii*. Growing 30 inches tall or less, it has kidney-shaped leaves that are 5 inches long by 11 inches wide, and saw-toothed along the margin. It flowers in summer, with daisies in a broad, flat-topped cluster. Plants with bright yellow flowers have green leaves and stems; those with orange flowers have purplish brown stems and leaves also flushed with purple on their underside. Native to Hokkaido and Honshu's northern district, the southern Kuriles and Sakhalin, this species is hardy to zone 5.

GOOSENECK LOOSESTRIFE

If you have room to let it ramble, gooseneck loosestrife, *Lysmachia clethroides,* is a wonderful plant for sunny informal gardens, preferring moist soil but amazingly tolerant of dry sites. Very commonly found in sunny hills and at low elevations on Hokkaido, Honshu, Shikoku, and Kyushu, and also Korea, Manchuria, China, and Indochina, the unbranched arching stems grow to 40 inches high. In summer, they're tipped with nodding spikes up to 12 inches long of densely clustered, small white flowers. It's not what you see above ground, but the tangled mass of pinkish runners, busily spreading underground into and through the crowns of adjacent perennials that make gooseneck loosestrife such a thug. If there is a rough area near a pond where you want a wild effect, turn gooseneck loosestrife loose, perhaps with other aggressive perennials such as beebalm. But for heaven's sake, keep it out of more refined, designed situations.

Patrinia

Patrinias are relatively new to Western gardens. The panicle-like clusters of small yellow flowers are excellent in combination with showier blooms such as the various daisies in the midsummer herbaceous border. Tidy, pinnately-lobed, jaggedly toothed, glossy foliage provides an attractive appearance when the plants are not in bloom. Vigorous and undemanding, slowly spreading by means of short, creeping rhizomes, patrinias are at their best with a moist soil high in organic matter and some light shade (especially at midday). Most widely available is *Patrinia gibbosa*. It grows about 2 feet tall, and in July and August bears many-flowered cymes (a more or less flat-topped flower cluster, the central flower opening first), 3 to 4 inches across, composed of tiny, ¼-inch, long-lasting, acid-yellow flowers. Native to the mountains of Hokkaido and the northern districts and Sado Island region of Honshu, it is hardy to zone 5.

Another species, *Patrinia triloba* var.

Lysmachia clethroides

palmata, has leaves palmately divided into 3 or 5 lobes on upright stems about 2 feet high. Found in the mountains of Honshu's central and western districts, and on Kyushu, it blooms in July and August. *Patrinia triloba* var. *triloba* (sometimes known as *P. palmata*) also has palmate leaves, irregularly toothed along the margins, and light yellow flowers. You would practically need to examine the flowers with a hand lens to see the differences. They are both hardy to zone 5.

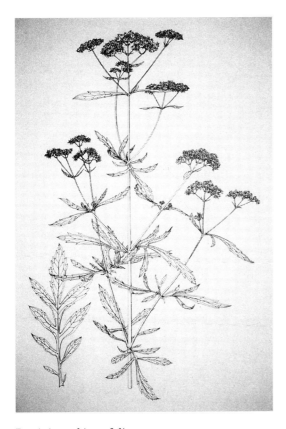

Patrinia scabiosaefolia

Patrinia scabiosaefolia grows 24 to 40 inches tall, with pinnately divided foliage, and flat-topped, many-flowered inflorescences of yellow flowers later in the season, from August to October. More tolerant of full sun and average (rather than constantly moist) situations, this widespread, common species is found in sunny meadows on the hills and mountains of Hokkaido, Honshu, Shikoku, and Kyushu, as well as the Kuriles, Sakhalin, Ryukyu, Formosa, Korea, China, Manchuria, and eastern Siberia. More tender than the preceding species, it is hardy to zones 6 or 7.

BALLOON FLOWER

Balloon flower, *Platycodon grandiflorum*, is another easy-care, long-lived perennial with a long season of bloom, from July to September. The common name refers to the flower buds, which look like swollen slate-blue balloons. Just before they are ready to open on their own, a gentle squeeze pops them open into a five-pointed, starlike, gently cupped flower. There is also a white form and a pink one so pale that the best I can say about it is that it is not white. A charming double form, really more of a hose-in-hose, has distinct appeal without the clumsiness of many double flowers. Upright stems, 2 to 3 feet tall, have saw-toothed edged, ovate leaves scattered along them. Older plants transplant poorly, as the heavy fleshy roots are intolerant of disturbance. If you are not meticulous about deadheading,

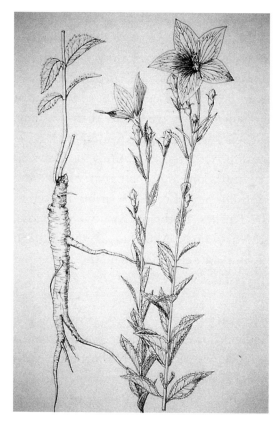

Platycodon grandiflorum

spicata, and cantaloupe-orange daylilies with the same period of bloom.

Ornamental Grasses

There are several ornamental grasses that have come to us from Japan. Their diversity includes diminutive species suitable for a container or rock garden setting, and tall species that can anchor the back of the border. Remember, grasses are, on the whole, sun lovers. Only one, Japanese wind-combed grass, *Hakonechloa macra* 'Aureola', prefers shade, and it will be found in the next chapter.

JAPANESE BLOOD GRASS
The plain green form of *Imperata cylindrica* is an invasive grass that frequently escapes from cultivation. Fortunately for gardeners, the exquisitely red-tipped cultivar 'Rubra' does not display the same dangerous characteristics. It is at its most ornamental when grown in large groups, sited where slanting late afternoon sun can shine through and illuminate the glowing red blade tips of the 12- to 18-inch-high culms. Charles Cresson grows this grass in his Swarthmore, Pennsylvania, garden together with red-and-green-flowered *Alstromeria psitticina* for an absolutely stunning combination. The grass is also attractive with the bronze foliage of dwarf red-leaved barberry, *Berberis thunbergii* 'Crimson Pygmy', and red-flowered snapdragons and nasturtiums.

seedlings will volunteer in the flower bed and can easily be moved to a new location. A fertile clay soil is best, as balloon flower resents dryness. It has long been cultivated in Japanese gardens for cut-flower use, and for the medicinal properties of its roots. In the wild, balloon flower is found on grassy slopes and in the mountains of Hokkaido, Honshu, Shikoku, and Kyushu, and also in Korea, northern China, and Manchuria. It is attractive in combination with the soft lavender-blue spikes of gayfeather, *Liatris*

MAIDEN GRASS

Eulia, maiden grass, or Japanese silvergrass, *Miscanthus sinensis*, is a large grass over 6 feet tall. It makes a dense clump of upright stems, crowned in August to October with white-haired, feathery seedplumes. Fumio Kitamura and Yurio Ishizu write in *Garden Plants in Japan*, "The spectacle of the plants waving their white spikes in the wind is a representative autumnal sight in Japan. There is an old Japanese custom to decorate with their cut flowers on the full moon night in mid-autumn." Some cultivars have been grown by the Japanese for centuries. It is a common native plant, widespread and variable, in the lowlands and mountains of Hokkaido, Honshu, Shikoku, and Kyushu, as well as the southern Kurile Islands, Korea, China, Ruykyu, and Formosa. This considerable diversity has allowed a broad selection of forms; some are dwarfer, others have variegated leaves or show variation in time of bloom. One of the oldest cultivars of maiden grass in the nursery trade is 'Gracillimus' or *M. sinensis* var. *gracillimus,* a fine-textured, narrow-leaved form with 2- to 3-foot-long, dark green leaves creating a 5- to 7-foot-high mound. Another popular cultivar, 'Zebrinus', has intermittent transverse whitish bands across the leaf blades, which is quite unusual, as most variegation follows a lengthwise pattern. A number of popular cultivars have been developed in Germany. They include 'Silberfeder' (silver feather) with showy, feathery white plumes on upright, closely clumping plants 6 to 9 feet tall; 'Silberpfeil' (silver arrow) with white-striped leaves and less tendency to flop than the older 'Variegatus'; 'Silberturm' (silver tower), an upright cultivar that can reach 8 to 10 feet tall; 'Kleine Fontaine' (little fountain) with a more compact form; 'Grosse Fontaine' (big fountain) with cascading fountainlike foliage; 'Herbstfeuer' (autumn fire) with good autumn color; and 'Rotsilber' (red-silver), which has red flowers and good fall color.

I have a clump of 'Gracillimus' planted on a moderately steep, gravely slope behind a cut-leaf sumac, *Rhus typhina* 'Laciniata'. Most of the year the grass is inconspicuous. Then in autumn, the combination of the sumac's flaming red and scarlet serrate leaflets, and the grass's smoke-plume seedheads creates a focal point in the garden. While my specimen grows satisfactorily in a dry site, Japanese silvergrass grows well in average to moist to positively wet sites, as long as they are sunny. Maiden grass is elegant reflected in the calm surface of a pond. Consider using it as a specimen, a screen, or a wind break. The foliage form, feathery flowers, and seedheads also combine attractively with tall late-blooming perennials such as fall asters, sunflowers, heleniums, and goldenrods.

Unless maiden grass is overfed with nitrogen resulting in lush, weak culms, it is generally self-supporting. The only maintenance necessary then is to cut the old growth off in late winter or earliest spring before new growth begins in March. The culms are rather tough. One technique is to tie a bungee cord around the clump and use a chainsaw to cut the growth down. The bungee cord also makes cleanup a simple matter, keeping all the culms in a tidy bundle for disposal.

FOUNTAIN GRASS

Fountain grass, *Pennisetum alopecuroides,* is one of the most popular, dependable, and useful grasses in the mixed perennial border. Forming a densely tufted mound 2 to 3 feet tall and as wide, it is native and quite common in grassy places and waste ground in the lowlands of Honshu, Shikoku, Hokkaido's southwestern districts, and Kyushu, as well as Korea, China, and Formosa on to the Philippines. There are three forms found in the wild, distinguished by the color of the bristles. These are *P. alopecuroides* f. *purpurascens,* which has dark purple bristles and is the most common; f. *erythrochaetum,* with red bristles; and f. *viridescens,* which has pale green bristles.

I like fountain grass best when it begins to flower in midsummer, forming numerous arching stems, each tipped with a 4- to 10-inch-long spike like an enraged cat's tail. Foliage fades from summer's green to a pale biscuit color in autumn. One of the loveliest combinations I've seen was at Wave Hill in the Bronx. Marco Stuffano had combined the grass with the silver, furry foliage of lamb's ears, *Stachys lanata,* and 'The Fairy', a small shrub rose that bears clusters of petite pink flowers. Another good late-season combination would be fountain grass, chrysanthemums, and ornamental kale.

THEMEDA

Perhaps more widely grown in Germany than in the United States, *Themeda triandra* is an ornamental grass with good garden potential. It makes a very leafy, erect clump 30 to 40 inches high and wide. The blades are densely haired, bright green, and arching, and they gradually turn red in summer, progressing from the base of the leaf blade to the tip. Though deciduous, the dry dead foliage retains a rich orange to coppery-red color late into winter. Native to the lowlands and low mountains of Honshu, Shikoku, and Kyushu, and also Korea, Manchuria, China, and India, themeda is hardy in zones 6 to 9. It flowers in September or October (thus its inclusion in the Seven Flowers of Autumn), and needs a warm climate to produce the outward-nodding branched panicles with numerous bright russet-colored, bristly-haired bracts rising a foot or two above the mass of foliage. Plants need a hot, sunny site with moist, fertile soil if they are to grow well and flower. Winter cold and damp can be harmful, making the plants difficult to winter over in zone 6.

With over 90 different genera, Japan is so rich in grasses that I expect new species to ornament our gardens in the not-far-distant future.

Bulbs

LILIES

Though not so rich in bulbs as the arid steppes of Central Asia, or the Cape of South Africa, Japan has definitely provided some choice additions to our gardens. Certainly the Oriental hybrid lilies confirm this, for they were developed from Japanese species—*Lilium auratum, L. speciosum, L. japonicum,* and *L. rubellum.* These tall, late-summer-blooming lilies include such stalwart selections as 'Empress of India', with 8 to 10 bowl-shaped, deep red flowers edged in white, each up to 10 inches across, on 4- to 5-foot stems; 'Imperial Crimson' with flat, fragrant, deep crimson flowers edged in white on 5-foot stems; and 'Imperial Gold' with flat, scented flowers, each white petal striped with a golden band down the center, on stately 6-foot stems. 'Journey's End' has deep pink flowers spotted with maroon and edged in white on 3- to 6-foot stems. The very popular 'Sans Souci', whose white flowers are flushed and spotted with red, and edged and tipped in white, grows to just 3 feet, making it a good choice for containers. The same is true of 3-foot 'Casa Blanca', whose flattish white flowers have petals that recurve at the tips.

In the wild, lilies are found throughout the temperate regions of the Northern Hemisphere. There is a concentration of species on the West Coast of the United States in California and Oregon; another in China extending into Korea, Siberia, and along the Himalayas; and a third encompassing Japan and Kamchatka. If you include the stately cardiocrinum, there are a baker's dozen of lily species found in Japan. Several are endemic, found wild

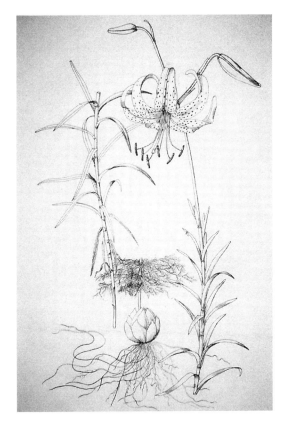

Lilium leichtlinii var. *tigrinum*

nowhere else in the world. One, the tiger lily, *Lilium lancifolium,* is a common garden escapee that has naturalized in other parts of the world. Like the tawny daylily, the tiger lily is a sterile triploid: it multiplies by offsets and through bulbils that form in the leaf axils. Others, such as *L. rubellum,* are difficult to keep in cultivation. Between these two extremes are to be found some elegant, exquisite lilies and their hybrid progeny, suitable for use in the average garden.

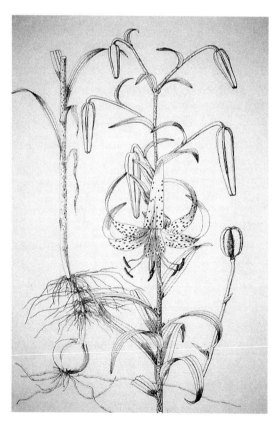

Lilium lancifolium

In general, these lilies prefer an open soil with good drainage, as they rot if the bulbs remain too wet, especially while dormant in winter. At the same time they do poorly in sandy, drought-prone situations. The ideal is a well-drained, slightly acidic soil high in organic matter, capable of retaining nutrients and some moisture. Lilies are not affected by late frosts since growth begins in late spring. Winter cold is not as much of a problem as summer heat and humidity, thus lilies are popular in Canadian gardens, but often difficult to grow in the Deep South. In the wild, lilies frequently grow among coarse vegetation or low shrubs, where their roots are shaded but stems, leaves, and flowers are in sunlight. Immature lily bulbs and seedlings should be planted relatively shallowly: contractile roots literally shorten in length and pull bulbs down to the correct depth. Fully grown bulbs are planted two to three times as deep as the bulb's height. Thus, if the bulb is two inches from tip to basal plate it should be planted with four to six inches of soil over its tip. If the particular species of lily is stem-rooting, with seasonal roots along the stem in addition to those at the base, plant it more deeply than a species that roots only from the base. The Oriental hybrids in particular are stem-rooting; check for this information in the catalog when ordering bulbs.

Gold-band lily, *Lilium auratum,* has been called "Queen of the Lilies" in homage to its huge, bowl-shaped, white flowers. The center of each petal is streaked with gold, and heavily spotted with gold and crimson red. In addition, the blossoms are very fragrant. A well-grown plant—6 feet tall, boasting 35 or more flowers to a stem—is a regal sight indeed. Its Japanese name, *yama-yuri* (mountain lily) refers to its habitat in the hills and lower mountain slopes of Honshu; it has naturalized on Hokkaido. It often grows in impoverished volcanic soil covered with a thin humus layer, where its growth is stunted and only a few flowers are produced per stem. The blooming period is late July or August. Bulbs are pale yellow, often 4 inches across and 3 inches high. This species is stem-rooting.

The gold-band lily arrived in Europe and the United States almost simultaneously. It was exhibited in England at a Royal Horticultural Society show in July 1862; von Siebold introduced it to Belgium at about the same time, and it was brought to North America, described, and named (invalidly) *Lillium dexteri* in August 1862.

If I were allowed to grow only one species of lily, then I think it would be the beautiful, fragrant, autumn-flowering *Lilium speciosum*. Though common in cultivation, it has a relatively limited natural distribution on Shikoku and Kyushu, rare even in its native haunts. It has been known in the West for three centuries. During his stay in Japan between 1690 and 1692, Kaempfer rendered a clearly recognizable drawing of it, making it one of the first Japanese lilies known in Europe. It was described by Thunberg and given its present, valid name a century later, in 1794. Appropriately, *speciosum* means "showy, splendid, good-looking." Bulbs were sent to Holland by von Siebold in 1830, and within the decade had reached England, where the species was rapturously received.

The bulb of this lily can be as much as 4 inches wide and high, made up of thick white, yellowish brown, or purplish brown scales. It is stem-rooting and so should be planted relatively deeply. However, good drainage must be assured, as this species is particularly prone to basal rot. If conditions in your garden are not suitable (if the soil is too heavy or too sandy, or the pH alkaline), this is an excellent lily to grow in containers. It is also a good choice for use as a cut flower. The stem grows 3 feet tall, sometimes higher, and in August and September has as many as 12 deliciously fragrant flowers on longish, somewhat nodding pedicels. The strongly reflexed petals are white or pale pink, flushed carmine-pink at the base, heavily spotted crimson or carmine, with raised warts or papillae toward the base of the petals. Several cultivars are available: 'Album Novum' is a good, vigorous, white-flowered form; 'Rubrum' is a vigorous, carmine-red flowered one with a purple-brown stem; and 'Uchida' is a form raised in Japan for commercial use as a cut flower and for pot culture, and widely available in the United States.

Though not generally grown in gardens, *Lilium longifolium* is still familiar to gardener and nongardener alike as the potted plant known as Easter lily. In Japan it is called *teppo-yuri,* or blunderbuss lily, for its wide trumpet like the primitive gun of that name. Coming as it does from the southerly islands of Yakushima and Tanegashima, and Rukuyu, it is too tender for outdoor cultivation in most places. Thunberg mentions it in his *Flora Japonica,* at first confusing it with the Mediterranean species, *L. candidum.* He finally recognized it as a distinct species and named it in 1794.

Easter lily bulbs are about 2½ inches wide, less than 2 inches tall, and made up of creamy white or yellowish scales. The lily roots along the stem, which grows from 3 to 4½ feet tall, though modern cultivars developed for container use have shorter stems. The pure white, trumpetlike flowers—up to six to a stem—are slightly recurved at the tips and accentuated by the golden pollen-bearing stamens. As well as being quite tender, this species is very susceptible to lily mottle virus and other diseases. Fortunately it comes quickly from seed (which is virus-free) and some strains reach flowering size just a year after sowing. Easy to force and good as a cut flower, this is a lily more useful as a temporary enhancement in your home than a permanent resident in the garden.

Lilium hansonii is an adaptable, easily grown lily that more often arrives in gardens as a hybrid. Crossed with the very dark-flowered *L. martagon* var. *cattaniae,* it has produced *L.* x *dalhansonii* with dark, reddish maroon, heavily spotted flowers. The results of crossing with *L. martagon* var. *album* produced the *L.* x *marhan* group, with dull, orange-yellow flowers. The Backhouse hybrids, including 'Mrs. R. O. Backhouse', are considered preferable. Jan de Graaff of the Oregon Bulb Farm raised a vigorous multihued strain known as the Paisley hybrids, with flowers colored white, very pale yellow, gold, orange, lilac, purple, tangerine, or mahogany, all with tiny maroon freckles and all flowering in June.

The husky stem of *Lilium hansonii* grows to 3 to 5 feet tall, with up to 12 very heavily fragrant, nodding, turk's cap flowers of a deep orange-yellow, spotted a dark purplish brown toward the base. The petals are quite thick, like orange peel according to the eminent lily authority Patrick Synge. In Japan *L. hansonii* is found on Hokkaido where it has naturalized, introduced from its native origins in Korea and Eurasia. The long-lived, yellowish white bulbs are 1½ to almost 3 inches in diameter and just over 2 inches high.

Tiger lily, *Lilium lancifolium*, has been in cultivation for over a millennium, and the bulbs are grown as an agricultural crop, for food, by the Japanese, Koreans, and Chinese. Commonly planted in gardens, this lily is native to Hokkaido, Honshu,

Shikoku, and Kyushu, as well as Korea, Manchuria, and China. It has naturalized in parts of the United States and Europe, happily growing wild along roadsides and in meadows and thickets. The astonishing thing is that tiger lily is a sterile clone, a triploid incapable of producing seed. Reproduction is accomplished vegetatively, by means of small black aerial bulbils that form in the leaf and stem axils. They fall to the ground, pull themselves below the surface, and rapidly mature to flowering size. So self-reliant a plant unfortunately has a major flaw. This lily is a carrier of a debilitating virus to which it is immune. Aphids carry the disease to other, more susceptible lilies, which are killed by it. If you are content to grow only this one species, then it is a fine choice.

Tiger lily's white bulbs, just over 3 inches in diameter and not quite as high, produce 4- to 6-foot purplish black stems furred with white hairs. Numerous flowers appear in July or August, with strongly reflexed, turk's-cap petals of a strong orange-red, heavily spotted with large purplish black freckles. In a cottage garden, combined with summer's many yellow daisies, ornamental grasses, and other informal herbaceous perennials, tiger lily is an admirable plant. Just be sure to keep it at least as far away from other lilies as aphids can fly.

Lilium concolor var. *partheneion* is a daintier lily, growing 1 to 3 feet tall. It flowers in June or July, with up to 10 orange-yellow to red flowers, usually spotted near the base of the petals. The upward-facing, star-shaped flowers are fragrant. Bulbs are small, barely 1 inch high and wide, with only a few white scales. It is stem-rooting. Other varieties of *L. concolor* are more common in China, North Korea, eastern Siberia, and along the Amur River. In Japan this species occurs as a rare inhabitant of mountain meadows on Honshu, Shikoku, and Kyushu. It tends to be rather short-lived in gardens (perhaps also in the wild) but is easily and quickly raised to flowering size from seed.

CARDIOCRINUM

Cardiocrinum, *Cardiocrinum cordatum* (= *Lilium cordatum*), is not quite a masochist's plant, but it comes close. It can take ten years to reach flowering size from seed, and soon after flowering drops dead. The saving grace is that before it dies, the bulb produces offsets that will reach flowering size in only a few years. At maturity the stem reaches 4 to 6 feet high, arising from a basal rosette of foliage. Four to 10, sometimes (though rarely) as many as 24, trumpet-shaped flowers have a lovely fragrance and are creamy white, the lower segments blotched with yellow and streaked and spotted with reddish purple markings. It was first described by Kaempfer in 1690, and was found again by Thunberg near Nagasaki in 1748. Cardiocrinum is widely distributed in Japan, found in moist woodlands of the lowlands and foothills of Honshu's Kanto district and westward, Shikoku, and Kyushu, where it blooms in July and August. While you are waiting for the plant to reach maturity, bloom, and die, you can enjoy the bronze-crimson color of the new growth as it emerges each spring. It should be given a site where the tender new growth will not be damaged by late spring frosts. Admittedly, the majestic Himalayan *C. giganteum* is more impressive. However, its 9-foot stems can make it awkward in a small garden.

Lycoris

Lycoris squamigera is called naked ladies, magic lily, rain lily, and surprise lily in the United States. Native to Honshu, Shikoku, and Kyushu, it is often grown in gardens in Japan. The bulbs, looking like those of some long-necked daffodils, send their straplike, gray-green leaves up in the spring. By early June they have gone dormant, only to surprise me in August and September when, like magic, the flower stalks suddenly appear after a summer rain. Each 20- to 28-inch stalk has 4 to 6 large, trumpetlike rose-pink flowers. Lycoris do not take well to disturbance, and often refuse to flower the first year or two after they are introduced to the garden. Then in subsequent years, if not intruded upon, they will make enlarging clumps. This is the only species of lycoris hardy in zone 6, and even so it needs a protected site.

It really thrives in the Southeast.

The lycoris that truly makes itself at home in the Southeast is red spider lily, *Lycoris radiata*. It sends up its narrow, dark green leaves with a central white stripe in autumn. Where winters are mild and summers not Mediterranean dry and hot, the spider lily sends up its flower scapes in September. The scarlet to carmine-red petals are narrow and deeply reflexed, and encircle long protruding stamens. Common in ditches around cultivated fields and in wet meadows in the lowlands and hills on Honshu, Shikoku, and Kyushu, this species is also found in Ryukyu and China. I saw some growing with crape myrtles in Texas in the parking area of an Austin mall. Edith Eddleman, senior curator of the perennial border at the North Carolina State University Arboretum in Raleigh, created a spectacular effect when she paired red spider lily with Japanese blood grass. Before its own leaves emerge, the lily's delicate red flowers arise on green scapes to float above the warm scarlet blades of grass.

Both species of lycoris make excellent cut flowers. Since they blossom without their leaves, be sure to plant them with other, leafier perennials that will conceal the naked lycoris scapes. Site them where they receive midday shade, or even lightly shaded conditions at all times.

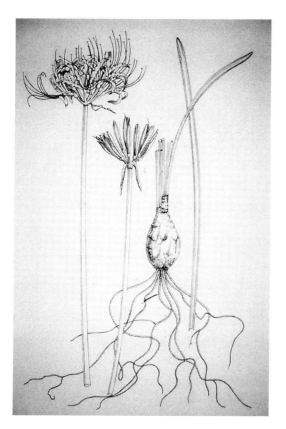

Lycoris radiata

A U T U M N

The end of summer need not mean the end of garden pleasures. Late-flowering perennials, grasses in their fall display, and trees and shrubs chosen for foliage and fruiting effects can be combined to create an attractive garden. Group these end-of-season plants together to strengthen their effect, and place them where the golden light of an autumn afternoon will warm the discerning gardener.

CHRYSANTHEMUM

Perhaps no other flower is as associated with Japan in Western minds as the chrysanthemum. Alas, the taxonomists have been at their revisionary work again, and the plant once known as *Chrysanthemum* x *morifolium*, must today be called *Dendranthema* x *grandiflorum,* which doesn't exactly trip off the tongue. But by any name, this beautiful autumn-flowering perennial is one of the representative plants used as autumn decoration, as garden plants, trained as a bonsai, or as a cut flower. Cultivated in Japanese gardens for centuries, numerous forms have been developed: some with large, many-petaled, nearly globular flowers; others with fewer narrow petals that give a spidery appearance; and still others with simple, daisylike flowers in white, yellow, bronze, pink, red, lavender, or wine.

When Dr. John Creech visited Japan in the autumn of 1956, he acquired 173 different varieties of chrysanthemum from nurseries and collected several species in the wild. Now commonly grown as an autumn-blooming annual, hybrid chrysanthemums are the product of crossing and recrossing *Dendranthema indicum* and other species. We purchase potted plants in full bloom, pop them into the garden in place of summer's marigolds and zinnias, then discard them with winter's snows (or spring thaws, depending on your level of activity). This is unfortunate because chrysanthemums, especially the Korean hybrids, are, on the whole, quite perennial. The difficulty lies in our treatment of them. Purchased in peak bloom, planted as the weather worsens, what else could we expect of them but their prompt demise? If they are purchased in spring with other hardy perennials, or removed after autumn planting to a cold frame's shelter their first winter, Korean hybrid chrysanthemums will come back year after year. I find the simpler flowered, single and semidouble daisy types more pleasing and more reliably perennial than the larger-flowered varieties. Numerous stems grow from the rootstock, reaching 2 to 3 feet tall unless manipulated by chemicals or by pinching. The lobed leaves have a spicy scent when crushed.

Blooming in October, Montauk daisy or Nippon daisy, *Nipponantherum nipponicum* (= *Chrysanthemum nipponicum*), is one of the last flowers to appear in my garden. Its somewhat succulent, glossy, rich green foliage makes a good contrast to its clean, clear white single daisies with golden centers. This is a sub-shrub that develops a leggy, woody base. For a neater, tidier appearance, cut back to only a few inches high before growth begins in spring. Endemic to Japan, it is found near the seashores of Honshu's Kanto district and northward. It thrives on sandy beaches, and one common name honors Montauk, Long Island, where the plant is tremendously popular. A correspondent in Rossdorf, Germany, notes that plants are damaged there by the winter climate.

Otherwise hardy to zone 5, Montauk daisy can be killed by winter wet and/or poor drainage.

Also found near Honshu's seashores, *Dendranthema pacificum* (= *Chrysanthemum pacificum*), is not much as far as flowers go, but excellent as a foliage plant. Green above, silver-haired beneath, the 1½- to 3-inch-long leaves appear to have a thin white line following the bluntly lobed margin.

Monkshood

Several species of wolfsbane, or monkshood, *Aconitum,* are found in Japan, with

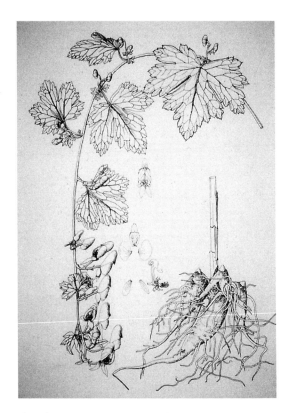

Aconitum sanyoense

flowers of typical violet-blue. The most popular species for gardens and cut flower use in Japan is *A. chinensis,* a native of China that grows 30 to 48 inches tall and has wonderful spikes of large, short-spurred, helmetlike, deep indigo blue flowers in September and October. Best in full sun, Chinese monkshood needs partial shade in warmer regions and requires cool nights and moist soil. Remember, all parts of the plant are poisonous—the tuberous roots especially so. If you have any cuts or scrapes on your hands, keep the wounds free of any juice when cutting flowers. Monkshood is hardy from zones 4 to 6, and the cooler parts of zone 7.

Adenophora

Ladybells, *Adenophora takedae*, is another of autumn's treasures. In the wild this Japanese endemic is found growing among the rocks in mountain ravines on Honshu. The slender stems, 12 to 24 inches long, scramble along the ground, clad with dark green, narrow, lanceolate leaves. In September and October ladybells produces a loose, open raceme of up to 10, dainty, bell-like flowers. They are a lovely blue and, indeed, can be easily mistaken for a campanula's flowers. Plant ladybells in a sunny, well-drained site but do not allow them to become parched since they cannot tolerate dry conditions. Select younger, smaller plants for purchase or transplanting since ladybells have thick, fleshy roots that resent

disturbance, and they move poorly as mature plants. There are some smaller species, discussed in chapter 9.

Japanese Anemone

Japanese anemone, *Anemone hupehensis* var. *japonica,* is another of those befuddling plants that are definitely Chinese and possibly Japanese, as it has been widely cultivated in Japan for hundreds of years. Numerous petals—silky and silvery outside, pale rose-purple inside—contrast

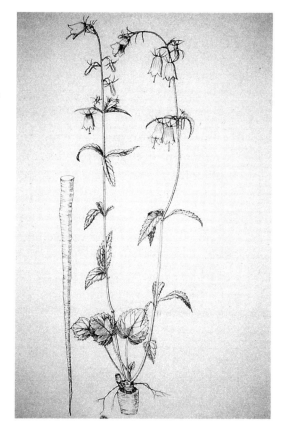

Adenophora triphylla var. *japonica*

beautifully with a central boss of golden stamens. A neat plant with tidy clumps of basal, maplelike leaves, it will range widely via underground roots once it has established in a site. It is usually the cultivars and hybrids (*A. japonica* "of gardens") that are available, rather than the straight species. In late summer sturdy but supple stems grow 20 to 30 inches tall, producing blooms of soft cerise-pink, rose-pink, pale silvery pink, or white. There are several readily available cultivars: white 'Honorine Jobert' and soft silvery pink 'September Charm' (usually in bloom by mid-August in my garden) are both singles. Semidoubles include white 'Whirlwind', cerise-pink 'Prinz Heinrich' (closest to the species), and deep cerise-pink 'Pamina'. Japanese anemones grow best in moist soil high in organic matter, in full sun with some midday shade in warmer regions or in light-dappled shade. Slow to establish, Japanese anemones are long-lived once they have settled into place. At the edge of a woodland they are elegant with taller ferns, while a perennial border pairing might bring together Japanese anemone with fall asters, monkshood, and late-flowering tall sedums.

BUSH CLOVER

Several species of bush clover, *Lespedeza* sp., are native to Japan. Somewhat shrubby, they function as perennials, usually dying back to the ground in winter. As their trifoliate leaves and pealike flowers suggest, they are legumes and can tolerate infertile, well-drained soil. Their late season of bloom makes a handsome display in September and supports their inclusion among the Seven Flowers of Autumn. Accordingly, find them companions that enhance the late season: grasses with feathery seedheads, silver-leaved artemisia that also like sunny sites, or colchicums that also flower as summer wanes.

Bush clover, *Lespedeza bicolor,* naturalizes easily in the southeastern United States. It is native to grassy places and thickets in the mountains and lowlands of Hokkaido, Honshu, Shikoku, and Kyushu, and also to Korea, Ussuri, Manchuria, and northern China. Plants may range from 2 to 6 feet tall, often woody at the base. In late summer rose-purple or rose-violet pealike flowers appear in loose axillary clusters or in terminal panicles. Once segregated as *L. bicolor* f. *acutifolia,* this species was grown not only as an ornamental but also as a utility plant to prevent landslides, or to be used as animal feed and fertilizer. In Japanese gardens bush clover is grown in a row to delineate a walkway, or as an attractive and informal hedge. 'Yakushima' is a dwarf form only a foot high, with small leaves and flowers.

Lespedeza thunbergii, is a handsome species growing 40 to 70 inches tall. Naturalized in Honshu's Hokuriku and Chugoku districts, it is widely cultivated in

Japan, and is native to China. The erect to arching stems, sometimes woody at the base, produce numerous pendulous racemes of rose-purple flowers in late summer. 'Albiflora' is the long-cultivated, white-flowered cultivar, while 'Versicolor' has white and rose-purple flowers.

BURNET

Perhaps you know burnet as a plant from the herb garden with cucumber-flavored leaves. There are burnets from Japan that also claim a place in the flower garden by virtue of their unusual, attractive blossoms in late summer and early autumn.

Great burnet, *Sanguisorba officinalis,* is a common native of the moist to wet lowland and mountain meadows of Hokkaido, Honshu, and Shikoku, and also Mongolia, China, Europe, and North America. The 3-foot-tall plant is somewhat spreading and weedy, occasionally grown for its upright, blood-red flower spikes that appear in late summer. Far better is the endemic *S. obtusa,* a native of alpine meadows on Honshu's Mount Hayachine. Each pinnately compound leaf has 13 to 17 grayed leaflets, giving plants a fine feathery texture. They grow only 12 to 20 inches tall. In August and September their nodding spikes of rich rose-pink flowers remind me of a cat's fluffy tail. This species is best suited to an informal planting in a sunny site with wet soil. *Sanguisorba obtusa* 'Alba' (= *S. obtusa* var. *albiflora*) is slightly taller and

has white flowers. When I was in Japan I became enchanted with *S. hakusanensis,* which grows up to 30 inches tall with 9 to 13 leaflets per leaf. In late summer the pendulous flower spikes, up to 4 inches long, are like trailing, deep rose-purple bottlebrushes. Native to alpine meadows on the Japan Sea side of Honshu's central districts, it seems quite happy in my garden.

Sanguisorba hakusanensis

SEDUM

Interest in the autumn garden has taken a quantum leap forward with the work of the Washington, D.C., landscape architecture firm of Oehme, Van Sweden. Mass plantings of black-eyed susans, fountain grass, and sedum are signatures of their designs. 'Autumn Joy' (= 'Herbstfreude') is probably a hybrid between *Sedum spectabile* and *S. telphium*. Brace yourself. The taxonomists have relocated both of these to the genus *Hylotelphium*. The Korean and Manchurian native *H. spectabile* is widely cultivated in Japanese gardens (as well as here) for its July to September blooming period. It is also grown as a cut flower. Flowering from August to September, *H. telphium* is native to Hokkaido, Honshu, and Kyushu, and is also widespread across Europe and Siberia. Both species grow to about 2 feet tall with thick erect stems, somewhat fleshy leaves, and broccoli-like flowerheads, that are pale apple-green in bud, rose-pink in bloom, and rusty-red in seed. *H. spectabile* has a number of cultivars: 'Stardust' has very pale green leaves and greenish-white flowers; 'Snowqueen' has white flowers; 'Brilliant' has deep pink flowers; 'Meteor' has deep carmine-red flowers; and 'Variegatum' has cream variegated leaves and deep pink flowers. All of these, species and cultivars alike, prefer a sunny site with a reasonably fertile soil and average to moderately dry conditions. They are hardy from zones 4 to 10. The flowers are very popular with butterflies and bees. Combine these end-of-season sedums with late-flowering Montauk daisies and ornamental grasses. Nerines would be charming companions in zone 7 and warmer.

CHAPTER SEVEN

Woodland Perennials

The natural landscape of Japan is heavily wooded, with broadleaved evergreens on the southern islands of Kyushu, Shikoku, and lower Honshu, and deciduous and coniferous forests on the northern islands and at higher elevations between 2,500 and 6,000 feet. Historically, many large forested tracts were controlled by the imperial household; others were in the custody of religious institutions. Both situations strongly restricted commercial activities such as logging and landclearing for farming or construction. Additionally, the steep mountainous nature of much of the land physically limits clearcutting for whatever reason, since erosion is an all too common result.

Just as there are excellent Japanese plants for sunny sites, there are perennials and bulbs that are superb additions to shady gardens across the country. Ozzie Johnson of Marietta, Georgia, gardens in zone 7B. With summer temperatures in the mid-90° Fahrenheit range for as long as three to six weeks, and an annual precipitation of 60 inches, gardening can be quite a challenge. Ozzie grows Japanese plants in traditional Japanese garden style. His soil varies from typical Georgia clay to sandy loam. His response to my question about his favorite plants: "At first I tried to limit my list. Then I started thinking, 'Terrible mistake!' The more I thought, the longer the list. I did stop at one page." Ozzie grows arisaema and asarum, calanthe and rohdea, and many, many others. Some, such as *Epimedium diphyllum,* are familiar landscape plants; just think how sparse our landscapes would be if they, along with astilbe, hosta, liriope, and pachysandra, were taken from our gardening palette. Everyone knows hosta. Cultivars, with tremendous variability in leaf size and coloration, number in the hundreds, if not thousands. Hybridists in Japan, the United States, and England are producing new variations on themes of green, gold, and glaucous blue, streaked or centered with white or yellow. Astilbe have been grown and hybridized in Europe and America for decades. The work of Georg Arends in Germany produced *Astilbe* x *arendsii* hybrids such as 'Fanal', 'Gloria', and 'Feur', still popular today close to sixty years after their introduction. Pachysandra is a ubiquitous ground cover, unfairly denigrated for its very utility. If these plants are so attractive, useful, and readily grown, what others are out there in the wings, waiting for their turn on our garden stage?

SPRING

ADONIS

Before winter is truly gone from the Northeast, the first herbaceous plant in my garden appears, the elegant *Adonis amurensis*. In its native haunts, Manchuria and the Japanese islands as far north as Hokkaido, adonis grows on moist northern and eastern hillsides under deciduous trees, and is cold-hardy to zone 4. Through icy snow in late February or early March, it puts forth satiny flower buds, wrapped with tightly furled fernlike foliage. Completely unaffected by cold or late snow, the lacy, olive-green leaves expand, and 2-inch, bright golden-yellow flowers, similar to large buttercups, quickly open. The only possible partners are such early flowering bulbs as winter aconite, *Eranthis hiemalis,* giant

snowdrops, *Galanthus elwesii,* and the equally early, deep plum-purple flowers of *Helleborus atrorubens* "of gardens" (not the valid name for this hellebore, but the one by which it is known by gardeners).

The site for adonis should be shaded, cool, and moist in summer, and rich, with a light loamy soil and a constant mulch of organic matter, such as shredded leaves. Many named forms, about fifty different types, are known in Japan, but even there they are scarce. The Jin-dai Botanic Garden in Tokyo now has only a few different kinds when once their collection held many more. I suspect that mine is the cultivar 'Fukujukai', which is described as large-flowered, semidouble, and sterile. Sterile plants are often very vigorous, as energy is not diverted into seed production.

My plants go dormant in late June. Because they never set seed, the only means of propagation is division. As the foliage is

These water lilies create an appropriately serene display at the Ekoji Temple garden in Utsunomiya-shi, designed by Furuhashi Yoshio.

Growing wild on Mount Taro in Nikko, *Adenophora nikoensis* flowers amidst the stony rubble of its native haunts. PHOTO BY NIHEI TAKEO

Happily spreading between the stone blocks of this wall, *Aquilegia flabellata* displays its jaunty blue and white flowers.

Ethereal, choice, and difficult to grow, the exquisite flowers of *Conandron ramondioides* make the effort worthwhile.

Photo by Nihei Takeo

Dicentra peregrina pusilla requires spartan conditions in barren, stony soil, replicating the volcanic slopes that are its natural habitat. Photo by Nihei Takeo

Japan, too, is home to edelweiss, as seen by the silvered, felt-leaved specimen of *Leontopodium hayachinense.* Photo by Nihei Takeo

Emblematic of Japan, the chrysanthemum figures in the emperor's crest. Its noble flowers enrich our gardens at summer's end.

Very like the outstretched wings of some great bird, *Pectilis radiata* fits its common name of "white heron-flowered orchid."

Cascading between the closely spaced stones of a wall, *Sedum sieboldii* begins to bloom in autumn.

yellowing I dig up a clump and shake off any loose soil before rinsing the root mass in a bucket of water. With a sharp knife I slice through the tangle of wiry black roots and dense rootstock, making two or three pieces, which I promptly replant. I have found adonis quite simple to grow. The hard part is obtaining it in the first place.

ANEMONE

Anemone flaccida is a quietly beautiful plant for the woodland garden, and is hardy to zone 6. In spring it sends up a tidy clump of three-parted leaves, the two outer ones themselves two-parted. At each lobe's indentation is a whitish spot, noticeable against the dark green leaf. Flowering is sparse: a few stems, each with two buds that will open to reveal a row of pure white petals surrounding a tuft of golden stamens. The thick creeping rhizomes make a congested clump, wilting promptly in hot weather and seeming to prefer constantly moist conditions in rather heavy shade. Native to eastern Russia and northern China, as well as Japan, anemone is very common in moist shaded places along streams and in ravines in the foothills.

Bulbous, Cormous, and Tuberous Plants

While we may think of bulbs as Dutch, they arose in any part of the world where cold winters or dry summers required

herbaceous plants to take a rest. Japan is home to some absolutely magnificent lilies. There is even a tulip, *Tulipa edulis,* common in wet lowland meadows along rivers on Honshu, Shikoku, and Kyushu, and in China. Some small ephemeral spring charmers also call Japan home.

WINTER ACONITE

Perhaps you have grown winter aconite, *Eranthis hiemalis*. Its golden buttercup-like flowers jostle snowdrops in their haste to be the first in bloom. *Eranthis pinnatifida* is a rather rare Japanese cousin from the woods of Honshu. Its Japanese name, *setsubun,* means the eve of the beginning of spring, a name I find poetically appropriate. White flowers easily distinguish it from the commonly offered species. The small tubers of aconites quickly desiccate, and often fail to grow when purchased in the dry state. Winter aconite comes easily from seed, and this might be a more satisfactory means of obtaining the Japanese species. Since winter aconites are ephemeral, they leave a bare spot in the garden when they go dormant. Combine them with plants that come later into growth, such as Japanese painted fern.

ERYTHRONIUM, OR DOGTOOTH VIOLET

Dogtooth violets are common in the Northeast, Southeast, Midwest, and even Pacific Northwest. The one I find in my Connecticut woods is the rich yellow trout lily or adder's tongue, *Erythronium ameri-*

canum. I also grow the rose-purple-flowered *Erythronium japonicum*, hardy to zone 3. The small whitish corms, with a marked resemblance to a dog's canine tooth, dislike disturbance. The first spring after planting they rarely flower, sending up only a pair of lightly mottled ovate or oblong leaves. Once they have settled in to their new location, each April they will produce their lovely flowers with the petals swept back like a badminton shuttlecock. The Japanese species is most commonly found in the lowlands and low mountain forests of Hokkaido and Honshu, is rare on Shikoku, and is also found in Korea. In time the bulbs will multiply to form a nice clump. Should you want to spread them around, dig as the flowers wither but while the foliage is still in prime condition. Separate the cluster of bulbs and replant promptly. Remember, bloom will be reduced the following spring. In olden days the Japanese made a starch from the corms of dogtooth violet that was used to thicken soup and as a medicine to cure colds.

FRITILLARIA

Many gardeners are familiar with the stately crown imperial, *Fritillaria imperialis* with its rather skunky odor, or the intriguingly checkered guinea hen flower, *F. meleagris.* There are fritillarias native to the west coast of North America, and there are several native to Japan. Black sarana, *Fritillaria camtschatcensis,* is one that inhabits both continents, and is found in rocky seashore sites in the eastern districts and alpine regions of Hokkaido's central districts, in the central and northern alpine regions of Honshu, and in Kamtchatka, the Kuriles, Sakhalin, Ussuri, and North America. Obviously, it is a plant that prefers cool climates. One to several stocky, bell-like, purple-black flowers top the 4- to 18-inch stems. In my garden black sarana flowers in late May or early June on stems perhaps 6 to 8 inches tall; in colder climates it would bloom later. It is difficult to establish, and once growing happily should not be disturbed. While I grow it in moderate shade in order to provide cooler conditions, gardeners in chillier places (Maine or New Hampshire) might well grow it in full sun. Black sarana is hardy to zone 5, perhaps even zone 4.

Fritillaria verticillata is a more amenable species. It is taller, with stems reaching 12 to 30 inches tall (mine grow to 15 or 18 inches), and is hardy to zone 5. The greenish flowers, usually several to a stem but occasionally solitary, are faintly checkered. By now my original few bulbs have made nice clumps. One group is set in a mass of Allegheny spurge, *Pachysandra procumbens.* The bulbs arise in spring, bloom, and then retire beneath their vegetative coverlet to sleep until the following spring. Others are interplanted with ferns, whose uncoiling croziers appear just as the fritillaria is in flower, than quietly expand to fill the gap.

Though it has occasionally naturalized in Japan, *F. verticillata* is actually a Chinese plant that has long been cultivated in Japanese gardens.

Paperwhite Narcissus
Another bulb found growing wild in Japan is the paperwhite narcissus, *Narcissus tazetta*. Although naturalized along the seashores of Kyushu, in Honshu's Kanto district and westward, and in China, the typical form occurs in the Mediterranean. It is likely that bulbs were carried eastward to China and Japan, as its distribution follows the old Silk Road overland caravan trading routes too closely for coincidence. Paperwhite narcissus is depicted in *Chieh Tzu Yuan Hua Chuan,* an illustrated Chinese handbook for art students published in several volumes between 1679 and 1701. In the United States this winter-blooming bulb is popular outdoors in southern gardens where it flowers before Christmas. Consider combining its fragrant white flowers with the silver foliage of dusty miller. Elsewhere it is popular for container use, blossoming indoors in winter. Simply plant in a bowl of pebbles and water. When the flowers fade, discard the depleted bulbs. No chilling period is necessary as is required with other narcissus.

Epimedium
Epimediums are discussed in chapter 5, for when massed they make a very functional ground cover, creating restful drifts and masses against which specimen plants can strut their stuff.

Jack-in-the-Pulpit
Another native North American perennial we have in common with Japan and China is the familiar jack-in-the-pulpit, *Arisaema* species. There are a dozen or more species that can be grown in cool temperate climates without protection. I have grown a number of these, and find them to be attractive and interesting. These Asiatic species are beginning to come into wider use, and are occasionally available as seed or tubers from commercial sources. Those described here are hardy to zone 6, possibly zone 5 with winter protection.

Perhaps the most elegant arisaema of all, impressing garden visitors the most, is snow rice-cake plant, *Arisaema sikokianum*. Native to Honshu, Shikoku, and Kyushu, this plant has been reliably hardy through several cold winters in my zone 6 garden with little protective snow cover. Growing about a foot tall, flowering-sized plants have 2 leaves whose 3- or 5-parted leaflets are often splashed with silver. In May, a showy purplish chocolate-brown spathe flares erect to make a wide-mouthed hood, displaying the snowy white club-shaped spadix. This is absolutely stunning with rose-pink forms of *Primula sieboldii* and the silver-gray fronds of Japanese painted fern, *Athyrium niponicum* 'Pictum'. This arisaema comes easily from seed, which mature plants produce in copious quantities. A friend once counted over 500 from one plant. Some young plants will begin flowering in their second year. Sow seed indoors under growlights in autumn; germination will take place only a few weeks later. Keep young seedlings growing through winter and early spring. As soon as the leaves show any signs of yellowing, gradually withhold water. Give the small tubers a dry dormancy period for about six weeks; then resume watering. This way you can crowd two growing seasons into the first year.

Unfortunately, *Arisaema sikokianum* is susceptible to a debilitating rust disease that can kill the plant. A light case can be treated with flowers of sulphur, using a spreader-sticker to help the solution adhere. (Arisaema's leaves are somewhat water repellent.) Apply weekly, or more frequently in humid, wet weather. Several people have told me that they obtained good results with Maneb or Zineb, two commercially available fungicides. It is recommended that severely infected tubers be burnt.

Arisaema ringens has large, glossy, 3-parted leaves that appear just after the flowers. In this species the spathe is folded over into a domelike hood, and has been likened to a cobra or the helmet of a cavalryman from the 1800s. Dark greenish or purplish brown, it has a slightly menacing

appearance. English authors write that this plant begins growth so early as to be cut back by late spring frosts, but in my garden it emerges late enough to avoid this problem. It is found in woods near the seacoast of Honshu's Kanto district and westward, Shikoku, and Kyushu, as well in Ryukyu, China, and South Korea. The bold foliage is handsome in combination with the lacier texture of ferns.

Arisaema thunbergii var. *urashima* is worth growing for the foliage alone. It has pedatisect leaves, which means palmately divided with the lateral lobes cleft into 2 or more segments, like the fronds of maidenhair fern. Twelve or more narrow dark green leaflets are arranged in a horseshoe. In addition, it has the strangest flowers I have ever grown. They appear in early May: each dark brown spathe or hood with a long extension at its tip, but not so long as on the spadix, whose whiplike flagella stretches out until it trails on the ground. Endemic to Japan, it is found in Honshu, Shikoku, and Kyushu. This is the most vigorous species I grow, producing many offsets on mature tubers and quickly forming a thriving colony. It also sets generous amounts of seed. Their germination is irregular, with about half sprouting reasonably promptly and the remainder taking a much longer time.

There are several other Japanese arisaema I enjoy growing. Somewhat tender, diminutive *Arisaema kiusianum* from

Kyushu has flowers that remind me of a little owl face. Hardy only to zone 7, it is an enchanting species that I grow in a container. Tall-stemmed *A. serratum* has a snake-spotted stalk and a simple green ruff of leaves below the flower. It is quite similar to *A. japonicum*. The expert on Japanese arisaema, Dr. Jin Murata of the University of Tokyo, feels that the two species can be regarded as identical.

PINELLIA

Also in the aroid family, pinellias have a close resemblance to their arisaema cousins. They too grow from a small tuber and cluster their flowers on a spadix wrapped in a sheathing spathe. The Japanese species, alas, are so rampant as to forbid them entry in our gardens. The Scott Arboretum of Swarthmore College in Pennsylvania and the T. H. Everett Rock Garden of the New York Botanical Garden are but two institutions where pinellias have made themselves only too thoroughly at home. *Pinellia ternata* is a common plant of roadsides and cultivated fields (read that as "weed") in Hokkaido, Honshu, Shikoku, and Kyushu, and also in Korea and China. Growing 4 to 6 inches tall, it has 3-parted leaves 6 to 8 inches long. Like a small cobra, a purple-flushed green spathe rises above the leaves, sticking out its tongue as the spadix extends beyond the hood. Every stalk makes bulbils just below the soil surface. Jim McClements of Dover,

Delaware, with some apparent dismay, notes that this species is "hardy, unfortunately." The catalog for Plant Delights Nursery in Raleigh, North Carolina, notes, "Do Not Grow *Pinellia ternata*." Don't say you weren't warned. Similar in appearance and behavior, *P. tripartita* is found in Shikoku, Honshu's Mino province and westward, and Kyushu.

The only pinellia I can recommend is *Pinellia cordata*, actually a Chinese species often grown in Japan. This has dainty lanceolate or cordate leaves 1 or 2 inches long, narrowing to an abrupt tail. Above, leaves are dark green with the veins picked out in silver, beefsteak red on the underside. Small, sweetly scented flowers appear in summer. The spadix extends beyond the spathe. Together they are scarcely more than a couple of inches high. In Japan it is common practice to grow *P. cordata* in a pot, to more readily pick it up and enjoy the fragrance. Aerial bulblets are borne at the juncture of the leaf and petiole. Marginally hardy in my zone 6 garden, this pinellia might need constraint in milder regions.

Orchids

CALANTHE

I think the easiest terrestrial orchids to cultivate, relatively speaking, are *Calanthe*. The genus contains a number of tropical or subtropical species, popular for greenhouse cultivation. The common misconception is that they all are tender. I have grown a few of the six or seven Japanese species in my garden, where the only winter protection I provide is a covering of evergreen boughs. Cold Connecticut winters keep the plants safely dormant until spring weather is settled and mild.

Ozzie Johnson of Marietta, Georgia (in the warmer portion of zone 7 with winter low temperatures of 10° to 15° Fahrenheit), grows both *Calanthe discolor* and *C. striata* (= *C. discolor* var. *bicolor* f. *sieboldii*) with-

out difficulty. Jim McClements in Dover, Delaware, also grows both species, but with difficulty. Eberhardt Fluche of Rossdorf, Germany (winter low temperatures of 5° Fahrenheit), found that both these species, though said to be hardy, died. I think this is an instance where slightly milder weather provides worse growing conditions, and I suspect the calanthes begin growth too soon and are damaged by late frosts.

Calanthes are evergreen, and by spring the old growth has a rather bedraggled appearance. My friend Nihei Takeo wrote, "Leaves last two years. But generally people cut old leaves to make it neat and tidy just before it blooms." That may be good aesthetics, but as long as the leaves look capable of photosynthesis, I leave them alone. These orchids have numerous fleshy roots that extend horizontally in the loose forest duff. The handsome oblong leaves have a pleated appearance. The species I grow flower in late April or May, depending on the season.

Once *Calanthe discolor* was seen everywhere in the lowland forests of Japan, growing in the shade of small-leaved, broadleaved evergreen trees. These days it is rarely seen. Plants have 2 or 3 evergreen leaves 6 to 8 inches long. The flower stalk is about 6 inches tall, with upwards of 10 flowers neatly arranged along the upper portion. There are several slight variations in color: the sepals are dark purple-brown

Calanthe discolor

to greenish, and the lip is rose or white. Relatively common, this species is found in the low foothills—under 1,600 feet—of Hokkaido's southwestern district, and on Honshu, Shikoku, and Kyushu. Growing as they do in woodland, especially under trees near streams, these orchids would be mulched naturally with leaf mold. Leaves and flowers appear together in May. There is an absolutely exquisite variation, *C. striata,* with larger leaves and bigger, clear yellow flowers. It grows in the western part of Japan and Korea. Again, according to Nihei-san, "People say it is not so hardy. But it grows in my garden okay. You'd better take care in winter, maybe by covering with fallen leaves."

Calanthe tricarinata was first introduced into European cultivation from Japan by the English firm of J. Veitch and Son in 1897. This species has 2 to 4 leaves, and a 12- to 20-inch-tall flower stalk with 7 to 15 attractive purplish brown flowers. Rather rare, this species is found on Hokkaido, Honshu, Shikoku, and Kyushu. It is more common at lower elevations in the north, and to 2,600 feet in the mountains in the south. Flowering occurs from May to June depending on how far north one goes. *C. tricarinata* prefers somewhat cooler conditions than *C. striata*. In summer the temperatures in its natural range are below 85° Fahrenheit, and in winter, plants are usually covered with as much as six or ten feet of snow.

Richard Weaver, Jr., former horticultural taxonomist at the Arnold Arboretum and associate editor of *Arnoldia,* now operates We-Du Nursery in Marion, North Carolina. In 1977 he and Dr. Steven Sponberg traveled to Japan collecting seed for the Arnold Arboretum. Weaver observed *Calanthe tricarinata* under cultivation in the center of Hokkaido. Although there is deep and reliable snow cover, winter temperatures of -40° Fahrenheit do occur. He obtained a specimen and brought it back to his garden in Boston. Though the leaves are unfortunately not reliably evergreen in Massachusetts, in its third season his plant produced ten flowers on a scape 15 inches tall. Flowers and new leaves appear together in the Boston area in early to mid-May.

Should you need to prepare a special site for these orchids, a mix (by volume) of ½ peat and ¼ each of coarse sand and partially rotted wood chips is suitable. I grow mine on a gentle slope where they get morning sun and midday shade. Rather than grow them with other plants, I mulch with reddish brown, punky wood, crumbled between my hands. Drainage is important, as soggy situations are sure death for these orchids. Conversely, they should never be allowed to become too dry. Moist but well drained is the balance you want to achieve.

In Japan these orchids are so popular that there is a Japan Calanthe Society.

Their general recommendation is to grow calanthes under evergreen trees in heavy shade. A slightly sloped bed provides the best conditions. Planting in clumps is also recommended (should you have enough to clump, that is!). Weaver suggests propagating calanthes by division of the pseudobulbs. In spring, before the new growth begins, dig an established plant, gently shake it free of soil, and carefully wash it clean. The underground portion, or pseudobulbs, looks like a cluster of beads. Old pseudobulbs, also called backbulbs, contain latent buds. Gently twist the backbulbs apart, and plant in a bulb pan in a mix of 2 parts peat moss, 1 part vermiculite, and 1 part perlite. The tops of the backbulbs should be just below the surface. Keep the potting medium moist, and guard against slugs, which avidly dine on the tender shoots. Winter under grow lights, and plant out the following spring. After division, you should promptly replant the leading, actively growing pseudobulb. I would probably sacrifice the flower scape should one be produced, to better reestablish the leading pseudobulb. Nihei-san says that nurserymen propagate calanthes by cutting the rhizome to one-joint sections.

CYMBIDIUM

Tropical cymbidium orchids are popular as container plants, grown on windowsills as well as in conservatories and greenhouses. *Cymbidium goeringii* is a charming little winter- or early-spring-blooming species found in the half sun, half shade of the forest floor in the foothills of Hokkaido's Okushiri Island, and on Honshu, Shikoku, and Kyushu, as well as in China and Taiwan. It is unusual in this terrestrial habit, as most cymbidiums are epiphytic. Sometimes fragrant, the small, 2-inch flowers (1, very rarely 2 to a scape) are greenish brown, flushed with red at the base, and speckled with reddish purple spots along the white lip. Narrow linear evergreen leaves are 8 to 12 inches long. This is, and has been for centuries, a plant that is part of Japan's traditional horticulture. Selection has been made for delicate varieties of tranquil beauty, rather than the larger, more brightly colored, showier flowers popular in Western horticulture. Cultivars with wavy leaves, variegated leaves, and flowers more fully flushed with red sell for extraordinary sums.

CYPRIPEDIUM

If Venus' slipper became the pouch of lady slipper orchids, she did not have very dainty feet. The large, showy flowers have a bloated pouch, underscoring the Greek relationship of *orchis* to *testis*. There are about forty species found in the temperate regions of the Northern Hemisphere, several in the United States and four in Japan. The only one with which I have any experience is *Cypripedium japonicum*. The plant seems imbued with a Japanese aspect, from

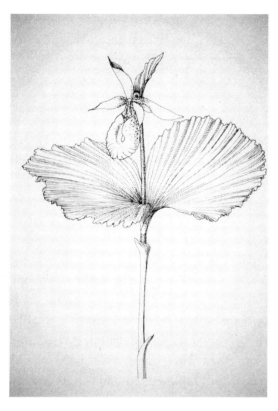

Cypripedium japonicum

from a single shoot to four. Based on the descriptions of the plant's native habitat, and his own experiences, he concludes that it prospers in community with other plants, rather than resenting the competition.

At least ten or fifteen years ago my friend Ed Leimseider of Westport, Connecticut, received a plant of *Cypripedium japonicum* from a correspondent of his in Japan. The plant grew nicely, and Ed requested a couple more, which were sent in due course. Within a year or two each plant was producing two or three shoots. Currently the three plants, growing closely together, produce a total of fifteen to eighteen shoots. Offsets have been shared, with perhaps as many as twelve given away to gardening friends. Divisions are taken from the outside of the clump, without digging the plants themselves. This is done either when they are in bud or right after they flower, depending on how the plants look that particular growing season. They are given "decent woodland soil . . . leaf mold, sand, peat." Leimseider feels this plant is not completely bud-hardy. In winter he covers the dormant crowns with pine needles or dry oak leaves, and inverts a plastic pot over them, weighed down with a rock to keep it from blowing away.

BLETILLA

While it is difficult to find a reputable commercial source for the two preceding genera, there is one Japanese orchid that regu-

the pair of large, 6- to 10-inch-broad, rounded, pleated, fanlike leaves to the solitary yellowish green flower with its purplish red lip. Though massive, very nearly 4 inches across, the flower has no suggestion of gross obesity. Owhi considers this plant rather common in the lowland woods and bamboo forests deep in the mountains of Hokkaido's Oshima province, Honshu, Shikoku, and Kyushu; it is also native to western China's upper Yangtze Valley. This plant proved hardy in the Boston area for Richard Weaver, increasing in seven years larly appears in garden centers and nurseries. Imported from Holland, pseudobulbs of a Chinese orchid, *Bletilla striata,* are offered along with hyacinths and daffodils, tulips and other so-called Dutch bulbs. Native to grassy slopes and the edge of thickets in the foothills of Honshu's Kanto district and westward, Shikoku, and Kyushu, bletilla is also native to Ryukyu and China. Though rare in the wild, it is frequently cultivated in gardens. It is easy to recognize as an orchid, for its flowers look like miniatures of the cattleya orchids sold for corsages. Canelike stems, 10 to 15 inches long, each with 4 or 5 lanceolate, conspicuously ribbed leaves, grow from tuberlike pseudobulbs several inches beneath the soil's surface. Five to 10 eye-catching rosy-purple or lavender flowers, each with 5 prominent, raised, white-frilled ridges on the lower lip, open in succession from late May through late June. The pseudobulbs are prone to desiccation; nursery stock should be carefully picked over to avoid any that look shriveled or damaged. A protected site, such as one against the shelter of a house wall, is probably a good idea in cold winter areas.

Blettila can be propagated in the same manner as calanthe. The pseudobulbs (which are separated by a section of rhizome) should be cut apart with clippers or a sharp knife. The new divisions can then be planted in a propagating frame, and covered with about 2 inches of soil, then lightly mulched with pine straw. Backbulbs up to five years old will produce shoots, and flower the second season.

Habenaria

Snowy heron grass, *Habenaria* (= *Pectilis*) *radiata,* grows in sphagnum-covered marshes; it is discussed in chapter 8 with other moisture-loving plants.

Glaucidium

Japan has a number of comely monotypic plants, where a genus contains only one species. A beautiful example is *Glaucidium palmatum,* whose enormous pale mauve flowers are a recurring delight each spring. Native to the high mountain woodlands, this Japanese endemic is found on Hokkaido and in the northern and central districts of Honshu. Sturdy 2-foot-tall stems appear in spring, each with 2 large leaves, toothed along their edges and palmately divided into 7 to 11 lobes. Each flowering stem has a third smaller leaf, and a single, 4-petaled, 3- to 4-inch-diameter flower. While the typical color is a delicate lavender, *G. palmatum* var. *leucanthum* (= *G. palmatum* 'Album') is a pure white form. Glaucidium is a stately perennial, producing numerous clustered stems from the sturdy rhizome. This year my ten-year-old plant had 22 stems, 12 of which flowered. Though the size of the plant might suggest placement at the back of a group of plants, I prefer to place glaucidium right at the edge of the path. That way, when it is in bloom I can more readily cup a flower in my hand and admire the tissuelike texture of the petals, centered with a short golden boss of stamens. Provide glaucidium with deciduous woodland conditions—a loamy soil high in organic matter, moist but well-drained, and reasonably fertile. Ferns are suitable partners; the delicate tracery of maidenhair fern, *Adiantum pedatum,* is especially attractive.

HYLOMECON

Hylomecon japonicum is a monotypic genus endemic to Japan. In early spring the rhizomatous, densely branched rootstock sends up masses of pinnately compound, serrate-edged, dark green leaves, followed in April or May by solitary, 4-petaled, 2-inch-diameter, rich golden-yellow flowers. Unfortunately, the flowers do not last very long, but the leaves make a tidy summer ground cover. These shade-loving plants grow best with adequate moisture and a rich woodland soil. Mine seed about, with new plants cropping up across the path. I like the contrast the leaves create with plain green hosta and evergreen ferns.

IRIS

Japan is certainly rich in iris, but we tend to think of them as plants for sunny situations. One that is happily at home in half shade is Japanese roof iris, *Iris tectorum.*

Short stout rhizomes produce a tuft of pale green swordlike leaves 12 to 18 inches long. Two to 6 flowers appear in May on scapes as high as the leaves. Most of the flowers I've seen are soft blue-lavender, usually spotted with a darker blue-lavender. Unspotted forms and clear white ones with a yellow beard are also available. This Chinese plant has long been grown in Japan on the straw-thatched roofs of houses. It grows quite well in the ground, and has naturalized. *Iris gracilipes,* native to the mountains of Hokkaido's southwestern district, Honshu's Kinki district and eastward, and Hokkaido, is even daintier. The slender, somewhat glaucous, pale green, grasslike leaves are 8 to 15 inches long. In May or June, two or three pale violet flowers appear.

JEFFERSONIA DUBIA

East Asian in origin, *Jeffersonia dubia* is a charming early spring woodlander. The young leaf growth is flushed coppery purple, creating a marvelous foil for the solitary 5- to 8-petaled lavender flowers, one to each stem. Mature plants transplant poorly. One must obtain a seedling plant that, when mature, will self-sow in reasonable numbers. The seed pod looks like a little jug on a wiry stem. When ripe, the lid flies open with sufficient force to set the stem swaying and to scatter the seed. Seed germinates poorly in containers, even when I have carried the container to the plant.

Named for our president Thomas Jefferson, there is an American counterpart, twinleaf, *Jeffersonia diphylla*. Twinleaf has angled, rather triangular leaves that appear to be joined point to point, and white flowers like those of a diminutive bloodroot, somewhat small for the length of the stem.

Peony

The peonies we commonly grow in our gardens are found in sunny perennial borders. There are two species native to Japan that grow as woodland plants. The typical form of *Paeonia obovata* has pale rose-pink flowers, and is found in woods and thickets in the mountains of Hokkaido, Honshu, and Shikoku, as well as Korea, Manchuria, China, Amur, and Sakhalin. I grow var. *alba*, with a single row of ethereal white petals around a central mass of golden stamens. In the deep shade provided by hundred-year-old white oaks, with black birch and dogwoods as the understory layer, the chalicelike flowers enhance my woodland garden in early May. Deep rose-red shoots, each with a single flower bud tightly clasped within, appear in early spring. They mature at 18 or 20 inches high, expanding to gray-green leaves flushed slightly with red that mature as the flowers open. As beautiful as these flowers are, I find the autumn display equally attractive. Fertile seed is pea-sized, and a lustrous metallic blue-black. Infertile seed is much smaller and bright red. Thus, as the capsule splits open, a wonderful contrast of colors is presented. I delay collecting the seed, simply because their appearance is so beautiful. Seeds should be sown the same autumn, and I simply push them into the soil around the parent plants. The next spring no growth will be visible, as peonies have delayed hypogeal germination, and only send a root down the first year. Shoots appear the second spring. Plants will reach flowering size in four or five years.

Paeonia japonica is another native Japanese peony, found in the thickets and open woods of the mountains of Honshu, Shikoku, and Kyushu, and also Korea and Manchuria. I must look closely to distinguish the two species, and the primary difference I can see is in the leaves. Those of *P. japonica* taper to a point. The leaves of *P. obovata* var. *alba* are, as the name suggests, obovate, rounded at the tip like the broad end of an egg. Both peonies have white flowers. With attractive flowers in spring, handsome foliage in summer, and beautiful fruiting effect, these peonies are high quality plants with three seasons of interest.

Solomon's Seal

Found in North American woodlands, Solomon's seals also grow in Japan. The thick, fleshy, ivory-white jointed rhizomes are marked with the leaf stem scars of previous years. Oval leaves alternate up the stem and green-tipped white bell-like flowers dangle beneath. *Polygonatum falcatum* is charming in the shelter of a rock or fallen log bordering a path. Growing 20 inches tall, in May or June plants bear one, sometimes more, drooping, green-tinged flowers below each leaf axil. Native to the hills and low mountains of Hokkaido, Honshu, Shikoku, and Kyushu, and also Korea, this Solomon's seal is hardy to zone 6, and to zone 5 in sheltered sites. The simple beauty of Solomon's seal enhances a grouping of epimedium, ferns, and other suitable plants. It slowly spreads to form a colony.

Even daintier is *Polygonatum humile,* which grows a scant 6 to 12 inches tall. The smaller plants are more erect, rather than drooping. Found in meadows and thin woodland from sea level to the mountain foothills of Hokkaido, central and northern Honshu, and Kyushu, and also in Sakhalin, Kuriles, Korea, and Manchuria to Siberia, it is probably hardy to zone 5, especially if there is winter snow cover. This species has only 1 or 2 green-tipped white flowers to each leaf axil, and in time also makes small colonies, quietly charming in the shaded rock garden. Both species need lightly shaded woodland conditions of moist but well-drained soil high in organic matter.

SMARTWEED

If the very mention of smartweed or knotweed sends you running for the flame thrower and harsh chemicals, take heart. Though Japanese knotweed, *Polygonum cuspidatum,* able to sprout through four inches of asphalt, is hardly a good neighbor perennial, the genus does have better-behaved species. For example, consider *P. virginianum* (= *P. filiforme*), found in the hills and lowland woods and thickets of Hokkaido, Honshu, Shikoku, and Kyushu, and also in the northeastern United States. The short, rather thick rhizomes produce hollow brown stems 16 to 30 inches tall, which carry large, oval, green leaves, each with 2 red-brown blotches. In late summer, plants have spikes of rose-pink to red flowers. This plant prefers a semishaded, somewhat moist site. It is hardy to zone 5. Rather than the species, most gardeners prefer the showier, variegated cultivars such as 'Variegatum', with broad leaves marbled and blotched with ivory and primrose yellow; or 'Painter's Palette', with gold-variegated leaves further marked with areas of pinkish brown. Or, consider *P. tenuicaule,* a stoloniferous perennial with short, thick rhizomes that grow 2 to 4 inches tall with broadly oval soft-green leaves that are purple on the underside. In flower from April to June, it has upright, 3- to 6-inch-high spikes of fragrant white flowers. Hardy to zone 6, it is found wild in Honshu, Shikoku, and Kyushu. Moist, humus-rich soil in partial shade suit *P. tenuicaule* best, suggesting its use in a large shady rock garden.

PRIMROSES

There is something about primroses that seems to announce, "It's spring!" There are hard-to-grow species from high alpine regions of the world, others that grow in woodlands, and some that prefer wet places. Several from Japan are among the most attractive species I've grown. One I have seen across the continent, growing in Vancouver, B.C., as readily as it does in Connecticut, is Japanese, or candelabra, primrose, *Primula japonica*. In a moist soil and a sunny or shady site, this primrose sends up a 16- to 30-inch-high flower stalk, with from 1 to as many as 5 tiered whorls of flowers in May to June. Typically the flowers are a bright rose-pink. 'Millar's Crimson' and 'Postford White' are self-descriptive names, whose seedlings come true. Native to wet places along streams in the mountains of Hokkaido, Honshu, Shikoku, Kyushu, and also Formosa, this species is hardy to zone 5. Once established, the fleshy thonglike roots seem proof against the currents of a not-too-vigorous stream where a small rock set over a portion of the roots helps anchor new transplants. Japanese primrose also accepts merely moist soil, and in such sites these precautions are not necessary. I have seen this self-sowing plant along a woodland streamside garden in Connecticut, where it happily mixed with sensitive fern and ostrich fern, skunk cabbage, and Welch poppy, *Meconopsis cambrica*.

Primula kisoana is a rare endemic of Shikoku, and Honshu's Kanto and south central district. Its large, rounded, gently lobed, pale green leaves, 2 to 4 inches across, are similar to those of coral bells but hairy rather than smooth. They cluster near the ground on short fuzzy petioles. New growth sometimes appears as much as a foot away, for this is a rhizomatous primrose. As such, it does best in a loose, open soil, high in organic matter, moist but well-drained, with a constant mulch of partially decayed leaf litter. In May a scape 4 to 6 inches tall appears, with 2 to 8 bright rosy-pink flowers clustered at the top. There is a pale pink and also a white form. Though reportedly difficult in England, I have no problems, nor do others in the North American Rock Garden Society who grow this species. Once you overcome the obstacle of first obtaining plants, and have planted in a suitable site, weeding, and watering in times of drought are all that's needed.

Cherry blossom primrose, *Primula sieboldii,* is found in wet grassy places along the lowland rivers of Hokkaido's southern district, Honshu, and Kyushu, as well as in Korea, Manchuria, and eastern Siberia. It is very much admired and cultivated in gardens, and even has a society devoted to it in Japan. Cherry blossom primrose is one of the easiest and most reliable of the woodland primroses, suitable for light, moderate, or even heavy shade, for this species grows and flowers in spring and then retreats underground with summer. Short creeping rhizomes, growing obliquely upward, allow plants to spread slowly to sizeable patches of crinkled, oval, light green leaves. An annual mulch of partially decayed compost or leaf litter is helpful. Since leaves are slow to appear, be cautious about digging in the area. In late spring 12-inch-tall stalks with as many as 10 or a dozen flowers are produced in abundance. Typically magenta-mauve, flowers may be clear pink, pale pink, white, or bicolor with a deeper color on the reverse. The petals may be rounded, tipped, or notched. I have seen a mass of bright pink cherry blossom primroses serving as "ground cover" for the dark chocolate spathes of *Arisaema sikokianum*. A good time to separate established plants is as they go dormant in early summer. Though cherry blossom primrose is increasingly being offered by specialty nurseries, it can hardly be described as common. When the tiny seed is available, perhaps through a rock garden society's seed exchange for members, germination is generally good and young plants begin to flower their second year.

Other primroses are discussed in chapter 8.

Ranzania

Ranzania japonica is a rare wildflower from the woodland mountains of the central and northern districts of Honshu, on the more sheltered Japan Sea side of the island, at elevations of 2,275 to 3,250 feet. Approximately 10 inches tall when it flowers, it continues to grow and matures at 15 to 20 inches, each stem with a pair of soft green, coarsely lobed, 3-parted leaves. At the point of the Y where the two leaf stems join the stalk, from 1 to 6 rose-pink flowers nod in a loose cluster on a long pedicel, appearing in April. This epimedium relative is the only member of its genus, named for Ono Ranzan, a celebrated naturalist who has been called the Linnaeus of Japan. A sheltered, light to moderately shaded woodland site, with a moist soil high in organic matter is most suitable. In spring 1993 my plants were affected by a late frost, resulting in disfiguring brown patches on the leaves. Though flowering was unaffected, the unsightly mottling remained throughout the growing season. I do not think this plant will grow well in regions with hot, humid summers.

Reineckia

Another member of the Lily family, *Reineckia carnea* has a superficial resemblance to lily turf, *Liriope muscari,* in that both have a tuft of linear, straplike, evergreen leaves. In Japan, reineckia is commonly planted in gardens. It is said that this plant, whose Japanese name *kichijo-so* means "good omen," does not bloom every year but only when the person who has the plant has good luck. This is fable rather

Reineckea carnea

Honshu's Kanto district and westward, Shikoku, and Kyushu. There is a variegated form, with handsome white stripes on the green leaf. This tends to revert to all green with some frequency. I trim out the more vigorous plain green shoots and pot them up separately. They root very readily.

TRILLIUM

Of the thirty or so species of trillium that exist, most are native to North America. Of the three species and one natural hybrid native to Japan, all are pedunculate, with a short stalk between the flower and the whorl of leaves. *Trillium kamtschaticum* is native to Hokkaido, also the Kuriles, Sakhalin, Korea, Manchuria, Ussuri, and Kamchatka. It has the typical tripartite trillium form—3 leaves, 3 sepals, 3 petals. *Trillium kamtschaticum* grows 12 to 15 inches tall and blooms in April or May with a white flower resembling that of great white trillium, *T. grandiflorum,* from North America. I grow this species in a good site, under dogwoods that leaf out later in the season, in moist but well-drained soil rich in humus. Plants are healthy and long-lived but shy about flowering for me. My experience with this plant is seconded by Jim McClements, who describes it as "surviving, not thriving." *Trillium tschonoskii,* from the mountains of Honshu and Shikoku, and also Korea, is said to be similar, but is only 8 inches tall. I've grown *T. smallii,* which has a flower

than fact, for reineckia flowers annually for my friend Nihei Takeo. Though the plant is hardy in my Connecticut garden, the flower buds are not. If I want to be lucky enough to have it bloom, I must grow it as a container plant and winter it over in my alpine house (more like a walk-in cold frame). Then in September or October, it sends up spikes of small, starry, pale pink flowers on reddish stems.

Reineckia is a forest dweller, found in the lowland and foothill forests of that aptly fits its name, with short or absent petals. (It used to be known as *T. apetalon*.) This trillium is hardly decorative, more interesting from a botanist's viewpoint than beautiful to a gardener.

SUMMER

ASTILBE

With good reason, astilbes are among the most popular herbaceous perennials. Once established they need little maintenance, not even deadheading, for their spent flower heads look attractive right though winter. Their tidy fernlike foliage and lovely plumey panicles of flowers add color and interest to the summer flower garden. They prefer a reasonably fertile soil that is constantly moist. Should conditions become too dry, their leaves will turn crisp and brown and die. Moderate to light shade is preferable, but given sufficient moisture, as along the banks of a pond, they will grow in full sun. What you will find at nurseries and garden centers are the Arendsii hybrids, *Astilbe* x *arendsii*, developed by Georg Arends of Ronsdorf, Germany, from three Japanese species: *Astilbe japonica*, which is found in the rocky mountain ravines of Honshu's Kinki district and westward, Shikoku, and Kyushu, and which has white flowers carried in short panicles, with densely packed, outward-arching, branched side-stalks; the common and variable *A. thunbergii*, from the sunny, grassy slopes of Honshu, Shikoku, and Kyushu, also with white flowers in looser, more open panicles, and unbranched, gracefully arching side-stalks; and *A. astilboides*, with white flowers in panicles, the branched side-stalks carried horizontally. It was a fourth, Chinese species, *A. chinensis* var. *davidii*, with upright panicles of magenta-pink to purplish flowers and erect side-stalks, that increased the color range of the hybrids beyond white. Such cultivars as 'Bridal Veil', 'Deutschland', 'White Gloria', and 'Feur' are as popular today as when they were developed sixty to seventy years ago.

In turn, the Arendsii hybrids were crossed with *Astilbe simplicifolia*, a rare native of Honshu's Suruga and Sagami provinces, which has dainty, arching, 8-inch-high flower panicles. Several small, vigorous cultivars with glossy dark foliage and open, airy sprays of flowers were developed: pale pink 'Sprite', salmon-pink, bronze-leaved 'Bronze Elegance', flesh-pink 'Inshriach Pink', and dark salmon-pink 'Atrorosea', among others. These are elegant in small spaces, equally charming where they can grow in drifts, perhaps intermingled with dwarf hosta; woodland sedges such as Japanese sedge, *Carex morowii*; candelabra primroses, *Primula japonica*; and other smaller, shade-tolerant, moisture-loving herbaceous plants.

Astilbe microphylla is a pale rose-pink

flowered astilbe from Honshu, Shikoku, and Kyushu, where it is commonly found in sunny, grassy places in the mountains. Growing 12 to 30 inches tall, it flowers in June or July. The Japanese name is *chidake-sashi,* for *chidake* is the name of a mushroom, and stems of the astilbe were used as a carrying device, threading chidakes to take them back home from the woods.

Deinanthe

To call *Deinanthe bifida* a coarse perennial herb with creeping woody rhizomes does not address its panache and distinctiveness. Erect leafy stems 16 to 28 inches tall appear in spring. Lovely large pebbly-textured leaves, 6 to 8 inches long and 3 to 6 inches wide, narrow a bit and then elegantly split like a mermaid's tail. Plants flower in July and August, with up to 20 white blooms in a terminal panicle; the fertile flowers are larger than the sterile ones. Native to Kyushu, Shikoku, and the Totomi, Yamato, and Kii provinces of Honshu, *D. bifida* has been perfectly hardy for me in zone 6, and even grows well in zone 5. Though a late frost can kill the new growth, the rhizomes are generally unfazed, sending up a new set of shoots. My plants have never set seed, but division is an easy means of propagation. Grow it in moderate to heavy shade in a moist soil high in organic matter and with a constant mulch of leaf litter. Ferns make elegant companions, as do glaucous blue-leaved hostas.

Hosta

There are more than forty species of hosta, and all but one or two of them are native in Japan. The permutations and combinations of leaf size and color are incalculable: size varies from daintily small to umbrella size, and color can be apple-green, forest-green, glaucous blue, sunny yellow, or variegated. Tiny *Hosta venusta* has green leaves about the size of my thumbnail, barely 1 inch long and less than 1 inch

Hosta montana

wide, while *H. sieboldiana* has glaucous green leaves nearly 14 inches long and 9 inches wide. *H. undulata* has green leaves with undulating, rather twisted edges with a broad white stripe down the center. *H. crispula* has large green leaves with slightly wavy, narrowly white-margined edges. August lily, *H. plantaginea,* has large, glossy, grass-green leaves and sweetly fragrant white flowers, and is a favorite of many gardeners. In August the plants produce tall spikes of deliciously fragrant, large, clean white flowers. The flowers may be cut and last quite a long time in arrangements. One combination I have used to brighten a shady corner paired this hosta with white impatiens and *Caladium* 'Candidum', a tender tuberous plant with large, arrowhead-shaped, green-veined white leaves. It was especially cool-looking and refreshing in hot summer weather. This species was brought from China to Japan, where it has long been cultivated in gardens.

There are other species of hosta, and even more cultivars. The earliest selections were made in Japan. Contemporary cultivars, literally hundreds of them, were and are being developed in the United States and England. Hostas are tough. I sometimes think they could be dug up, left lying around for several days, and replanted, and they would still thrive. Naturally, proper care and a moist fertile soil will result in the most vigorous, beautiful plants. They are appealing to slugs, who munch holes in the unfurling leaves of the softer, less glossy-leaved species, and to deer, who dine with enthusiasm on leaves and flowers alike. Hostas have fleshy thonglike roots that spread in a horizontal fashion. In autumn plants develop purple, conical shoots below ground on the crown, which emerge and expand the following spring. Since they come up relatively late, hostas can combine effectively with spring bulbs. Their bold leaf shape pairs well with lacy astilbes, cimicifuga, aruncus, or ferns. Hostas are equally elegant with the linear form of sedge or iris leaves. When flowers are sparse in summer, hostas can provide interest with colorful foliage in the shady garden. A single plant of some large-leaved cultivar can serve as a bold focal point, while a row of medium or small hostas can edge a path. Remember, though, that assembling a variety of different hostas and planting them together can result in a hosta collection, and not a well-designed garden.

FERNS

We associate ferns with the dappled shade of woodlands where, under the high canopy of deciduous trees, their lacy fronds provide a graceful pattern. In general ferns prefer a moist site, and one with at least moderate fertility. In nature, fallen autumn leaves provide a natural mulch, which should be replicated in the garden. Some Japanese ferns are akin to European or North American forms. Of sensitive fern, *Onoclea sensibilis* var. *interrupta,* Owhi notes, "The typical variety occurs in North America." Ostrich fern, *Matteuccia struthiopteris,* is found throughout Japan and elsewhere in the region, as well as in Siberia, Europe, and northern North America. *Polystichum lonchitis,* a very rare fern of Honshu's Mount Kitadake's alpine slopes, northern Europe, and Asia, is also found along the border between Canada and the United States, where it is called northern holly fern. Japan has a wonderful diversity of ferns and fern allies: approximately 600 species in 90 different genera!

In a landscape containing Japanese plants, design criteria are not necessarily those of a traditional Japanese garden. An informal woodland garden can incorporate ferns as a natural component of the forest floor plant community. Combined with primroses and spring bulbs, the ferns will add interest later in the season. Think of ferns with jack-in-the-pulpit, bloodroot, hellebores, and hosta. Evergreen species provide visual appeal in winter. Ferns that grow in tidy clumps or crowns make good neighbors for other plants, while expansive spreading species can serve as a ground cover or be combined with other vigorous perennials. Remember to match the lacy fronds of ferns with bold or linear foliage. If placed near a similarly dissected leaf, such as

astilbes, the airy appeal of the ferns will be lessened.

Growing 18 inches high, Japanese maidenhair fern, *Adiantum aleuticum* var. *japonicum,* is very similar to our native northern maidenhair fern, *A. pedatum.* Both are exquisite plants for damp woods with humus-rich soil. They have glossy, deep purplish black stipe (leaf stem) and rachis (stem of a compound leaf), and 5 to 9 fingerlike pinnae (leaflets) in a pedatisect (horseshoelike, palmately divided) arrangement. When I saw the Japanese variety in the botanic garden and forest research station of Tokyo University at Nikko, I was very taken with the deep rosy-red color of the new growth. Nihei-san tells me that the color persists for a long time as the fronds unfold. The fern was growing near some *Rodgersia podophylla,* which also has bronze foliage in spring. Japanese maidenhair fern would look handsome, I think, with the yellow flowers of the celandine poppy, *Stylophorum diphyllum.* This fern is rarely offered for sale in the United States; the people I know who are growing it have raised their plants from spore. In Japan the fern is very common, found in the damp, humus-rich soils of mountain forests of Hokkaido, Honshu, and Shikoku, and elsewhere in the cooler regions of Asia. It is easily grown in gardens from zones 2 to 8.

Upside-down fern, *Arachnoides standishii,* is rather common, found on wooded mountainsides in Hokkaido, Honshu,

Shikoku, and Kyushu, and also Korea. This fern is easy to grow in zones 4 to 9. It thrives in shade, and prefers moist conditions and fertile, humus-rich soil. In such sites, the short, creeping rhizomes develop into compact colonies. Lacy, tripinnate, erect to arching semi-evergreen fronds are 1 to 3 feet long and a handsome rich green color. "Upside-down" refers to prominent veins on the upper surface of the fronds, something more typically seen on the underside.

Found in shaded lowland sites, *Athyrium niponicum* is common in Hokkaido's southwestern district, Honshu, Shikoku, and Kyushu, as well as Korea, Manchuria, China, and Formosa. It is easy to grow, widely available, and suitable for gardens from zones 4 to 9. The attractive gray-fronded cultivar, Japanese painted fern, *A. niponicum* 'Pictum' (= *A. goeringianum* 'Pictum'), is most frequently cultivated, adding a cool, silvery note to shady sites. (Most plants with gray foliage are sun-lovers, having developed a hairy coat to protect against evaporative water loss. Think of lamb's ears, sage, or lavender.) With adequate moisture Japanese painted fern sends up fronds right through the growing season. The greatest color contrast, burgundy stipe to silver pinnae, develops in light shade: too much sun will bleach the fronds. Widely available, this cultivar is easily grown in moist, humus-rich soil, in partial shade in cooler regions and heavier shade in

southeastern and southern gardens. I especially enjoy it in combination with a glaucous-blue-leaved hosta such as 'Blue Cadet' or 'Halcyon', perhaps accenting the pairing with the silver-netted leaves of *Lamiastrum* 'Herman's Pride'.

Eared lady fern, *Athyrium otophorum,* is found on Honshu, Shikoku, and Kyushu, and also China. Readily available and hardy from zones 5 to 9, this is an easy fern to grow. In spring, croziers unroll to pale lime-green young fronds, with a burgundy stipe and rachis. The triangular fronds grow 12 to 18 inch long, and the dark burgundy-red color of the stipe remains at maturity, a handsome contrast to the medium gray-green frond color. Eared lady fern makes a fine addition to a planting of medium-sized, glaucous-blue-leaved hosta.

Semievergreen, large-leaved holly fern, *Cyrtomium macrophyllum,* is a plant found in Honshu, Shikoku, and Kyushu, as well as Formosa, and China to the Himalayas. The yellowish green, gracefully arching fronds reach 10 to 20 inches long, growing in a compact group. Readily available and easily cultivated, this fine fern should be more widely grown in gardens; it is suitable for zones 8 and 9.

The dwarf holly fern, *Cyrtomium caryotidum,* has 3 to 6 pairs of light green, leathery, long-pointed, hollylike pinnae on arching, evergreen fronds 12 inches long. It is found in limestone areas of Honshu's Kanto District and westward, Shikoku, and

Kyushu, as well as from China to India and Hawaii. The glossy, upright, dark green fronds of Japanese holly fern, *C. fortunei,* grow 18 to 30 inches long, with dark, blackish stipe and rachis. As the croziers unroll in spring the new, narrow pinnae are a pleasing, pale pea-green. This species is common in low mountain and hillside thickets of Hokkaido's Okushiri Island, and on Honshu, Shikoku, and Kyushu, where it is common. It also grows in southern Korea and China. As might be expected with natural populations in Hokkaido, Japanese holly fern is more cold-tolerant than the other species, and is the only reliable holly fern in the Northeast, successfully grown in New York and Massachusetts in zone 5. It has even escaped and become naturalized in the southeastern states, as far north as South Carolina. Japanese holly fern is superb as a ground cover—elegant among rocks or the paving of a patio, and a good companion with bold-textured shrubs such as large-leaved rhododendrons in cool climate gardens or fatsia in southern areas. It is readily available, as is another Japanese holly fern, *C. falcatum,* which is popular in southern and southwestern gardens but unreliable in the Northeast. *Cyrtomium falcatum* is attractive, with lustrous, dark green fronds that resemble a branch of Oregon grape holly, *Mahonia aquifolium,* and a stem covered with shaggy brown scales.

Rather rare in the wild, beaded wood fern, *Dryopteris bissetiana* (= *D. varia* var.

setosa), is found in central and southern Honshu, Shikoku, and Kyushu, and also in Ryukyu, Formosa, China to Indochina, and the Philippines. Hardy in zones 5 to 8, this easily cultivated fern, frequently available from specialty nurseries, should find its way into wider use. The small leathery segments roll over at the edges, adding a delightful, distinctly beaded appearance to the arching, 1- to 2-foot fronds. Though the triangular fronds are evergreen, new croziers do not emerge until early summer. Given moist, humus-rich soil in shade, the short, creeping rhizomes will develop into a tidy clump.

Champion's wood fern, *Dryopteris championii,* is a favorite of John Mickel, senior curator of ferns at the New York Botanical Garden. Found on Honshu from southern Kanto south and west, and on Shikoku and Kyushu, and southern Korea and China, it is hardy from zones 5 to 8. Champion's wood fern is easily grown, but unfortunately infrequently available. Evergreen fronds, erect to arching and 1 to 3 feet long, provide a handsome appearance year-round. Most other evergreen ferns have fronds that soften at the base in cold weather, giving the plants a more horizontal habit in winter. Champion's wood fern remains boldly upright. Like beaded wood fern, it is slow to wake in spring; new croziers unroll in early June in John Mickel's home garden. Black-scaled croziers give rise to new fronds that begin a delicate apple green, and later become dark green, glossy, and leathery at maturity.

Thick-stemmed wood fern, *Dryopteris crassirhizoma* (= *D. buschiana*), is locally common on the wooded slopes of Hokkaido, Honshu, and Shikoku, as well as in Sakhalin, the southern Kuriles, Korea, and Manchuria. It is hardy from zones 5 to 8, and easy to grow, but infrequently available. Forming a massive crown up to 4 inches across, plants produce an imposing display of erect to arching semi-evergreen fronds 2 to 3½ feet long. Abundantly brown-scaled croziers develop into thin-textured blades tapering at both ends, in a vaselike array. A single plant might serve as a focal point in the garden. Use caution with its companions, for in autumn with the first cold weather the fronds literally play "all fall down" and collapse. They remain mostly green through the winter, however, so avoid using low-growing evergreen plants, small bulbs, and other dainty spring ephemerals as inappropriate neighbors.

Autumn fern, or copper fern, *Dryopteris erythrosora,* is found in the damp low-mountain and hillside forests of Honshu, Shikoku, and Kyushu, as well as in Korea, Ryuku, Formosa, and from China to the Philippines. Easily grown and generally available at neighborhood garden centers and nurseries, autumn fern is a welcome addition to gardens in zones 5 to 8. In spring short, creeping rhizomes produce arching, evergreen fronds, 18 to 30 inches

long. Coppery-pink croziers unroll to a glowing, glossy, rosy-brown color when young. Then fronds turn a deep, glossy green. The spore cases, or sori, on the underside of the fronds are scarlet red, the characteristic that provided the species name. *Dryopteris erythrosora* var. *prolifica* (or cultivar 'Prolifica') has fronds only 12 to 15 inches long, less upright than the species. Now and then, especially under humid conditions, it is viviparous, producing new plantlets along the upper surface of the rachis. 'Prolifica' is, however, not as reliably hardy as the typical variety.

Formosan wood fern or limelight shield fern, *Dryopteris formosanum,* is found on Kyushu and in the Totomi province and Kinki district westward on Honshu, as well as on Formosa. It is hardy and easily grown from zones 6 to 9. Formosan wood fern has a neat crown with erect to arching, semi-evergreen, triangular fronds that are 18 to 30 inches long (usually smaller in cultivation). Fronds are a beautiful glowing lime-green, especially when young. It would be elegant in combination with golden hosta and the narrow, straplike, dark green leaves of liriope. I'm sure this fern will be more widely grown once it becomes more widely available, and gardeners become more aware of it.

Dryopteris lacera is found on Honshu, Shikoku, and Kyushu, as well as in Korea and Manchuria on open hillsides, in moist woodlands, and on stream banks in the mountains. Hardy from zones 5 to 8 and easy to grow, it is, unfortunately, infrequently available. The apple green, leathery semi-evergreen fronds range from lance-shaped to triangular, and from erect to arching. They grow 12 to 24 inches long, forming a tidy clump. Only the outer third of the frond is fertile; these fertile pinnae are often deciduous, giving fronds a curious truncated appearance in winter. With its acceptance of varied habitats, *D. lacera* would be a useful addition to our gardens.

Tokyo wood fern, *Dryopteris tokyoensis,* is found in the forests of Hokkaido, Honshu, Shikoku, and Kyushu, and also Korea. Hardy from zones 5 to 8 and easily grown, this fern is more readily available than several others discussed in this section. Stiffly erect narrow fronds, 18 to 36 inches long, develop into a vaselike plant. Though vigorous in growth, it branches only infrequently, so propagation by division is slow. Fortunately, Tokyo wood fern has abundant, large sori, and is readily raised from spore.

Looking more like some sort of vine than a fern, Japanese climbing fern, *Lygodium japonicum,* has a Connecticut counterpart, the Hartford climbing fern, *L. palmatum.* Growing in thickets and hedges of the lowlands and low mountains of Honshu's Kanto district, Shikoku, and Kyushu, Japanese climbing fern is also found in Ryukyu, Formosa, Korea, and China. The twining fronds reach an amaz-

Lygodium japonicum

ing 5 to 20 feet from a short, creeping rhizome. The Japanese species is easier to cultivate than the American native, but still somewhat difficult. Hardy in zone 6 only in mild winters, Japanese climbing fern is frequently grown as a houseplant in colder regions. It is more reliable in zones 7 to 10, and in the southeastern coastal United States it has naturalized in lightly shaded open woodland sites. If you wish to try Japanese climbing fern in colder locations, a winter mulch of evergreen boughs or dry oak leaves is vital to protect the roots. John Mickel mulches plants in his garden well, and finds they die only in cold, open, snowless winters where the frost strikes most deeply in the ground, or if he becomes overconfident and neglects to mulch. For a more attractive appearance, the old deciduous fronds should be pruned away before new growth begins in spring, so cut them down when you mulch.

Gathered as a spring vegetable, Japanese royal fern, *Osmunda japonica,* is a common fern found on Hokkaido, Honshu, Shikoku, and Kyushu, as well as southern Sakhalin, Korea, Ryukyu, Formosa, and China to the Himalayas. This plant would be better admired as an ornamental than a vegetable, for the fronds contain carcinogenic compounds. One or two meals are unlikely to be harmful, but this definitely should not be a regular part of your diet. Similar to North America's royal fern, *O. regalis,* Japanese royal fern grows more compactly, and is only 18 to 36 inches tall, with erect, deciduous fronds. Individual fronds are fully dimorphic; that is, either fertile or sterile, rather than a mix as on royal fern. All osmundas are an excellent choice for moist sites, thriving along the banks of a stream or a pond edge. Easily grown in zones 6 to 9, Japanese royal fern is rarely commercially available.

There is a clear family resemblance among the holly ferns, *Polystichum* species. Evergreen except in severe winters, their hollylike leaves are elegant additions to the woodland garden. They like a loose, organic soil, moist but well-drained. Since holly ferns tend to lift themselves out of the soil, I find that maintaining a mulch of coarse compost keeps them in good condition. Of course, when they are periodically lifted and divided, plants should be reset at the proper level. In general I prefer to transplant and separate ferns either early in the spring before the croziers begin to unroll, or after the new growth has hardened off. September is also a possibility, except where winter comes early.

Braun's holly fern, *Polystichum braunii,* has upright to arching, lustrous deep green, semi-evergreen fronds that are 8 inches wide and up to 30 inches long, sometimes more. Next year's croziers are formed by late summer, densely covered with silvery scales and looking like a cluster of fleecy eggs in a nest of the current year's fronds. As they unroll, the new fronds slump backward, looking rather wilted. With maturity they regain stiffness and present a more upright appearance. The scales age to golden tan as the new fronds mature, giving a delightfully shaggy look. Braun's holly fern is found on Hokkaido and the northern and central districts of Honshu, and in Korea, Manchuria, China, the Kuriles, Sakhalin, Kamchatka, and Siberia, to Europe and North America. Quite cold-hardy, this readily available fern prefers cooler locations and can be easily grown in zones 4 to 8. Remember that it is rare in the wild. Be sure that any plants you purchase are of propagated origin.

Makino's holly fern, *Polystichum makinoi,* is found in Honshu's Kanto district and westward, and on Shikoku and Kyushu. Another of John Mickel's favorites, this easily grown, frequently available fern is hardy in zones 6 to 9, and worth trying in a protected site in zone 5. Arching and lustrous, the 20- to 30-inch-long evergreen fronds grow in an erect crown. This is a handsome plant for damp, shady, deciduous woodlands, perhaps in combination with golden-leaved hosta and dark green liriope to accentuate the fern's bright olive-green fronds.

Japanese tassel fern, *Polystichum polyblepharum* (= *P. setosum*), is a good choice for gardens with dappled shade and consistently moist, fertile soil high in organic matter. The 12- to 24-inch-long arching, dark green, glossy, wide-spreading, evergreen fronds are paler on the underside. Growing in a tight clump, the croziers begin to unroll in a familiar manner, then droop backward, eventually righting themselves and finishing in a typical ferny posture. The new growth is susceptible to damage from late frosts so plant in a sheltered location. Common in nurseries and garden centers, Japanese tassel fern is easily grown in zones 6 to 8; try it in zone 5 in a protected microclimate.

Polystichum tsussimense is often sold as a houseplant, as its dainty, deciduous to semi-evergreen fronds, perhaps 8 to 12 inches long and 4 to 5 inches wide, are attractive in terrariums or dish gardens. Hardy in the Southeast, it has understandable difficulty with my Connecticut winters, given its native range: Honshu's Kanto district and westward, Shikoku, and Kyushu, as well as Korea, China, and Formosa. You might try this commonly available fern in sheltered sites in zone 6, but it is most reliable in zones 7 and 8. Good drainage, rich soil, and a shaded rock garden setting is best.

Japanese beech fern, *Thelypteris decursive-pinnata* (= *Phegopteris decursive-pinnata*), is common and adaptable, growing on rocks and stone walls in the lowlands and lower mountain slopes of Honshu's Kanto district and westward, Shikoku, and Kyushu, as well as in Korea, Ryukyu, Formosa, China to Indochina, and India. Although it is amply hardy, from zones 4 to 10, this easily cultivated, frequently available fern is just not grown very often. I hesitate to think that gardeners would be so suspicious of something new, but Judith Jones, proprietor of Fancy Fronds, a nursery exclusively devoted to ferns, tosses huge numbers of this fern on the compost heap because they simply do not sell. Like its close relatives from America, broad beech fern, *T. hexagonoptera,* and narrow beech fern, *T. phegopteris,* the Japanese beech fern is deciduous. Unlike the American species, however, the runners on which new plants are produced are short, so that Japanese beech fern spreads in a more refined manner. It is easily propagated by division—lifting and separating plants, and replanting each piece individually. Once you have this fern you will, I think, want more. The 12- to 24-inch upright fronds remain a consistent vivid green throughout the growing season, even through the first autumn frosts. Only after a hard freeze will they finally consent to winter dormancy.

GRASSES

Grasses are primarily plants of sunny places. In woodland shade, it is usually left to sedges and rushes to present a grasslike appearance. However, there is one shade-tolerant Japanese grass, hakone grass, or wind-combed grass, *Hakonechloa macra*. It is found in the wild as a rather rare endemic of wet, rocky cliffs in the mountains of the Tokaido district of Honshu, from Sagami to Kii province. Spreading slowly by means of creeping rhizomes and stolons, its culms grow 12 to 24 inches tall, but present a much lower appearance since the foliage bows in a graceful, horizontal manner. Its habit of arching in only one direction gives the plant the tidy, combed appearance referred to in its English common name. While the plain green form is attractive in its own right, the cultivar generally available is the golden yellow form, 'Aureola'. In Japan, variegated forms are cultivated as ornamental potted plants. A dark green glazed container is a good choice for 'Aureola', making a harmonious contrast to the golden, narrowly green-striped blades. Full sun will discolor and burn the leaves. Plants have been perfectly hardy for me in Connecticut, turning beige-tan in winter dormancy, and then sending up pink-flushed new shoots in spring. So elegant is 'Aureola' that it can function alone as an accent plant, perhaps set against a water-worn stone at the bend of a path. I've used this grass with 'Kabitan' and 'Wogan Gold', two small golden-leaved hostas, and a rather slow-growing little ivy with gold-freckled leaves for a warm, sunny combination in the shade. One marvelous alliance I saw in Seattle was a substantial clump of hakone grass growing in an open grove of black-stem bamboo in a courtyard setting. The contrast between the softly arching golden grass blades and the vertical thrust of the bamboo's polished ebony culms could not be improved upon. I have seen references to other variegated cultivars: 'Albo-variegata' with white-striped leaves showing only very narrow green bands, and 'Albo-aurea' with leaves striped lengthwise with cream and yellow, again finely banded with green. I have not yet found any sources for these.

RODGERSIA

Moisture-loving *Rodgersia podophylla* is a beautiful, stately, 3-foot-tall perennial from woodlands on the mountains of Hokkaido,

Honshu, and Korea. Bold, palmately compound leaves are 20 inches wide and irregularly, jaggedly toothed along the edges. Bronze when young, they retain a dark, coppery flush over the mature green leaf color. In late June or early July the free-blooming plants have fluffy, creamy-white panicles of flowers reminiscent of astilbes. Plants are wonderful in combination with perennials of similar scale and equal vigor, such as big hostas and the larger ferns. Though the foliage of the larger astilbes creates a good effect, the flowers of the two plants, blooming as they do at the same time, are too similar for effective display. In a sunny site consider using eulalia grass, *Miscanthus sinensis,* which is of similar scale yet with delicate linear foliage texture. As you might expect, plants of this stature need a very fertile, humus-rich soil, and ample, constant moisture. There are several German selections slowly making their way into American nurseries: 'Pagode' has white flowers in large pagoda-like inflorescences, greening as they age; 'Rotlab' has coppery-red leaves; and 'Smaragd' has emerald-green leaves.

Meadowrue

Thalictrums are charming plants with airy foliage, and even taller, more statuesque species appear refined and graceful. They are impressive in formal structured perennial borders in sunny sites; equally delightful in lightly shaded, informal woodland plantings. *Thalictrum rochebrunianum* is a stately yet airy plant growing 3 to 5 feet tall. Native to grassy places in Honshu's central district highlands, it is rather rare in the wild. The cultivar 'Lavender Mist', with its small but numerous bell-shaped violet-lavender flowers centered with a tuft of golden stamens, is at home in semishaded gardens with cool, humus-rich, moist soil. *Thalictrum aquilegiifolium* is found throughout the cooler regions of the Northern Hemisphere, including Japan and Europe. Its light green, columbine-like foliage makes a dense clump, giving rise to tall glaucous stems that branch into a wide head of fluffy, rose-lilac flowers.

AUTUMN

All too often gardens come to a raggedy halt in late summer. School starts up again after the summer vacation, and we think about planting bulbs for next spring, and sigh, anticipating autumn's leaf-raking chores. Nowhere is this more obvious than in shady areas that may have been neglected for the opulence of sun-loving, summer-blooming perennials. But even as the first leaves begin to turn color, let loose, and spiral to the ground, a handful of shade-loving perennials from Japan still flower.

ANEMONOPSIS

I could never pick a favorite plant, or make a list of favorites. Partiality fluctuates with the garden's seasons, with what is new and thus of special interest to me, and other such subjective criteria. Still, anemonopsis is surely something special. *Anemonopsis macrophylla* is a rare plant in the woods of Honshu's central district mountains. This plant has a genus all to itself. Its leaves resemble those of a coarse astilbe: rich dark green, twice or thrice divided into 3 parts, each 3-lobed leaflet toothed along the edge. Vigorous plants in loose, open, humus-rich moist soil can reach 30 inches tall. Beginning in late July or more often August, and continuing into September, flowers like the ethereal waxy ghosts of spurless columbines, translucent lilac in color, dangle in a loose, open raceme, trembling at the slightest breeze. Plants seem to prefer a slightly raised position, perhaps a site on a gentle slope, or between rocks. Summer drought and heat are both harmful. The plant is apparently hardy to zone 5, even zone 4 in sheltered sites with reliable snow cover. Unfortunately, it's hard to come by. Anemonopsis can be raised from seed but, as with other plants in the family *Ranunculaceae,* fresh seed germinates best, older seed only poorly.

JAPANESE CIMICIFUGA

Cimicifuga japonica var. *acerina* (= *C. acerina*) is found on Honshu, Shikoku, and Kyushu. All the dark green leaves are at the base of the plant, making a dense, compact mound through the growing season. Plants have a refined look, as leaves are once or twice 3-parted, and each leaflet has 3 to 5 long-pointed lobes. In September or October, numerous small, fluffy, white flowers open, clustered at the upper portion of 4-foot-high stems. As they fade, the flowers shatter, dusting whatever is beneath with white threads of stamens.

There is a second, very familiar, and well-liked autumn-flowering cimicifuga from Japan, *Cimicifuga simplex*. Found in mountain meadows and alpine regions of Hokkaido, Honshu, Shikoku, and Kyushu, as well as in Sakhalin, the Kuriles, and Kamchatka, *C. simplex* produces 30- to 36-inch-tall stems with 2 to 4 slender candlelike panicles of white-petaled flowers in September and October. Leaves are bipinnate and pale green. In my garden this plant flowers three or four years out of five, when heavy frosts hold off long enough for the buds to open. I consider this a sufficient return, since the plants themselves are reliably hardy and we can try again next year. 'White Pearl' is a popular cultivar with exceptionally pale green leaves and white flowers.

HOSTA

Hosta are grown primarily for their foliage, and flowers are regarded as mostly incidental. Then there is *Hosta tardiflora,* with a very late period of bloom, from late September into October in my garden. I've seen the flowers displayed against a carpet of freshly fallen yellow birch leaves. Plants make a 10-inch-tall mound of thick, firm, glossy green leaves, and have dense, compact spikes of purple flowers. It is attractive paired with liriope, which also blooms at this time. The grasslike liriope leaves contrast with the broader shape of the hosta throughout the growing season. Add Christmas fern, *Polystichum achrostichoides,* and a pleasing trio will result. Another possibility would be one of the smaller, pinkish lavender, fall-flowering colchicums such as *Colchicum autumnale,* or its white form, 'Album'. It is possible that *H. tardiflora* is a plant of garden origin: Owhi's *Flora* mentions it as "cultivated in Honshu (near Nagoya)."

Kirengeshoma

What would you say to a herbaceous plant that grows in the shade with maplelike leaves and yellow bell-like flowers in autumn? Look no further. Resembling an abutilon, *Kirengeshoma palmata* is native to Honshu's southern Kinki district, Shikoku, and Kyushu. Somewhat shrublike in appearance, it produces numerous 24- to 30-inch-tall stems, and 7- to 10-lobed, fresh green leaves that range from 4 to 8 inches long and wide. In August arching sideshoots produce terminal clusters of elegant, nodding flowers. They are soft yellow, and

look like open bells. In my garden, winter comes too soon and kirengeshoma rarely matures seed, but just a few miles away, it self-sows. Moist but well-drained, humusrich, acid soil is necessary for its healthy growth. I have seen kirengeshoma paired with Japanese cimicifuga for a lovely result. You might also want to try planting it with Japanese anemone.

Liriope

Evergreen, attractive in winter, fall flowering—liriope performs well as a ground cover and, accordingly, will be found in chapter 5.

Salvia

Preconceptions are very difficult to cope with, in gardening as elsewhere. If asked to guess about the habitat needs of sage, I'd probably think a sunny, reasonably well-drained site most suitable. A pretty, lax-stemmed, yellow-flowered, autumn-blooming sage came to me from a friend who'd gotten it from Richard Weaver of We-Du Nursery in Marion, North Carolina. Weaver, who introduced the sage to this country, knows his plants and recognizes a good one when he sees it. (He was previously horticultural taxonomist at the Arnold Arboretum.) The name that came with the sage was *Salvia koyamae.* This is a rare plant from Honshu's Shinano province that closely resembles *S. nipponica.* In fact, I wonder if it might actually be

S. nipponica, a rather common plant found in woods and thickets on the mountains of Honshu, Shikoku, and Kyushu, with pale yellow flowers in August to October. It is described in Owhi's *Flora* as having decumbent, trailing stems, hastate (arrow-shaped, with 2 outward pointing lobes at the base) leaves, and deliciously soft, pale yellow, 1-inch-long flowers that bloom in autumn. The *RHS Index of Garden Plants* lists neither, so I'm not going to fret over this too much, but intend to continue to enjoy the late flowers. As I would expect of a woodland plant, mine seems happy in a shady place with a humus-rich, somewhat moist soil. This charming autumn-flowering sage has been perfectly hardy in zone 6, and you could always take cuttings to over-winter it if you garden in a colder climate.

Tricyrtis hirta

TRICYRTIS

Perhaps most familiar of the late-flowering Japanese plants are toad lilies, *Tricyrtis* spp. I wonder where the English common name came from, as I can think of no link between the flower and any froggy cousin. Much more sensible and appropriate is the Japanese name of *hototogisu,* which means cuckoo, for the dotted pattern of the flower petals is like the markings on the cuckoo's breast feathers. The most common, and likely the most available, is Japanese toad lily, *T. hirta.* Endemic to Japan, it is common on Honshu, Shikoku, and Kyushu. Plants grow 16 to 30 inches tall, sometimes

higher; softly hairy leaves clasp the upright stem on the upper portion. Upward-facing, purple-spotted white flowers appear in September to October on the upper portion of the stem. They have an unusual shape, slightly cupped but with the segments splayed like a starfish. There is also a pure white, green-flushed, unspotted cultivar, *T. hirta* 'Alba'. 'Alba' makes a charming trio with white-margined, green-leaved *Hosta decorata,* and dark green Christmas fern, *Polystichum achrostichoides.*

I have seen *Tricyrtis macranthopsis* perfectly placed, with the arching stems trailing over a low stone retaining wall as though pulled by the weight of the clear yellow bells, freckled with brownish purple spots on the inside. Beverly Nichols, the fey English garden writer, divided his friends into those who could, and those who could not, shrink small enough to peer up into the bell of a snowdrop. Were he to have seen this plant in autumn bloom, I'm sure the distinction would have been those who could, and those who could not, hear faintly the chiming music to which the fairies dance. Sixteen to 30-inch-long stems grow from short rhizomes. Narrow oblong-ovate leaves are paired up the stem. The pendulous flowers sway from pedicels in the leaf axils and at the tip of the stem. With limited distribution in the mountains of the Kii province of Honshu, this is a rare plant in the wild, and is occasionally planted in Japanese gardens.

Deer do dine on tricyrtis, usually waiting until the flower buds are well formed.

Tricyrtis latifolia

WINTER

Winter's aspect varies throughout the country. The north is under snow, while gardeners in the Southeast are enjoying pansies and may see the first daffodils and perennials in bloom shortly after the new year. Evergreen foliage can still be enjoyed on a walk in the garden or viewed from indoors even when—perhaps especially when—flowers are absent from the landscape. A number of evergreen perennials are suitable for the woodland garden.

GINGER
There are some superb gingers in Japan. Dr. John Creech collected eight different variations from the woods along the Miyanoura River on Yakushima in 1956. Altogether, there are thirty different ginger species in Japan. Many are found on

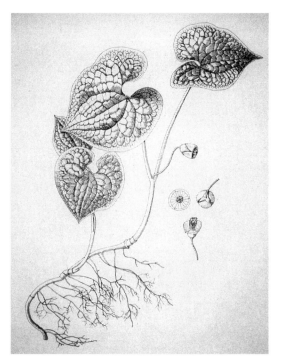

Asarum caulescens

There are several evergreen species native to the American Southeast, placed in *Asarum* by some botanists, while others classify them as *Hexastylis*. The Japanese species—beautiful, exotic, evergreen—are something new to us. Their leaves may be rounded, heart-shaped, or kidney-shaped, and vary from 3 to 5 inches wide. Their very dark green color is highlighted by silver veining or blotches. The few species I have grown in my garden survive but do

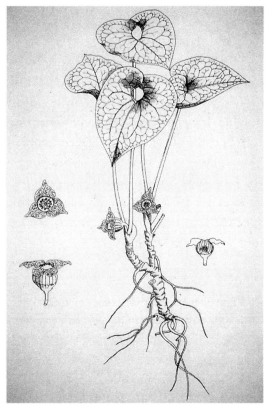

Asarum sieboldii

Honshu, and several on Shikoku and Kyushu. (These are not related to the tropical ginger that we use for seasoning.) Flowers are concealed beneath the leaves, and often have a fetid odor that is attractive to the beetles that pollinate them in the wild. Where they thrive, gingers enhance gardens with the beauty of their leaves in winter.

Perhaps you've grown evergreen European ginger, *Asarum europeum,* often used in shady gardens, or Canada ginger, *A. canadensis,* a deciduous North American species grown by wildflower enthusiasts.

not expand into large patches as do European and Canada ginger, nor do they make large clumps as do *A. ariifolia* and *A. shuttleworthii* from the southeastern United States. With devilish persistence, slugs attack the leaves. It is safer, and still effective, to grow them in containers. I prefer deep, round, blue-glazed bonsai pots, which make a beautiful contrast to the leaves. Use a moisture-retentive mix, but do not allow it to become soggy. The plants need a winter rest and cannot survive as houseplants. The pots can be plunged into sand in a cold frame or alpine house in winter.

Many of the Japanese gingers have striking flowers. Most, *Asarum megacalyx* for example, flower in spring in March, April, or May. A few flower in winter, most notably *A. nipponicum,* which blooms from October to February. Jim McClements of Dover, Delaware, has had *A. kumagianum* for five years and finds it slow-growing. Flowering in February or March, this species has thick, lustrous leaves and is found on Yakushima.

PACHYSANDRA

Pachysandra is discussed in chapter 5, which describes vines and ground covers.

NIPPON LILY

Sam and Carleen Jones grow Nippon lily, *Rohdea japonica,* at Piccadilly Farms, their home and nursery in Athens, Georgia. Sam

Rohdea japonica

says it is a mainstay of their north-facing, dry, poor-soil winter garden. The glossy green leaves look fresh and elegant through the worst of winter, coming through one exceptional low of -6° Fahrenheit. It's a great plant for dry summer conditions, too. In 1993 rainfall was so meager that farmers could only cut one hay crop, rather than the typical four or five. Nippon lily never flagged, never turned brown, and was never given any supplemental watering. At Piccadilly Farms, Nippon lily is propagated by seed. Sales are moderate, with most going to retail nurseries in North and South Carolina. Sam and Carleen have a few each of a pleated-leaf and a variegated form, which were given to them by Fred Galle, the noted azalea expert, who brought them back from Japan. These must be propagated by division, as their seedlings have plain green leaves. The Joneses are also cosseting four plants of a mottled-leaved form that came from the estate of Ben Pace, propagator at Callaway Gardens, after his death.

My Japanese friend Nihei Takeo wrote me that Nippon lily is a classic plant developed during the Edo period and cultivated by the feudal nobility, along with peonies and chrysanthemums. Many forms were selected representing a variety of leaf shapes, sizes, and coloring. Today there is a Nippon lily society, devoted to the cultivation of this plant. In May 1992, at the Jin-dai Botanic Gardens in Tokyo, I saw an exhibit of the society. To accommodate the long fleshy roots, and to accentuate the display, plants were grown in deep pots glazed black or rich blue. Three forms especially impressed me: one with pale ivory variegations on chartreuse leaves, producing a very soft, light effect; another with not-quite-white blotches on green leaves; and yet another with curly leaves. Mature, nicely grown, rare forms can fetch as much as one thousand dollars. At a garden center in Takanezawa-machi I saw some very attractive varieties, but at approximately two hundred dollars apiece I did not purchase them.

The Japanese name, *omoto,* is written in three kanji letters and its literal meaning is "ten thousand years blue." *Ten thousand* connotes long life, and this is thought to be a plant of good omen. Traditionally, when someone is about to move to a new house, he will personally take a pot of Nippon lily to the new house on a particularly auspicious day and place it in the front entry area. After that, all the household belongings are sent to the new dwelling.

Nippon lily is native to thickets and woods in the warmer Tokaido district and westward of Honshu, Shikoku, and Kyushu. My first plants came from the rare plant auction of the Arnold Arboretum in Boston. They are hardy there and have proven so in my garden. I find the glossy green leaves elegant, and a handsome contrast to the lacy texture of evergreen autumn fern, *Dryopteris erythrosora,* and the lustrous rounded leaves of European ginger, *Asarum europeum.* As well as the plain green-leaved form, I have one with a pleated green leaf, another that is a dwarf pleated-leaf form, and a third with crisply defined white stripes on the leaf margin. They all seem equally cold-hardy, getting only a covering of evergreen boughs in late December.

In May or June established plants develop an odd, dense, congested spike of creamy, pale yellow flowers tucked down in the center of the leaf cluster. Then in autumn the plants produce a spike of handsome red fruits reminiscent of that of jack-in-the-pulpit. Individually, each berry is about ¼ inch in diameter. There is usually one large, beige-tan seed per berry. But, as was noted before, seedlings tend to be of the plain green-leaved form, regardless of the appearance of the seed parent.

CAST IRON PLANT

Beloved of Victorian England, cast iron plant, *Aspidistra elatior,* is an introduced Chinese plant long cultivated in Japanese gardens. It is barely hardy with protection in my zone 6 garden, but makes a sturdy, carefree houseplant that I move outdoors in summer. The most common form has pointed, oval, dark, glossy evergreen leaves, 15 inches long and 4 inches wide, on a 10-inch-high stalk. There is also a white variegated form with handsomely striped leaves. J. C. Raulston, of the North Carolina State Arboretum, brought still another interest-

ing form back from Korea: its new leaves come up with a pale ghostly white tip on the upper third of the leaf. However, plants must be well established before this marking appears.

Aspidistras are excellent for the dimmest, darkest corner, indoors or out. In southeastern states such as North Carolina and Georgia, they add superb textural interest to the outdoor garden. I very much admired one combination at the Atlanta Botanical Garden that paired aspidistra and its blocky foliage with the linear tracery of horsetail, *Equisetum* sp. I asked horticulturist Mildred Pinnell if the wide-ranging roots of the horsetail were confined in a buried pot, as I'd seen recommended. No, she said, someone just periodically headed it back. If such maintenance seems more than you want to take on, a more mannerly fern would also be a suitable partner for aspidistra.

CHAPTER EIGHT

Plants for Rock and Water Gardens

The small treasures we assign to the rock garden are often plants originally from mountain or alpine sites. Some are self-sufficient, able to carry on with a modicum of care; others need precisely the right conditions, cosseting, and constant attention. If miniatures appeal to you, then you will enjoy rock gardening. There are Japanese plants for rock gardeners at every level of expertise, from easily grown lilliputian beauties like columbines to persnickety plants like conandron, which will take your horticultural hubris down a peg or two. There are even counterparts of that epitome of the Swiss Alps, edelweiss.

SPRING

COLUMBINES

Columbines are found throughout the temperate regions of the Northern Hemisphere. In spring their graceful flowers float over attractive foliage. Easy to grow but short-lived, columbines do provide a self-perpetuating colony of volunteer seedlings. Plants are easily raised from the glossy black seed.

Remember, though, that columbines are flagrantly promiscuous; if you grow more than one species their seed-produced offspring will be hybrids, often attractive but different from their parents.

Perhaps the most attractive Japanese species is *Aquilegia flabellata,* whose height varies from 5 to 12 inches. The taller plants are

described in chapter 6. A dwarf form, more suitable for the rock garden than the perennial border, *A. flabellata* var. *pumila* (= *A. akitensis*) is only 6 to 8 inches tall. In April or early May each flowering stem produces from 1 to 3 large showy flowers, 1½ inches in diameter. The sepals are purplish blue or lilac in color, and the petals, lilac at the base and pale to ivory at the tip. The spurs at the flower's base may be blunt or charmingly curved. Found in sunny rocky outcrops in the alpine regions of central and northern Honshu, Hokkaido, the southern Kuriles, Sakhalin, and northern Korea, *A. flabellata* var. *pumila* is a delightful addition to the rock garden. In Japan it is frequently grown as a container plant. There are several named forms: 'Alba' has white flowers; 'Nana Alba' is a dwarf form with gray-green leaves and creamy-white flowers; and 'Ministar' is a vigorous form that has bright blue sepals and white petals.

CAMPANULA
Bellflowers are a marvelous group of plants offering possibilities for a range of habitats: rock garden, perennial border, and lightly shaded woodland garden. One Japanese species, *Campanula lasiocarpa,* is a small charmer particularly suited to the rock garden. Forming neat tufts of smooth, pale green, slightly toothed, rounded leaves, it produces an opulent display in August of shapely, large, clear-blue bells, each solitary on a 3-inch stem. It is found growing on

sandy, gravelly alpine slopes, between stones or in rough cindery volcanic lava, with an adequate flow of underground water. Native to Hokkaido, northern and central Honshu, and also Sakhalin, the Kuriles, Kamchatka, the Aleutian Islands, and Alaska, it needs moraine conditions (rocky, gravelly, quick-draining soil and flowing underground water) in the rock garden. At lower elevations, the flowering period will be earlier, and the plants tend to be short-lived, succumbing to summer heat and humidity. *Campanula chamissonis* is found in similar sites. The numerous glossy leaves form a neat rosette, which in turn produces short stolons terminating in yet other rosettes of foliage. Many 2- to 3-inch-high stems appear in August, each with a single, nodding, deep violet flower; that is, in the wild. In cultivation the plants are often reliably perennial yet only bloom grudgingly. Sharp drainage, relatively fertile soil, flowing subsurface water, and protection from blistering heat are the optimal conditions. 'Oyobeni' has flowers striped blue and white, and there is a rare white-flowered form.

CONANDRON
Imagine an enchanting, almost hardy relative of the African violet with pendulous, crinkly, pale green leaves, and orange-eyed lavender flowers, 10 to 40 per plant. This is *Conandron ramondioides.* I had this plant once. Slugs, those slimy hell-spawn,

Conandron ramondioides

off, and the plant forms a densely haired, resting bud. In the wild, snow cover would provide some moisture and insulation. The plant should not dry out at this time, nor should it be kept so wet as to rot—a difficult tightrope. During the growing season keep the plants evenly moist, and in light to moderate shade. Propagation is from the minute, dust-fine seeds, or by leaf cuttings. Plants are sometimes available from specialty nurseries.

DICENTRA

There are bleeding-hearts native to North America, and certainly *Dicentra spectabilis* from Korea, Manchuria, and China is a perennial garden favorite, in Japan as well as in the United States. The gem of them all is *D. peregrina pusilla*. Found mainly in the harsh environment of volcanic slopes of Hokkaido and central and northern Honshu, as well as Sakhalin, the Kuriles, Kamchatka, and eastern Siberia, this dainty plant can only be described as rare, and possessed of an equally rare beauty. Glaucous, silver-blue, fernlike foliage forms a hoar-frost tuft. The locketlike flowers, 3 to 6 on a stem scarcely 4 inches high, are rosy pink; there is an even rarer white form. This special bleeding-heart needs a sunny site, sharp drainage, and unaggressive neighbors. In Japan it is often cultivated in pots. H. Takeda, in his *Alpine Flowers of Japan*, gives fussily precise directions on how this might be accomplished:

climbed up the bench where I kept it and devoured the plant overnight. Just how do they know which are your rarest, most irreplaceable plants, and then home in on them? Conandron is native to steep, wet, shaded, rocky cliffs in the mountains of Honshu, Shikoku, and Kyushu, where it is rather common. In cultivation the biggest problem is winter wet. Those rock gardeners I know who have grown this plant keep it in an alpine house (a glasshouse kept at just above freezing) over the winter. Using a humus-rich, lime-free compost, position the thick, fleshy, brown-haired rhizomes between a couple of rocks arranged to form a vertical crevice. In autumn the leaves die

"Put in large lumps of red clay at the bottom, then large granite chips, and then fill the pot up with a mixture of 2 parts of leaf-mould and 8 parts of grit or volcanic cinders. Very good drainage is essential. Expose the plant to full sun. It is rather difficult to grow. Little watering. When it takes root give plenty of fertilizer, there being no fear of over-feeding. Propagation from seed. Disinfect the plant frequently, as the leaves are apt to be infested by red-spiders on the underside." I have grown this plant on a very sandy, gravelly west-facing slope in my Connecticut garden, and it did self-sow to a small extent. Seed should be sown fresh, while still green. The seed ripens so fast, you almost have to camp out beside the plant to catch it. Friends in the Pacific Northwest have also done quite well with *D. peregrina pusilla* as a container plant.

HELONOPSIS

Helonopsis orientalis is a relatively hardy little evergreen plant suitable for a shady rock garden where summers are cool, and the soil is moist and rich in organic matter. Found in mountain thickets and meadows, occasionally reaching up to alpine zones, this is a plant common to Hokkaido, Honshu, and Shikoku, rarely found in Kyushu, and also found in Sakhalin and Korea. Summer heat is detrimental to this plant, which is simply not widely grown except by rock garden aficionados. From experience I know it is hardy in zone 6, and from its natural range would expect it to be so in zone 5, possibly even zone 4. A rosette of lanceolate leaves like those of a broadleaved sedge develop from a short, somewhat woody rhizome. A 6- to 8-inch-tall scape carries a loose cluster of 3 to 10 carmine-red to rose-purple flowers, like miniature lilies, that appear from April to June depending on local conditions. A winter mulch of pine boughs or pine needles is advisable if snow cover is lacking. *Helenopsis orientalis* var. *breviscapa,* found in the mountains of Kyushu, has pale pink to white flowers that do not nod. This variety also has an interesting means of reproduction: new plants will be produced viviparously where the scape touches the ground.

VIOLETS

If anyone knew his plants it was H. Lincoln Foster, doyen of rock gardeners, who lived and gardened in Connecticut. Yet even he hesitated to answer an innocently phrased "What's that?" when it came to violets. In his book *Rock Gardening*, published in 1968, Foster wrote, "Vast and varied is the race of violets." So if you regard these plants as obnoxious weedy invaders of your lawn, think again. There are attractive violets for the woodland and rock garden, some of which come from Japan.

Viola crassa is a rare summer-blooming

violet from gravelly sites in alpine regions of Hokkaido, central and northern Honshu, and also the Kuriles and Kamchatka. Short, creeping rhizomes produce stems 2 to 5 inches long, each with 3 or 4 deep green, kidney- to heart-shaped leaves flushed with reddish brown. Dark yellow flowers, the lower lip penciled with dark brown stripes, appear in July and August, each not quite 1 inch across. This captivating plant needs a site in the sunny well-drained rock garden, or showcased in a trough. Bury part of the stem under the gravelly soil mix. Takeda suggests 6 parts fine gravel, 2 parts crushed brick, 1 part fibrous loam, and 1 part peat, ample water and midday shade.

Viola dissecta (= *V. eizanensis*, *V. dissecta* var. *chaerophylloides* f. *eizanensis*) is an elegant plant that is 4 to 5 inches high, with long-stemmed 3-parted leaves gracefully dissected into linear segments. In April or May large, slightly fragrant flowers, white with purple striations or pale rose, appear individually just above the leaves. To flower well this violet needs moist, acidic soil high in organic matter and woodland conditions of partial shade. Rather common, *V. dissecta* is native to the mountains of Honshu, Shikoku, and Kyushu. I grow this in the woods, and also in the perennial garden where the violet will be shaded by taller plants later in the season.

With lilliputian stature of 1 inch high, *Viola verecunda* var. *yakusimana* (= *V. yakusi-*

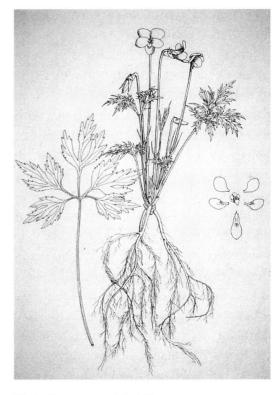

Viola dissecta var. *sieboldii*

manum) is small and dainty, even for a violet. In spring or summer, tiny heart-shaped, pale green leaves cluster under a nosegay of ⅓-inch white flowers delicately veined in purple. From the high mountains of Yakushima, this little plant is perfectly hardy, but I think it's best grown in a container so you can lift it up and admire its diminutive perfection. While it lives happily in moist, well-drained woodland, the sort of site where mosses thrive, the fine mats of ¼-inch leaves are rather inconspicuous. Jim McClements of Dover, Delaware, writes,

"Bijou, in the woodland rockery, seems to do well in a bed of moss."

Viola variegata var. *nipponica* is more commonly found in cultivation than the straight species. Quite showy, plants form flattened rosettes of dark green leaves with silver markings and purplish undersides. Foliage is the main attraction; the small, light purple flowers that appear in spring are secondary features. Cleistogamous (hidden, self-pollinating) flowers are produced in summer, so this violet does self-sow generously in both sunny or semishady sites. Growing about 2 inches tall, plants are charming where they distribute themselves about a gravel terrace or in the garden. Hot, dry summers and cold, snowless winters are damaging. This variety is a rare native of Honshu and Shikoku, while the ordinary form is found in Korea, Manchuria, and Siberia.

SUMMER

ADENOPHORA

Rock gardens tend to peak in spring, so plants that have a later period of bloom are to be treasured. Two dainty ladybells from Japan flower in summer. Native to alpine regions of Honshu, *Adenophora nikoensis* has a lustrous rosette of dark green leaves. In August or September the plants produce a number of flower stems from 7 to 12 inches tall. The somewhat chubby blos-soms are often a dark azure blue but color is frequently variable. Somewhat short-lived, new plants are easily raised from seed. From Kyushu and southern Korea, *Adenophora tashiroi* is even smaller—from 4 to 10 inches tall. Flowers are a clean, cool white or pale blue, as well as violet.

DIANTHUS

While the typical form of *Dianthus superbus* would only be suitable for a large rock gar-

Dianthus superbus var. *longicalycinus*

den, *D. superbus* var. *speciosus* is a dwarf alpine phase from the same region. It is lower-growing with the same large, fragrant, extravagantly frilled flowers. There is a tendency for clumps to die out in the center. Should this begin to happen, top-dress in spring with a mix of gritty sand and a little loam worked into the bare center. *Dianthus superbus* var. *longicalycinus* has large, deeply fringed, pale lilac flowers with a noticeably long throat that appear from July to October. Native to Honshu, Shikoku, and Kyushu, as well as Formosa, Korea, and China, it differs from the species and other varieties in its preference for moist sites such as wet meadows and lowlands.

EDELWEISS

Woolly-haired against cold, dry alpine conditions, edelweiss, *Leontopodium alpinum,* is the embodiment of a high-mountain plant from the European Alps. Japan, too, has several species of edelweiss. From Mount Hayachine on Honshu, *L. hayachinense* is a dainty, 4- to 8-inch plant with lanceolate leaves with woolly undersides. In July and August it bears densely silver-haired flowers. Even smaller, only 3 to 6 inches high, *L. fauriei* is found in the alpine regions of northern Honshu. Plants are densely haired all over—on both sides of the leaves, the stems, and even the flowers, which appear in July and August. By comparison, *L. japonicum* is a veritable giant,

with 10- to 18-inch-long stems. The narrow leaves are covered with white woolly hairs beneath, sparsely covered above. *Leontopodium japonicum* is found on Hokkaido and Honshu, and also in China. At lower elevations these alpines are not long-lived, and their leaves may lack the flannel-like coat of woolly hairs that protects them from excessive water loss in the dry conditions at high elevations. All these alpine edelweiss need full sun and very gritty, freely draining, but not droughty, conditions; in other words, they need water, but the water must move rapidly through the soil. A soil mix of 4 parts gravel to 1 part loam is suitable.

POPPY

Papaver fauriae is a very rare, darling miniature perennial poppy from the gravelly alpine slopes of Hokkaido's Rishiri Island. Growing a scant 4 inches tall, with many divided, hairy leaves, it produces relatively large, cool lemon-yellow flowers in summer. Like other poppies it transplants poorly, so either plant seedlings, or, better, scatter seed where you want the poppies to grow. Choose a sunny, open site that has good drainage but is not parched.

TANAKEA

Picture a miniature white-flowered astilbe, and you have a good image of *Tanakea radicans*. A 4-inch-high evergreen carpet of dark green, coarsely toothed, leathery leaves develops from the creeping rhizomes below ground and the stoloniferous runners above. In summer plants produce 8-inch plumes of greenish white blossoms. A rare native of Honshu's Tokaido district, Shikoku, and Kyushu, it grows in the wild on wet, shaded rocks. In gardens try a moist but well-drained shady site with acid loamy soil. Maintain a mulch of leaf litter to encourage stoloniferous spread, and a winter mulch of pine boughs if snow cover is not reliable. Not grown widely enough to be certain, but *T. radicans* is probably hardy to zone 6.

MEADOWRUE

A dainty meadowrue suitable for the rock garden, native only to southern Japan, *Thalictrum kiusianum* grows a scant 3 to 4 inches tall. Its fluffy mauve-pink to purple flowers bloom for a long period, beginning in early summer. It prefers a humus-rich, gravelly, well-drained, lightly shaded site and loose soil conditions to encourage spread of the stoloniferous roots. Where happy, *T. kiusianum* will make a small colony. This particular meadowrue is often slow to begin new growth in spring, so be patient and don't dig too soon, or you'll be sorry.

Two other species, also native to Japan, have a wider distribution. Alpine meadowrue, *Thalictrum alpinum,* is native to temperate Asia, Europe, and North America. Suitable for a sunny rock garden in regions

with cool summers, this plant makes diminutive, 6-inch-high cushions of gray-green leaves resembling a miniature maidenhair fern, with violet-lavender flowers appearing in early summer. *Thalictrum minus* grows from temperate Asia to Europe, and is taller, from 1 to 3 feet high. In summer it produces very open panicles of greenish yellow flowers that are of negligible interest. With its finely cut, fernlike, glaucous foliage, 'Adiantifolium', growing 15 inches tall, is preferable.

AUTUMN

ORNAMENTAL ONION

If you want something pleasing for the end of the gardening season, consider *Allium thunbergii*. Found in the low mountains of Honshu, Shikoku, Kyushu, and southern Korea, the bulbs produce a grasslike mound of glossy, darkish green, somewhat floppy foliage. This plant may be rather inconsequential through spring and summer, but from September to October, its tussock produces dainty tight heads of rose-purple flowers on reasonably numerous 12-inch-tall scapes. It is an attractive companion to fall-blooming crocus such as *Crocus speciosus*. Well-behaved, this little onion does not seed about in my garden, so periodically I dig up a clump in spring, divide it into thirds or fourths, and replant. The white-flowered form grows so slowly I haven't been able to divide it.

AUTUMN CHRYSANTHEMUM

A dainty gem, *Dendranthema* (= *Chrysanthemum*) *yezoense* is a stoloniferous plant with long, creeping rhizomes. It is native to rocks along the seashore of Hokkaido and to Honshu's northern Kanto district. In September to December the mats of plants are spangled with starry little white daisies, just under an inch across, that occur alone or in pairs or trios. Quite cold-hardy, this species is useful to zone 3. Another marvelous chrysanthemum is fleshy-leaved, mat-forming *Dendranthema* (= *Chrysanthemum*) *weyrichii*. Found on the rocks near the seashores of Hokkaido, and also on Sakhalin, it blooms with pink or white daisies from August to October. This species is hardy to zone 4. Because of their spreading, mat-forming habit, both of these chrysanthemums are useful for the larger rock garden where they have ample room to sprawl. They would also be suitable for gravelly or sandy sunny banks. Other chrysanthemums are discussed in chapter 6.

GENTIANS

If ever there was a flower admired by all, it would be the gentian with its flowers of electrifying blue. *Gentiana scabra* var. *buergeri* is fall-blooming gentian, flowering in September to November. It is common in wet meadows, grassy places, and thickets in lowlands and at low elevations in the mountains of Honshu, Shikoku, and Kyushu. Erect stems reach 12 to 15 inches tall, making a compact bushy plant. Other forms of this gentian have decumbent stems that lie flat to the ground. These are elegant splayed over a rock where they can trail in a delightful fashion. Several bright campanula-blue flowers, each over 1 inch long, cluster together at the ends of the stems. Partial shade and a moist fertile soil give best results. A site on the north side of a house, bright and open to the sky but with little direct sun, worked well for me. *Gentiana triflora* var. *japonica* blooms in August and September. Found in the lowlands of Hokkaido, and in Honshu from the north to the northern Kinki district along the Japan Sea, it also occurs in the southern Kuriles and Sakhalin. Deep sky-blue to purple flowers, each nearly 2 inches long, are clustered in the upper leaf axils and at the tips of stems that can reach 18 inches. Moist, acid, humus-rich soil and semishade are the most suitable conditions. *Gentiana makinoi* is found in alpine pastures and bogs, and on wet slopes in the alpine and sometimes subalpine regions of high mountains in Honshu's central district. Pale blue, richly spotted, 1½-inch-long flowers cluster in August and September at the ends of the erect, unbranched, 12- to 24-inch stems and in the upper leaf axils. This species would be a good choice for a suitable waterscape garden site.

Mother of Thousands, or Strawberry Geranium

It fascinates me how we develop preconceived ideas about plants and their hardiness or garden suitability, only to have the plant prove otherwise. Mother of thousands, or strawberry geranium, *Saxifraga stolonifera,* is typically grown in containers. A popular houseplant for hanging baskets, you've no doubt seen its little plantlets dangling from long, thin, red stolons. The

Saxifraga nipponica

rosettes of bristly leaves—medium- to olive-green, silver-veined above, and flushed with red beneath—are handsome in their own right. Imagine my surprise when I first saw this plant outdoors, elegantly festooning a rock outcrop in a Larchmont, New York, garden. Checking Owhi's *Flora,* I learned that strawberry geranium is native to wet soils and rocks in Honshu, Shikoku, and Kyushu, and also China, and is frequently planted in gardens. So it is sufficiently hardy for a protected, rather shady, rock garden situated in zone 6. I've seen it in Atlanta, Georgia, where winters are significantly milder. In July and August plants produce 12-inch-long stems with loose airy panicles of white flowers. 'Cuscutiformis' has leaves marbled in maroon and green with red undersides, and is reportedly somewhat hardier; 'Tricolor' (= 'Magic Carpet') has prettily variegated dark green, gray-green, and ivory-white leaves, with a soft overlay of pink to rose, but flowers poorly.

Saxifraga stolonifera is recognizable by the uneven length of the narrow flower petals. If this species can be grown in zone 6 gardens, adding its starry sprays of lopsided flowers to the summer rock garden, what other species might also be suitable for semishaded sites with soils high in organic matter? The typical species for the Diptera section (those saxifrages with uneven petals) is *S. cortusaefolia*. Rounded to kidney-shaped, the fleshy, green, hairy leaves, from 1 to 6 inches long and from 1 to 7 inches wide, are often deeply cleft into 5 to 11 lobes. The plants make tidy rosettes and have no stolons. Rather rare in the wild, plants are found in wet shaded places, especially on rocks and along mountain streams in Honshu's Kanto district and westward, and on Shikoku and Kyushu. Choose a site with moist acid soil high in organic matter, where the plants will be sheltered from early frosts that can damage the flowers. Plants bloom in September and October, sending up 16-inch-high stems with a shower of starry white flowers.

Saxifraga fortunei is native to wet rocks in the mountains of Hokkaido, Honshu, Shikoku, and Kyushu, and also to southern Sakhalin, the southern Kuriles, Korea, Manchuria, Ussuri, and China. Its large, fleshy, shiny basal leaves are up to 4 inches across, rounded, 7-lobed, and somewhat toothed along the margin. Leaves are green above, reddish brown beneath. In late autumn plants produce a 15-inch red flower stalk, with a loose panicle of starry white flowers. There are several selections: 'Rubrifolium' has reddish brown leaves for a handsome contrast to the white flowers; 'Wada's Variety' has shorter mahogany-red flower stems and mahogany-red leaves.

Saxifraga fortunei var. *incisolobata*

SEDUM

Taxonomists have shifted most of the species in the genus *Sedum* to *Hylotelphium*. I'm sure they have their reasons, but to my mind, sedum is still sedum. *Sedum sieboldii* is the neatest autumn-flowering succulent, found on Shodoshima in Shikoku's Sanuki province. The arching, trailing stems, 6 to 12 inches long, have glaucous to purple fleshy leaves that are attractive in their own right. The purple color appears strongest in cool weather. Plants bloom rather late, in October or November; the dense clusters of pale pink flowers at the tips of the stems are accented with reddish purple to purple anthers. Choose a sunny site with good drainage. I combine this sedum with blue sheep's fescue, *Festuca ovina* cultivars with intense silver-blue tussocks of leaves, the little autumn-flowering onion discussed earlier, and a fall-blooming crocus such as *Crocus speciosus*, with lavender flowers. 'Mediovariegatum' has leaves with a yellow-white blotch at the center; 'Variegatum' has glaucous blue leaves marbled with cream. Both of these have proven less hardy for me.

PLANTS FOR WET SITES

Water may present itself as an open pond, a shaded wet swamp, a sunny reed-filled marsh, or even a poorly drained meadow with constantly wet soil. The quantity of water, and whether the site is sunny or shady, directly influences which plants will grow there. Familiar herbaceous perennials such as astilbe and rogersia grow best with consistently moist soil and do not tolerate dry conditions. Chapters 3, 4, 6, and 7 include plants that would also be suitable for moist to wet soil.

Pond Plants

WATER LILIES
Pond plants are true aquatics, with a year-round need for open, standing water. The classic aquatic for gardens is the water lily.

Pygmy water lily, *Nymphaea tetragona* var. *tetragona,* is a dainty, hardy, dwarf water lily with 4-inch-wide leaves and somewhat fragrant 2-inch-wide white flowers that float on the water's surface. The flowers appear from July to October, opening in the morning and then closing at night. The young leaves are streaked, splashed, or entirely blotched with brown. Even mature leaves are red on their underside. Found in ponds and shallow lakes, this plant has a wide distribution: Hokkaido, Honshu, Shikoku and Kyushu in Japan; and eastern Siberia, Manchuria, China, Korea, India, and North America. It is suitable for container use, in man-made pools, or any similarly confined space, growing happily in water only 2 to 6 inches deep. It is hardy in zones 2 to 9. This species was used by Marliac of France to produce his dwarf 'Laydekerii' hybrids: 'Laydekeri Fulgens' has 4-inch-diameter wine-red flowers with red stamens; 'Laydekeri Lilacea' has fragrant lilac-pink flowers with orange-red stamens; 'Laydekeri Purpurea' has green leaves and carmine-red flowers with orange-red stamens; and 'Rubra' has purple-tinted leaves and dark red flowers with orange stamens.

Lotus
There are two different genera commonly called lotus: the sacred lotus, *Nelumbo,* and yellow pond lily, *Nuphar.* Both are aquatic perennials with stout, creeping, invasive rhizomes.

Sacred Lotus

Sacred lotus, *Nelumbo nucifera,* is a large perennial with leaves up to 20 inches across, and flowers 8 inches in diameter. The slightly cupped, bluish green leaves are held above the water on stems from 3 to 6 feet tall. Raindrops collect in the hollowed leaf until their gathered mass tips the leaf. The water rolls off, and the dry leaf, upright once more, begins the collection process again. It has been suggested that the tilting bamboo pipe that repeatedly fills with water and empties, striking a wooden block with a hollow *tock*, is based on this natural occurrence. In autumn the leaves stiffen as they turn brown and dry, rustling together on their long stems as breezes scatter autumn foliage on its descent. The flowers are a deep rose-pink, sometimes white. The seeds are held in a spongy receptacle, peeping out like peas embedded in Swiss cheese. This receptacle hardens as it matures, and is popular in dried flower arrangements. Native in Asia from Iran to Japan, and in south Australia, sacred lotus is frequently cultivated in ponds and shallow lakes.

Yellow Pond Lily

There are several species of *Nuphar* in Japan. Though common, these tend to be a little too vigorous for most garden ponds. Yellow pond lily, *Nuphar japonica,* is found in the ponds, lakes, and shallow streams of Honshu, Shikoku, and Kyushu, and Hokkaido's southwestern district. Its creeping rhizomes lie in the muck of the pond bottom; its 2-inch-wide golden-yellow flowers float at or just a few inches above the water's surface from June to September. The tough, leathery floating leaves are narrowly oval, up to 1 foot long, and 5 inches wide, while those submerged in spring are narrower and thinner in texture. *Nuphar japonica* is hardy to zone 5. *Nuphar pumila,* also called yellow pond lily, is native to Hokkaido's eastern districts and Honshu's northern districts, and to Europe, Russia, and Siberia. It is hardy to zone 4. The broadly oval floating leaves are 4 inches long and wide, sometimes larger, with small, 1-inch starlike, floating yellow flowers appearing in July and August.

Fox Nuts

Fox nuts, *Euryale ferox,* is a giant aquatic with puckered, sparsely spined, olive-green leaves up to 5 feet across. The young leaves are especially wrinkled and rumpled, and prominently marked with veins in a tidy geometric pattern. The smallish, 2-inch red, purple, or lilac flowers appear from August to October, weather permitting, and are partially to entirely immersed in the water. Native to ponds and lakes in the lowlands of Honshu and Kyushu, fox nuts are also found growing wild in India, China, and Formosa. They are tender, and can best be grown as a perennial in warm summer regions such as zone 8 and higher. Elsewhere they should be grown as enormous aquatic annuals.

Wet Meadows, Marshes, and Swamps

In addition to the plants suggested in this section, you should keep in mind other likely candidates for sites with wet soil, discussed elsewhere in this book. Certainly there are shrubs and trees you should consider, as well as perennials such as ferns, astilbe, and rodgersia.

MEADOW SWEET

Japanese meadow sweet, *Filipendula purpurea* (= *F. palmata*), has long been cultivated in Japan. A handsome plant for deep, fertile, moist soils adjacent to a pond or in a wet meadow, it grows 2½ to 4 feet tall. Plants often have purple stems and attractive pinnately compound leaves with the last leaflet palmate. In summer numerous small pink to purple-red flowers in dense clusters top the stems. Hardy in zones 3 to 8, flowering begins in late May in warmer gardens, mid-June in Connecticut, late June in colder regions. When choosing a place in your garden for Japanese meadow sweet, consider constancy of moisture and whether your location is in a southern or northern region. Full sun is suitable for cooler gardens with moist soil, partial shade for average moisture in warmer sites. 'Alba' (= f. *albiflora*) has white flowers; 'Purpurascens' has strongly purple-tinted leaves.

HOSTA

Hostas, discussed in chapters 5 and 7, offer myriad possibilities for shaded sites with damp soil.

KAMCHATKA SKUNK CABBAGE

If this plant's common name puts you off, think again. "Rose is a rose is a rose is a rose," according to Gertrude Stein, but this is a skunk cabbage with panache. To begin with, Kamchatka skunk cabbage, *Lysichiton camtschatcense,* is in a different genus than the well-known eastern skunk cabbage, *Symplocarpus foetidus.* Kamchatka skunk cabbage is common in swampy places in Hokkaido and Honshu's central and northern district, and is also native to the Kuriles, Kamchatka, Sakhalin, and Ussuri. A large perennial for gardens to zone 5 with wet places and adequate room, this plant has paddlelike leaves up to 40 inches long and 12 inches wide. In May or June plants have pristine white, 10-inch-high spathes that wrap around the flowers, in a very showy fashion. In the wild these grow in imposing colonies, their fleshy roots happy in the oozy mud of periodically flooded wet meadows. Related to the Kamchatka skunk cabbage, *L. americanus* from the Pacific Northwest has yellow spathes. The two species can interbreed, producing offspring with delicious, ivory to creamy-yellow spathes.

BUTTERBUR, OR SWEET COLTSFOOT

Butterbur, *Petasites japonicus,* is a plant of bold scale, with kidney-shaped basal leaves up to 30 inches in diameter. It is found in moist woods and thickets along streams in the hills and mountains of Honshu, Shikoku, and Kyushu, as well as Korea, China, and Ryukyu. Hardy to zone 5, milky-white flowers appear in late winter to early spring, long before the leaves emerge. They cluster in a dense head, like a bouquet erupting from the bare ground. This is a plant with an attitude: large leaves, spreading roots, and an aggressive nature reaching out for new territory. Butterbur is gathered as a wild vegetable, and also cultivated for the same purpose. Young, unopened leaves are briefly steamed and served with a dipping sauce or prepared as tempura. More mature stems are simmered in soy sauce thinned and flavored with sake and mirin, until the liquid has been absorbed. It is then refrigerated and served cold. 'Variegatus' has leaves attractively splotched and streaked with cream to milky-yellow markings. *Petasites japonicus* var. *giganteus* is gigantic indeed, with leaves up to 5 feet in diameter supported on 6-foot-long petioles. It is native to Hokkaido and Honshu's northern districts, and can also be found in Sakhalin to the southern and central Kuriles.

PRIMROSES

Primula japonica is an easily grown cande-labra primrose suitable for damp sites on the banks of a pond, along a stream, in wet woods, or in any boggy site in sun or shade. It is discussed in chapter 7.

Primula modesta is a charming little primrose from the rocky subalpine mountains of Hokkaido, Honshu's central and northern districts, Shikoku, and Kyushu. Only 4 to 5 inches tall, this treasure has leaves whose undersides are powdered with gold dust. The yellow-eyed flowers are pale lavender, pink, or, rarely, white. As few as 2 or 3, often 7 or 8, cluster at the top of a 2- to 6-inch-high stem. A moist, fertile, gritty soil in a sunny meadow is ideal for *P. modesta,* if competition will not overwhelm it, or grow it on a gravel bar near a gentle streamlet. As it is likely to be short-lived, it is a good idea to keep new plants coming from seed.

BURNET

As discussed in chapter 6, there are Japanese burnets suitable for wet meadow situations: *Sanguisorba obtusa;* its white form, *S. obtusa* 'Alba' (= var. *albiflora*); and *S. hakusanensis.*

ORCHIDS

Snowy heron grass, *Habenaria* (= *Pectilis*) *radiata,* is widespread over Honshu, Shikoku, and Kyushu, where it grows in open, sunny, wet marshes covered with grass or sphagnum. It is a plant of lower elevation, at altitudes of 325 to 975 feet. In the past it has been sold through mail-order catalogs, mixed in with perennials and bulbs. As an orchid it currently falls under the protection of the Convention on the Internation Trade of Endangered Species, Appendix II, which regulates its exportation from Japan, and importation into other countries. Easy to cultivate, this charming plant does well in containers or in a suitable garden—sunny, with moist to wet, well-drained soil in zone 7. The orchid produces small, pea-sized, hairy-looking resting tubers. Pot the tubers in a sphagnum and gravel blend and keep moist. Turface, an expanded clay product used on golf courses, can be substituted for the gravel. Water daily while in growth, and tip the excess moisture out every second or third day. The tubers contain enough energy to produce several slender grasslike leaves about 12 to 15 inches long. Two or three crystalline white flowers will appear, fringed along the outer edge and resembling in miniature the outspread wings of a great white heron. The tricky part is satisfying the plant's need for a winter dormant period. Leave the tubers in the pot, but do not allow the medium to dry out. In Japan, some enthusiasts grow the tubers in straight, live sphagnum without any gravel. If live sphagnum is used, water must not contain chlorine or high levels of calcium as these can kill the moss. In winter the tubers, still in their container, should be kept just above freezing, perhaps in the refrigerator. Repot the plant in spring. Where winters are mild enough so that the ground does not freeze deeply, and summers not hot and humid, the snowy heron grass can be grown in a suitably wet swale or bog garden.

Nursery Sources

I f this book whets your appetite, start looking for plants that catch your fancy. Well-known plants native to Japan (balloon flower, chrysanthemum, peony, black pine, and chamaecyparis, for example) are found at many nurseries. They are usually cultivars. It is when you seek the wildflowers of Japan that availability is limited. The nurseries listed here do not specialize in Japanese plants. Rather, they have an uncommon selection of plants that includes some from Japan. Mail-order sources ship small plants. Do not expect specimen-size trees to be crammed into your mailbox or lugged up the driveway by a grunting United Parcel Service deliverer. Often specialty nurseries have modest quantities of each item, and what is currently listed may not be in the next year's catalogue. My mother used to say that if you saw something you really wanted you'd better get it, as next time it would either not be available or cost twice as much. Remember that catalogues cost money to print. Send $2 or $3 with your request, for printing and mailing costs. I have not yet ordered from all these nurseries, but I'm working on it.

Kurt Bluemel, Inc.
2740 Greene Lane
Baldwin, MD 21013-9523
tel: (410) 557-7229

> Well-known specialist in ornamental grasses and grasslike plants: acorus, bamboos, carex, equisetum, hakonechloa, imperata, miscanthus, pennisetum, themeda, and more. Additionally, the nursery offers a selection of ferns and perennials that includes a few Japanese species/cultivars.

Burt Associates
P.O. Box 719
Westford, MA 01886
tel: (508) 692-3240

> Albert Adelman sells bamboos large and small, intended for indoor use. Container-grown, their rhizomes are in a more compact mass than that of free-range specimens.

Camellia Forest Nursery
125 Carolina Forest Road
Chapel Hill, NC 27516
tel: (919) 967-5529

> David Parks's nursery offers camellias and a wide range of rare Asian trees and shrubs. Camellias include hybrids and older, historical cultivars of *Camellia japonica; C. sasanqua* selections; and *C. oleifera* hybrids. Other shrubs and trees include clerodendrum, cleyera, eurya, *Prunus* x 'Okame', and more.

Collector's Nursery
16804 NE 102nd Avenue
Battle Ground, WA 98604
tel: (360) 574-3832

> How many choice plants can be collected in a finite space? Plant connoisseurs Bill Janssen and Diana Reeck possess enviable skills in growing and propagating plants. Their enticing list includes peren-

nials from acorus to *Viola dissecta* var. *sieboldii,* and selected trees and shrubs.

Fairweather Gardens
P.O. Box 330
Greenwich, NJ 08323
tel: (609) 451-6261

> Robert Hoffman and Robert Popham run a relatively new nursery (opened in 1989) that already offers a diverse selection of woody plants. Their list includes Japanese maples of several species, calli-carpa, camellias, clerodendrum, crape myrtles, magnolias, crab apples, *Prunus* x 'Okame', stewartia, and styrax.

Fancy Fronds
1911 4th Avenue West
Seattle, WA 98119
tel: (206) 284-5332

> Judith Jones's specialty nursery offers ferns, ferns, ferns, and yet more ferns. Some are from Japan, described in a catalogue with an impassioned viewpoint.

Foliage Gardens
2003 128th Avenue SE
Bellevue, WA 98005
tel: (206) 747-2998

> Sue Olsen has a remarkable listing of ferns and their cultivars, including a few of Japanese origin.

Forest Farm
990 Tetherow Road
Williams, OR 97544-9599
tel: (503) 846-7269

> Ray and Peg Prager mostly sell woody plants, primarily in small sizes (the kind you'd grow on a nursery row for a couple of years). They also offer a few items in 1-gallon or 5-gallon size. Plants

include: Japanese fir, many kinds of maples, Japanese alder, plum yew, dogwoods, cryptomeria, loquat, hydrangeas, kerrias, crape myrtles, Japanese larch, magnolias, crab apples, spruces, pines, cherries, Japanese hemlock, grasses, sedges, and perennials.

Gossler Farms Nursery
1200 Weaver Road
Springfield, OR 97478-9691
tel: (503) 746-3922

> This nursery offers a wonderful array of selected woody plants: dogwoods, hydrangeas, maples, an especially diverse selection of magnolias, *Prunus* x 'Okame', rhododendrons, schizophragma, stewartia, styrax, *Vitis coignetiae,* and more.

Heronswood Nursery Ltd.
7530 288th Street NE
Kingston, WA 98346

> Dan Hinkley and Robert Jones list a wide range of woody plants and a potpourri of perennials. They offer a diversity of chamaecyparis, Japanese larch, pines, podocarpus, sciadopitys, maples, magnolias; beautyberry, camellias, eurya, hydrangeas, skimmia, spirea; several vines; and a number of perennials.

Limerock Ornamental Grasses
R.D. 1, Box 111-C
Port Matilda, PA 16870
tel: (814) 692-2272

> Norm and Phyllis Hooven specialize in ornamental grasses and grasslike plants: acorus, carex, variegated Japanese grass, a nice selection of miscanthus and pennisetum, Japanese themeda, and more. They also offer a selection of fall-flowering perennials and ferns to compliment the grasses.

Plant Delights Nursery
9241 Sauls Road
Raleigh, NC 27603
tel: (919) 772-4794

> Tony Avent offers an astonishing array of primarily herbaceous plants, with a few woody goodies tucked in here and there. Japanese plants include several acorus, cryptomeria, ferns, grasses, lycoris, lysmachia, ophiopogon, reineckia, rohdea, salvia, tricyrtis, and more.

Roslyn Nursery
211 Burrs Lane
Dix Hills, NY 11746
tel: (516) 643-9347

> Dr. Philip Waldman is interested in rhododendrons, and offers a diverse selection of species and cultivars. Among the other available plants are pieris, camellias, dwarf and slow-growing conifers, some maples, and magnolias.

Siskyou Rare Plant Nursery
2825 Cummings Road
Medford, OR 97501
tel: (503) 772-6846

> Baldassare Mineo specializes in small, low-growing plants suitable for the rock garden and woodland garden. In his catalogue are such elegant Japanese plants as columbines, arisaemas, chrysanthemums, *Lysichiton camtschatcense,* nandinas, primulas, rhododendrons, and thalictrum. He also offers dwarf conifers, small and miniature trees, and ferns.

Steve Ray's Bamboo Gardens
909 79th Place South
Birmingham, AL 35206
(205) 833-3052

> Steve and Janie Ray dig and ship bamboos from September through

March. They also offer container plants available for year-round local pickup. Their catalogue gives cultural information along with plant descriptions, and they invite you to make an appointment to visit their groves and help select your own bamboo.

Tradewinds Bamboo Nursery
28446 Hunter Creek Loop
Gold Beech, OR 97444
tel: (503) 247-0853

Gib and Diane Cooper sell all types of bamboo: clumping and running, hardy and tender, tall and small. They propagate their plants and offer a very nice selection of dwarf, shrub, hedge or screening, and timber bamboo.

We-Du Nurseries
Route 5, Box 724
Marion, NC 28752
tel: (704) 738-8300

Dick Weaver and Rene Duval are particularly interested in the Asian counterparts of our native wildflowers, and also specialize in nursery-propagated plants native to the Southeast. Their offerings include mosses, ferns, carex, cimicifuga, *Hemerocallis* sp., iris, lycoris, ophiopogon, patrinia, polygonatum, reineckia, violets, and more.

United States Hardiness Zones

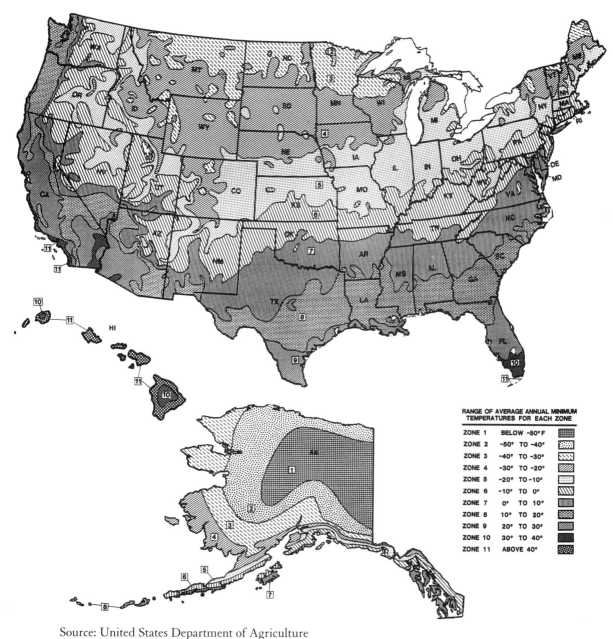

RANGE OF AVERAGE ANNUAL MINIMUM
TEMPERATURES FOR EACH ZONE

ZONE 1	BELOW -50° F	
ZONE 2	-50° TO -40°	
ZONE 3	-40° TO -30°	
ZONE 4	-30° TO -20°	
ZONE 5	-20° TO -10°	
ZONE 6	-10° TO 0°	
ZONE 7	0° TO 10°	
ZONE 8	10° TO 20°	
ZONE 9	20° TO 30°	
ZONE 10	30° TO 40°	
ZONE 11	ABOVE 40°	

Source: United States Department of Agriculture

Zone	Range of Average Annual Minimum Temperature	Example
Zone 1	below -50° Fahrenheit	*Empetrum nigrum*
Zone 2	-50° to -40°	*Cornus canadensis*
Zone 3	-40° to -30°	*Abies veitchii*
		Berberis thunbergii
		Rosa rugosa
Zone 4	-30° to -20°	*Malus floribunda*
Zone 5	-20° to -10°	*Chamaecyparis pisifera*
		Cornus kousa
		Deutzia gracilis
		Ginkgo biloba
		Taxus cuspidata
Zone 6	-10° to 0°	*Acer palmatum*
		Ilex crenata
		Ligustrum ovalifolium
		Pieris japonica
Zone 7	0° to 10°	*Acuba japonica*
		Camellia sasanqua
		Rhododendron Kurume hybrids
Zone 8	10° to 20°	*Eriobotrya japonica*
		Pittosporum tobira
Zone 9	20° to 30°	*Ardisia crenata*
		Cycas revoluta
Zone 10	30° to 40°	

Recognize that zone ratings are just the beginning. They only identify the range of average annual minimum temperatures, and do not include information on duration. A nightly drop in temperature, with warming the following day, is quite different from steady low temperatures for several weeks. When reliable snow cover shelters herbaceous plants, they may survive in a colder zone than might be expected. Soil moisture can be critical; generally, plants survive better on sites with good drainage than on those that stay moist to wet in winter. Plants, especially ever-green perennials and broadleaved evergreen shrubs, suffer leaf damage when exposed to drying winds and early sunlight in winter in zone 6 and colder.

Heat tolerance is another factor. Athens, Georgia, and central California both fall within zone 8. Their average annual minimum tem-perature is the same, but humidity, rainfall, and (most especially) sum-mer nighttime temperatures are very different. Summer heat and humidity in zones 8, 9, and 10 will kill plants unable to tolerate those conditions, especially where there is little if any variation between day-time and nighttime temperatures.

Every garden has microclimates, pockets that are more sheltered, or more exposed, than elsewhere on the property. These sites provide an opportunity to experiment with plants whose hardiness goes beyond that suggested by zone rating alone.

Bibliography

Coats, Alice M. *Garden Shrubs and Their Histories.* New York: Simon and Schuster, 1992.

Creech, John Lewis. *Plant Explorations: Ornamentals in Southern Japan.* Washington, D.C.: Agricultural Research Service of the U.S. Department of Agriculture in cooperation with Longwood Gardens of the Longwood Foundation, Inc., 1957.

——. *Ornamental Plant Explorations—Japan 1961.* Washington, D.C.: Agricultural Research Service of the U.S. Department of Agriculture in cooperation with Longwood Gardens of the Longwood Foundation, Inc., 1966.

den Boer, Arie F. *Ornamental Crabapples.* The American Association of Nurserymen, 1959.

Engel, David H. *Japanese Gardens for Today.* Rutland, Vt.: Charles E. Tuttle Co., 1969.

Fairchild, David. *The World Was My Garden.* New York: Charles Scribner's Sons, 1938.

Fiala, Fr. John L. *Flowering Crabapples: The Genus* Malus. Portland, Ore.: Timber Press, 1994.

Foster, H. Lincoln. *Rock Gardening.* Boston: Houghton Mifflin Co., 1968.

Glattstein, Judy. "Hardy Aroids in the Garden." *Arnoldia* 47, no. 2 (Spring 1987): 27–34.

Gothein, Marie Luise. *A History of Garden Art.* Vol. 2. Edited by Water P. Wright. Translated from the German by Mrs. Archer-Hind. New York: E. P. Dutton & Co., 1928.

Grenfell, Diana. *Hosta: The Flowering Foliage Plant.* Portland, Ore.: Timber Press, 1990.

Griffiths, Mark. *Index of Garden Plants.* Portland, Ore.: Timber Press, 1994.

Halfacre, R. Gordon, and Anne Rogers Shawcroft. *Landscape Plants of the Southeast.* 5th ed. Raleigh, N.C.: Sparks Press, 1989.

Hansen, Richard, and Friedrich Stahl. *Perennials and Their Garden Habitats.* 4th ed. Portland, Ore.: Timber Press, 1993.

Haworth-Booth, Michael. *The Flowering Shrub Garden.* London: Country Life, 1938.

———. *The Hydrangeas.* 5th ed. London: Constable and Co., 1984.

Ihei, Ito. *A Brocade Pillow, Azaleas of Old Japan.* Translated by Kaname Kato. New York: Weatherhill, 1984.

Ingram, Collingwood. *Ornamental Cherries.* New York: Charles Scribner's Sons, 1948.

Jelitto, Leo, and Wilhelm Schacht. *Hardy Herbaceous Perennials.* 3rd ed. 2 vols. Portland, Ore.: Timber Press, 1990.

Johnson, Arthur T. *Rhododendrons, Azaleas, Magnolias, Camellias and Ornamental Cherries.* London: My Garden, 1948.

Kaempfer, Engelbert. *A History of Japan.* 3 vols. Glasgow: James MacLehose and Sons, 1906.

Kitamura, Fumio, and Yurio Ishizu. *Garden Plants in Japan.* Tokyo: Kokusai Bunka Shinkokai, 1963.

Klaber, Doretta. *Primroses and Spring.* New York: M. Barrows & Co., 1966.

Krussmann, Gerd. *Manual of Cultivated Conifers.* Rev. ed. Portland, Ore.: Timber Press, 1985.

Kudo, Yushan. "The Vegetation of Yezo." *Japanese Journal of Botany* (Tokyo) 2, no. 4 (1925).

Mickel, John. *Ferns for American Gardens.* New York: Macmillan Publishing Co., 1994.

Oakes, A. J. *Ornamental Grasses and Grasslike Plants.* New York: Van Nostrand Reinhold, 1990.

Ohashi, Hiroyoshi, and Jin Murata. "Taxonomy of the Japanese *Arisaema* (Araceae)." *Journal of the Faculty of Science* (University of Tokyo), Sect. 3, 12 (31 March 1989): 281–336.

Ohwi, Jisaburo. *Flora of Japan.* Washington, D.C.: Smithsonian Institution, 1984.

Onoe, Kochi, with Kazuko Fujii and Kazuo Mori. *The Wild Flowers of Japan.* Hyogo-ken: n.p., 1981.

Sansom, George. *A History of Japan 1615–1867.* Palo Alto, Calif.: Stanford University Press, 1963.

Sargent, Charles Sprague. *Forest Flora of Japan.* Boston and New York: Houghton, Mifflin and Co., 1894.

Siren, Osvald. *Gardens of China.* New York: Ronald Press Co., 1949.

Stout, A. B. *Daylilies.* New York: Macmillan Co., 1934.

Takeda, H. *Alpine Flowers of Japan.* Tokyo: Sanseido Co., 1938.

Thunberg, Charles Peter. *Travels in Europe, Africa, and Asia, performed between the years 1770 and 1779. Containing a Voyage to Japan and Travels in Different Parts of That Empire in the years 1775 and 1776.* Vol. 3. London: F. and C. Rivington, 1795.

Van Melle, P. J. *Shrubs and Trees for the Small Place.* New York: Charles Scribner's Sons, 1943.

Weaver, Richard E., Jr. "Exotic Orchids in the Garden." *Arnoldia* 41, no. 4 (July/August 1981): 128–149.

———. *Orchids for Everyone. Arnoldia* 44, no. 1 (Winter 1983–84).

Wiley, Peter Booth, with Korogi Ichiro. *Yankees in the Land of the Gods.* New York: Viking Penguin, 1990.

Wilson, Ernest Henry. *The Conifers and Taxads of Japan.* Publications of the Arnold Arboretum: no. 8. Cambridge: Cambridge University Press, 1916.

Yoshikawa, Isao. *Elements of Japanese Gardens.* Translated by Christopher D. Witmer. Tokyo: Graphic-sha Publishing Co., 1990.

Index of Plant Names

Abies
    Abies firma, 61
    Abies homolepis, 61
    Abies veitchii, 36, 61–62, 210
Acer, 14. *See also* maple
    Acer buergerianum, 44
    Acer circinatum, 43
    Acer ginnala, 44
    Acer griseum, 78
    Acer japonicum, 43–44, 45–46
    Acer maximowiczianum, 36
    Acer palmatum, 33, 42–43, 45–46, 210
    Acer pensylvanicum, 44
    Acer pseudosieboldianum, 46
    Acer rufinerve, 44
    Acer shirasawanum, 43–44, 46
    Acer sieboldianum, 45
Aconitum chinensis, 144–45
Aconitum sanyoense, 144
Acorus gramineus, 32
Actinidia kolomikta, 104
Adenophora
    Adenophora nikoensis, 192
    Adenophora takedae, 144
    Adenophora tashiroi, 192
    Adenophora triphylla var. *japonica,* 145
Adiantum aleuticum var. *japonicum,* 170
Adonis amurensis, 150–51

Agastache rugosa, 126–27
Ajania pacifica, 39
Akebia quinata, 33, 104
Albizzia julibrissin, 46, 47
Alcea rosea, 28
alder, 17, 18
Allium thunbergii, 194
Alnus maximowiczii, 17
Amaryllis hallii, 34
Ampelopsis brevipedunculata, 33, 105
Anemone
    Anemone caroliniana, 121–22
    Anemone flaccida, 151
    Anemone hupehensis var. *japonica,* 145–46
    Anemone narcissiflora, 17
Anemonopsis macrophylla, 19, 179
anisetree, 72
Athyrium nipponicum, 171
Athyrium otophorum, 171
apricot, 59–60
Aquilegia. See also columbine
    Aquilegia buergeriana, 124
    Aquilegia flabellata, 124, 187–88
    Aquilegia flabellata var. *pumila,* 188
    Aquilegia oxysepala, 124
Arachnoides standishii, 170–71
Ardisia, 18, 90
    Ardisia crenata, 90, 111, 210

Ardisia japonica, 111

Arisaema (jack-in-the-pulpit), 153–55

    Arisaema draconitum, 19

    Arisaema japonicum, 155

    Arisaema kiusianum, 154

    Arisaema niponicum, 153–54

    Arisaema ringens, 154

    Arisaema serratum, 155

    Arisaema sikokianum, 153, 154

    Arisaema thunbergii var. *urashima,* 28, 35, 154

    Arisaema triphyllum, 19

artemisias, 4

Arundo donax, 18

Asarum

    Asarum ariifolia, 183

    Asarum calulescens, 183

    Asarum canadensis, 183

    Asarum europeum, 183, 185

    Asarum kumagianum, 184

    Asarum megacalyx, 184

    Asarum nipponicum, 184

    Asarum shuttleworthii, 184

    Asarum sieboldii, 183

ash, 17, 18

Aspidistra elatior, 186

Aster x *frikarti,* 127

Astilbe, 12

    Astilbe astilboides, 167

    Astilbe chinensis var. *davidii,* 167

    Astilbe japonica, 167

    Astilbe microphylla, 167–68

    Astilbe simplicifolia, 167

    Astilbe thunbergii, 167

    Astilbe x *arendsii,* 167

Aucuba japonica, 13, 18, 29, 32, 36, 90–91

Aucuba japonica var. *borealis,* 91

azaleas, 5, 8, 10–11, 25, 29, 73–102

    Glen Dale azalea, 76

    Hirado azalea, 75–76

    Kaempferi azalea, 78–79

    Kurume azalea, 77–78

    Mollis azalea, 77

    snow azalea, 77

balloon flower, 8, 133–34

bamboo, 7, 18–19, 37, 47–48. *See also Pleioblastus, Sasa, and Semiarundinaria*

    dwarf bamboo, 112–13

    heavenly bamboo, 18, 98–99

beautyberry, 87

bellflower, 127–28. *See also* campanula

Berberis thunbergii, 210

Betula

    Betula ermanii var. *nipponica,* 17

    Betula maximowicziana, 36

    Betula plantyphylla var. *japonica,* 38

bigleaf hydrangea, 19

birch, alpine, 17

bittersweet, 110

black pine, 18

black sarana, 16

bleeding heart, 125

bletilla, 159–60

blood grass, 39, 134–35

Boston ivy, 33, 109

bunchberry, 17

burnet, 147–48, 201

bush clover, 7–8, 19, 146–47

butterbur, 201

Calanthe, 155–58

    Calanthe discolor, 156

    Calanthe discolor var. *bicolor* f. *sieboldii,* 156

    Calanthe striata, 156, 157

    Calanthe tricarinata, 157

Callicarpa dichotoma, 87

Callicarpa japonica, 87

camellia, 10, 18, 25, 69–70

    Camellia japonica, 69

    Camellia sasanqua, 69, 210

Campanula

    Campanula carpatica, 82

    Campanula chamissonis, 188

    Campanula glomerata var. *dahurica,* 127

    Campanula lasiocarpa, 188

    Campanula punctata, 127–28

    Campanula punctata var. *hondoensis,* 127

Cardiocrinum cordatum, 141–42
Cardiocrinum giganteum, 142
Carex morrowii var. *expallida,* 39
carpet grass, 37
cast iron plant, 186
cedar, 14, 18, 63–64
Celastrus orbiculatus, 110
Celastrus scandens, 110
Cephalotaxus harringtonia, 91–93
Chaenomeles
    Chaenomeles japonica, 80–81
    Chaenomeles japonica f. *alba,* 81
    Chaenomeles japonica var. *alpina,* 81
    Chaenomeles speciosa, 33, 80
Chamaecyparis obtusa, 62–63, 93
Chamaecyparis pisifera, 63, 94, 210
cherry trees, 5, 6, 8, 10, 37, 55–59. *See also Prunus*
chestnut, 18
Chinese juniper, 96–97
Chrysanthemum, 6–8, 12, 143–44, 195
    Chrysanthemum indicum, 29
    Chrysanthemum nipponicum, 144
    Chrysanthemum pacificum, 39
    Chrysanthemum x *morifolium,* 143
Cimicifuga
    Cimicifuga japonica var. *acerina,* 179
    Cimicifuga simplex, 179
clematis, 25, 105
    Clematis florida, 105
    Clematis fusca, 106
    Clematis japonica, 106
    Clematis patens, 106
    Clematis terniflora, 106
Clerodendrum trichotomum, 83
clethra, 18, 19
    Clethra alnifolia, 87–88
    Clethra barbinervis, 88
cleyera, 70–71
    Cleyera japonica, 70–71
climbing fig, 107
climbing hydrangea, 18, 108
Colchicum autumnale, 180
columbine, 124, 187–88
common camellia, 13

Conandron ramondioides, 188–89
Convallaria, 32
coralberry, 13
Cornus
    Cornus alternifolia, 49
    Cornus canadensis, 210
    Cornus controversa, 49
    Cornus florida, 48–49
    Cornus kousa, 48, 210
Corylopsis pauciflora, 56
crab apples, 53–54
crape-myrtle, 38
creeping fig, 38
Crocus speciosus, 87, 194, 198
cryptomeria, 27
    Cryptomeria japonica, 63–64
    Cryptomeria japonica var. *elegans,* 64
Cycas revoluta, 30, 32, 94–95, 210
Cymbidium goeringii, 158
Cypripedium japonicum, 158–59
Cyrtomium
    Cyrtomium caryotidum, 171–72
    Cyrtomium falcatum, 172
    Cyrtomium fortunei, 172
    Cyrtomium macrophyllum, 171

day lily, 128–30
dead nettle, 119
Deinanthe bifida, 19, 36, 168
Dendranthema, 195
    Dendranthema indicum, 143–44
    Dendranthema pacificum, 143–44
    Dendranthema weyrichii, 195
    Dendranthema yezoense, 195
    Dendranthema x *grandiflorum,* 143
Deutzia, 81–82
    Deutzia crenata, 81–82
    Deutzia gracilis, 38, 81–82, 210
    Deutzia scaba, 82
Dianthus
    Dianthus barbatus, 128
    Dianthus superbus, 8, 128, 192–93
    Dianthus superbus var. *longicalycinus,* 192–93

Dianthus superbus var. *speciosus,* 193

Dicentra peregrina pusilla, 189–90

Dicentra spectabilis, 125, 189–90

dogtooth violet, 151–52

dogwood, 19, 48–49

Dryopteris

    Dryopteris bissetiana, 172

    Dryopteris championii, 172–73

    Dryopteris crassirhizoma, 173

    Dryopteris erythrosora, 173, 185

    Dryopteris erythrosora var. *prolifica,* 193

    Dryopteris formosanum, 173

    Dryopteris lacera, 173–74

    Dryopteris tokyoensis, 174

    Dryopteris varia var. *setosa,* 172

dwarf bamboo, 112–13

dwarf stone pine, 14, 16–17, 100

dwarf water lily, 18

Echinacea purpurea, 83

edelweiss, 193

Empetrum nigrum, 210

Epimedium, 12, 153

    Epimedium diphyllum, 114

    Epimedium grandiflorum, 114

    Epimedium x *youngianum,* 114

Eranthis hiemalis, 151

Eranthis pinnatifida, 151

Eriobotrya japonica, 71, 210

Erythronium americanum, 151–52

Erythronium japonicum, 152

Euonymus

    Euonymus fortunei, 18, 36

    Euonymus fortunei var. *radicans,* 106–7, 114–15

    Euonymus fortunei var. *vegeta,* 107

    Euonymus radicans, 33

Eurya japonica, 71, 72

Euryale ferox, 18, 199–200

false cypress, 62–63

fan palm, 94–95

Fatsia japonica, 13, 18, 95

Ficus pumilia, 107

Filipendula purpurea, 200

fir, 16, 27

    Nikko fir, 14, 18

    Veitch fir, 14

flowering apricot, 59–60

flowering cherries, 5, 6, 8, 10, 37, 55–59

flowering crab apples, 53–54

flowering quince, 80–81

Forsythia, 82

    Forsythia japonica, 82

    Forsythia suspensa, 82

fountain grass, 136–37

fox nuts, 199–200

Franklinia alatamaha, 69

Fritillaria

    Fritillaria camtschatcensis, 152

    Fritillaria imperialis, 152

    Fritillaria verticillata, 152, 153

full-moon maple, 18

gentians, 195

    Gentiana makinoi, 195

    Gentiana scabra var. *buergeri,* 195

    Gentiana triflora var. *japonica,* 195

giant hyssop, 126–27

ginger, 182–83

ginkgo, 49–50

    Ginkgo biloba, 49, 210

Glaucidium palmatum, 19, 39, 160–61

Glaucidium palmatum var. *leucanthum,* 160

Glen Dale azalea, 76

gloryvine, 18

gooseneck loosestrife, 131–32

grasses, 12, 38–39, 177

    blood grass, 39, 134–35

    fountain grass, 136–37

    maiden grass, 135–36

Habenaria radiata, 201–2

Hakonechloa macra, 177

hardy kiwi, 104

harlequin glory bower, 83–84
heavenly bamboo, 98–99
Heloniopsis orientalis, 190
Heloniopsis orientalis var. *breviscapa,* 190
Hemerocallis
    Hemerocallis aurantiaca, 39
    Hemerocallis aurantiaca var. *littorea,* 39
    Hemerocallis dumortierii, 39, 129–30
    Hemerocallis fulva, 39, 128–29
    Hemerocallis fulva var. *kwanso,* 129
    Hemerocallis lilioasphodelus, 130
    Hemerocallis littorea, 130
    Hemerocallis middendorffi, 39, 130
    Hemerocallis minor, 130
    Hemerocallis thunbergii, 39
hemlock, 16, 18, 19, 69
hemp palm, 101–2
hibiscus, 8
hills-of-snow hydrangea, 34
hinoki false cypress, 93–94
Hirado azalea, 75–76
holly, 13–14, 95–96
holly fern, 112
holly-grape, 82
hollyhocks, 28
honeysuckle, 34, 110
hops, 108
hornbeam, 18
Hosta, 12, 200
    Hosta caerulea, 32
    Hosta decorata, 115, 181–82
    Hosta lancifolia, 115
    Hosta longissima, 115
    Hosta montana, 168
    Hosta plantaginea, 32, 169
    Hosta pulchella, 115
    Hosta sieboldiana, 115, 169
    Hosta tardiflora, 179–80
    Hosta tardiva, 115
    Hosta undulata, 169
    Hosta venusta, 168–69
Humulus japonicus, 108
hydrangea, 25, 35, 84–86
    Hydrangea anomala ssp. *petiolaris,* 84

Hydrangea involucrata, 86
Hydrangea macrophylla, 37
Hydrangea macrophylla var. *macrophylla,* 84
Hydrangea macrophylla var. *normalis,* 84
Hydrangea paniculata, 33–34, 85, 86
Hydrangea petiolaris, 108
Hylomecon japonicum, 161
Hylotelphium
    Hylotelphium sieboldii, 197
    Hylotelphium spectabile, 148
    Hylotelphium telphium, 148
Hypnium (moss), 120
hyssop, 126–27

Ilex crenata, 95–96, 210
Illicium anisatum, 72
Imperata cylindrica, 134
Ipomoea, 8
    Ipomoea nil, 107
    Ipomoea x *imperialis,* 107
iris, 5–6, 8, 12, 161
    Iris gracilipes, 161
    Iris tectorum, 161

jack-in-the-pulpit. *See Arisaema*
Jeffersonia diphylla, 162
Jeffersonia dubia, 161–62
jetbead, 33
Juglans ailanthifolia, 33
juniper, 96–97, 115–116
    Juniperus chinensis, 96–97
    Juniperus conferta, 115
    Juniperus procumbens, 115
    Juniperus sabina, 97
    Juniperus sargentii, 116
    Juniperus x *media,* 97

Kadsura japonica, 108–9
Kaempferi azalea, 78–79
katsura tree, 14
Kerria japonica, 19, 28, 32, 86

Kirengeshoma palmata, 19, 180
Korean mountain ash, 18
Korean pine, 18
kudzu, 111
Kurume azalea, 77–78

larch, 14, 18, 64
Larix kaempferi, 64–65
Leontopodium
    Leontopodium alpinum, 193
    Leontopodium fauriei, 193
    Leontopodium hayachinense, 193
    Leontopodium japonicum, 193
Lespedeza, 7–8, 19, 146
    Lespedeza bicolor, 8, 146
    Lespedeza thunbergii, 146
Leucothoe keiskei, 97
Ligularia, 12
    Ligularia dentata, 130–131
    Ligularia hodgsonni, 131
    Ligularia przewalskii, 131
    Ligularia stenocephala, 131
Ligustrum
    Ligustrum japonicum, 97–98
    Ligustrum lucidum, 98
    Ligustrum obtusifolium, 98
    Ligustrum obtusifolium var. *regelianum,* 98
    Ligustrum ovalifolium, 98, 210
    Ligustrum x *ibolium,* 98
lilies. *See Lilium*
Lilium, 10, 12, 137–38
    Lilium auratum, 137, 138–39
    Lilium concolor, 141
    Lilium concolor var. *partheneion,* 141
    Lilium dexteri, 139
    Lilium hansonii, 140
    Lilium japonicum, 27, 137
    Lilium lancifolium, 138
    Lilium leichtlinii var. *tigrinum,* 137
    Lilium longifolium, 27, 138, 140–41
    Lilium maculatum, 27
    Lilium martagon var. *album,* 140
    Lilium martagon var. *cattaniae,* 140

Lilium rubellum, 137–38
Lilium speciosum, 26–27, 137, 139
Lilium x *dalhansonii,* 140
Lilium x *marhan,* 140
lilyturf, 116–117
liriope, 32, 180
    Liriope exiliflora, 117
    Liriope muscari, 116–17
    Liriope platyphylla, 117
    Liriope spicata, 116, 117
Lonicera japonica, 110–11
loquat, 33, 71–72
lotus, 8, 18, 198–99
Lycoris radiata, 34, 142, 143
Lycoris squamigera, 34, 142
Lygodium japonicum, 174
Lysichiton americanus, 200
Lysichiton camtschatcense, 200
Lysmachia clethroides, 131–32
Lysmachia nummularia, 118–19

magnolia, 11, 19, 34, 50–53
    Magnolia denudata, 52
    Magnolia kobus, 14, 51–52
    Magnolia kobus var. *kobus,* 52
    Magnolia kobus var. *loebneri,* 52
    Magnolia kobus var. *stellata,* 51–52
    Magnolia liliflora, 52
    Magnolia salicifolia, 52
    Magnolia sieboldii, 52
    Magnolia stellata, 50
    Magnolia virginiana var. *australis,* 14
Mahonia aquifolium, 172
Mahonia japonica, 82
maiden grass, 135–36
Malus. See also crab apples
    Malus floribunda, 53–54, 210
    Malus hupehensis, 54
    Malus sargentii, 54
    Malus sieboldii, 54
    Malus toringo, 54
    Malus tschonoskii, 54
Malva mauritiana, 28

maples, 6, 8–11, 18, 29–30, 42–46. *See also Acer*
marlberry, 111–12
Matteuccia struthiopteris, 170
meadowrue, 178, 194
meadow sweet, 200
Meehania urticifolia, 119
mimosa, 46–47
Miscanthus
    Miscanthus saccariflorus, 18
    Miscanthus sinensis, 8, 39, 135, 178
    Miscanthus sinensis var. *gracillimus,* 135
Mollis azalea, 77
monarch birch, 18
moneywort, 118–19
monkshood, 144–45
morning glory, 8, 107–8
moss, 5, 119–21
mother of thousands, 196
mountain ash, 17

Nandina domestica, 29, 98–99
Narcissus tazetta, 152
Nelumbo nucifera, 8, 18, 198–99
Nikko fir, 14, 18
Nipponanthemum nipponicum, 144
Nippon bells, 20–21
Nippon lily, 184–85
Nuphar, 198
    Nuphar japonica, 199
    Nuphar pumila, 199
Nymphaea tetragona var. *tetragona,* 198

oaks, 18
Occonee bells, 20
Onoclea sensibilis var. *interrupta,* 170
Ophiopogon
    Ophiopogon jaburan, 117–18
    Ophiopogon japonicus, 32, 118
    Ophiopogon planiscapus, 118
orchids, 155–58, 201–2
ornamental onion, 194–95
Osmunda japonica, 175

pachysandra, 10, 184
    Pachysandra procumbens, 152
    Pachysandra terminalis, 121–22
Paeonia
    Paeonia japonica, 162
    Paeonia lactiflora, 125
    Paeonia obovata, 162
    Paeonia obovata var. *alba,* 162
Papaver fauriae, 193
paper plant, 13, 18, 95
paperwhite narcissus, 152
Parthenocissus quinquefolia, 109
Parthenocissus tricuspidata, 109
Patrinia, 8
    Patrinia gibbosa, 132
    Patrinia scabiosaefolia, 8, 133
    Patrinia triloba var. *palmata,* 132–33
    Patrinia triloba var. *triloba,* 133
Peltoboykinia watanabei, 19
Pennisetum
    Pennisetum alopecuroides, 136
    Pennisetum alopecuroides f. *erythrochaetum,* 136
    Pennisetum alopecuroides f. *purpurascens,* 136
    Pennisetum alopecuroides f. *viridescens,* 136
peony, 8, 10, 12, 125–26, 162
Petasites japonicus, 201
Petasites japonicus var. *giganteus,* 201
Phyllostachys nigra, 48
Picea
    Picea glenhii, 64–65
    Picea jezoensis, 65
    Picea torano, 65
Pieris floribunda, 11
Pieris japonica, 11, 99–100, 210
pine, 7, 16, 27, 65–67
    dwarf stone pine, 14, 16–17, 100
    umbrella pine, 18, 67–68
Pinellia, 155
    Pinellia cordata, 155
    Pinellia ternata, 155
    Pinellia tripartita, 155
Pinus
    Pinus densiflora, 65
    Pinus parviflora, 66

Pinus pumilia, 66, 100
Pinus sylvestris, 28, 29
Pinus thunbergii, 66
Platycodon, 12
Platycodon grandiflorum, 133–34
Platycodon mariesii, 8
Pleioblastus
Pleioblastus auricoma, 112
Pleioblastus argenteostriatus, 112
Pleioblastus gramineus, 113
Pleioblastus humilis, 113
Pleioblastus humilis var. *pumilis,* 113
Pleioblastus pygmaeus, 112
Pleioblastus pygmaeus var. *disticha,* 112
Pleioblastus simonii, 47–48
plum, 7
plum yew, 62, 91–92
Podocarpus macrophyllus, 67
Polygonatum, 163
Polygonatum falcatum, 163
Polygonatum humile, 163
Polygonum, 163
Polygonum cuspidatum, 163
Polygonum tenuicaule, 163
Polygonum virginianum, 163
Polystichum
Polystichum achrostichoides, 180
Polystichum braunii, 175–76
Polystichum lonchitis, 170
Polystichum makinoi, 176
Polystichum polyblepharum, 176
Polystichum tsussimense, 176
Polytrichum commune, 119
poppies, 193
porcelain berry pine, 105
primroses, 164–65, 201
Primula
Primula cunefolia var. *hakusanensis,* 17
Primula japonica, 164, 201
Primula kisoana, 164
Primula modesta, 201
Primula nipponica, 17
Primula sieboldii, 164
privet, 13, 97–98

Prunus, 14, 18, 57
Prunus apetala, 57
Prunus campanulata, 58
Prunus incisa, 58
Prunus japonica, 58
Prunus maximowiczii, 59
Prunus mume, 59
Prunus nipponica, 59
Prunus persica, 8
Prunus sargentii, 56–57
Prunus serrulata, 8, 55–56
Prunus serrulata var. *spontanea,* 55
Prunus speciosa, 57
Prunus subhirtella, 57
Prunus subhirtella var. *autumnalis,* 57
Prunus x *sieboldii,* 57
Prunus x *yedoensis,* 57
Pueraria lobata, 111

quince, 80–81

Ranzania japonica, 19, 165
red spider-lilies, 33
Reineckia carnea, 165–66
Rhaphiolepis umbellata, 33
rhododendron, 14, 17, 18, 20, 73–102
Rhododendron fauriei, 17
Rhododendron indicum, 75–76
Rhododendron japonicum, 77
Rhododendron kaempferi, 76, 78–79
Rhododendron keiskei, 79
Rhododendron kiusianum, 78, 79
rhododendron Kurume hybrids, 210
Rhododendron metternichii var. *yakushimanum,* 80
Rhododendron molle, 77
Rhododendron mucronatum, 74, 76–77, 79
Rhododendron obtusum, 77–78, 79
Rhododendron poukhanesis, 79
Rhododendron yakushimanum, 79–80
Rhododendron x *kosteranum,* 77
Rodgersia podophylla, 170, 177–78
Rohdea japonica, 184

Rosa multiflora, 33
Rosa rugosa, 14, 19, 210

sacred lotus, 8, 18, 198–99
sago palm, 94–95
Salvia koyamae, 180–81
Salvia nipponica, 180–81
Sanguisorba
    Sanguisorba hakusanensis, 147
    Sanguisorba obtusa, 147, 201
    Sanguisorba obtusa var. *albiflora,* 147, 201
    Sanguisorba officinalis, 147
Sargent cherry, 18
Sasa palmata, 113
Sasa veitchii, 113
satsuki, 75–76
satsuki hybrids, 75–76
Saxifraga
    Saxifraga cortusaefolia, 196
    Saxifraga fortunei, 197
    Saxifraga fortunei var. *incisolobata,* 197
    Saxifraga nipponica, 196
    Saxifraga stolonifera, 196
scarlet kadsura, 108
Schizophragma hydrangeoides, 109
Sciadopitys verticilata, 18, 67–68
sedgegrass, 39
Sedum sieboldii, 197
Sedum spectabile, 148
Semiarundinaria fastuosa, 48
Shiba, 37
Shortia galacifolia, 20–21
Shortia uniflora, 20
single-flowered keria, 31–32
skimmia, 18
    Skimmia japonica, 100–101
smartweed, 163
snow azalea, 77
snowbell, 18
Solomon's seals, 162–63
spirea, 19, 82–83
    Spirea japonica, 82–83
    Spirea nipponica, 83

Spirea x *bumalda,* 82
    Spirea x *bumalda* var. *bullata,* 83
spruce, 64–65
stewartia, 19, 60
strawberry geranium, 196
Styrax japonicum, 60
sundew, round-leaved, 17
sweet coltsfoot, 201
Symplocarpus foetidus, 200
Syringa reticulata, 86–87
Syringa suspensa, 82

Tanakea radicans, 193–94
Taxus
    Taxus baccata, 69, 101
    Taxus cuspidata, 68–69, 92, 101, 210
    Taxus cuspidata var. *nana,* 68–69, 92, 101, 210
    Taxus x *media,* 101
ternstroemia, 70–71
    Ternstroemia gymnanthera, 71
Thalictrum
    Thalictrum alpinum, 194
    Thalictrum aquilegiifolium, 178
    Thalictrum kiusianum, 194
    Thalictrum minus, 194
    Thalictrum rochebrunianum, 178
Thelypteris
    Thelypteris decursive-pinnata, 176
    Thelypteris hexagonoptera, 176–77
    Thelypteris phegopteris, 176–77
Themedia triandra, 8, 136–37
Thuja dolobrata, 28
Thuja japonica, 36
tiger lily, 25
Tofeldia japonica, 17
Trachycarpus fortunei, 101–2
tree lilac, 86–87
tree peony, 25
Tricyrtis
    Tricyrtis hirta, 181
    Tricyrtis latifolia, 182
    Tricyrtis macranthopsis, 181–82
Trillium

Trillium grandiflorum, 166
Trillium kamtschaticum, 19, 166
Trillium smallii, 19, 166–67
Trillium tschonskii, 19, 166
Trollius japonicus, 17
Tsuga diversifolia, 69
Tulipa edulis, 151

umbrella pine, 14, 18, 67–68

Viburnum, 88–89
    Viburnum carlesii, 89
    Viburnum dilatatum, 88
    Viburnum macrocephalum, 89
    Viburnum plicatum, 88–89
    Viburnum plicatum f. *tomentosum*, 88–89
    Viburnum tomentosum, 33, 88
    Viburnum x *carlcephalum*, 89
Vinca minor, 51
violets, 190–91
    Viola crassa, 190–91
    Viola dissecta, 191
    Viola dissecta var. *sieboldii*, 191

Viola variegata var. *nipponica*, 192
    Viola verecunda var. *yakusimana*, 191
Vitis coignetiae, 18

water lilies, 7, 198
white birch, 38
windmill palm, 101–2
winter aconite, 151
wintercreeper, 18
wisteria, 8, 19, 33, 34
    Wisteria floribunda, 109–10
witchhazel, 19

X *Fatshedera lizei*, 95

Yakushima rhododendron, 79–80
yellow pond lily, 199
yew, 14, 18, 68–69, 101

Zelkova serrata, 33
Zoysia matrella, 37